D1142989

Cecil William Turpie Gray was born in Edinburgh in 1895, into a prosperous Scottish family. He was educated in England and took an arts degree from Edinburgh in 1913. During the First World War he lived in London and Cornwall, near D. H. Lawrence, and wrote for the *New Age*; but his career as a music critic really began when he founded *The Sackbut* in 1920, with Philip Heseltine. His outspoken criticism in the *Manchester Guardian* and *Daily Telegraph* won him a controversial reputation which was reinforced by his books – *A Survey of Contemporary Music* (1924), *Carlo Gesualdo* (1926), with Philip Heseltine, and a biography of Heseltine himself, *Peter Warlock* (1934). Later essays were collected in *Predicaments* (1936) and *Contingencies* (1947). His own compositions include the *Symphonic Prelude* (1945) and three operas – *Deirdre* and *The Temptation of St Anthony* (both 1937), and the *Women of Troy* (1939).

Gray's character, as *Musical Chairs* suggests, was an ebullient mixture of cantankerousness, extravagance and charm. As well as being musically enlightening, his memoirs convey the unique personality that made him such a figure of his time; he lived in the bohemian world of Fitzrovia, the world of Anthony Powell's *A Dance to the Music of Time*, and his close friends included the leading writers, artists and dancers of his day, as well as the musicians. His romantic relationships were as enthusiastically conducted as the rest of his life – he married three times and his daughters were 'all over the place'. They include Pauline, the daughter of his first wife, Tasha, and Perdita, the poet Hilda Doolittle's only child. In later life Cecil Gray retired to Ischia and Capri, but returned to England, seriously ill, in 1951. He died that same year in Worthing, aged fifty-six.

MUSICAL CHAIRS

or
Between Two Stools

Cecil Gray

New Afterword by
Pauline Gray

THE HOGARTH PRESS
LONDON

Published in 1985 by
The Hogarth Press
40 William IV Street, London WC2N 4DF

First published in Great Britain by Home & Van Thal 1948
Hogarth edition offset from original British edition
Copyright the Executors of the Estate of the late Cecil Gray
Afterword copyright © Pauline Gray 1985

ACKNOWLEDGEMENT
Thanks are due to Messrs. Heinemann Ltd., and the literary executors of
D. H. Lawrence, for permission to quote from his letters to the author.

British Library Cataloguing in Publication Data

Gray, Cecil, 1895-1951
Musical chairs
1. Gray, Cecil, 1895-1951   2. Music critics – Scotland – Biography
I. Title
780'.92'4   ML403.G7
ISBN 0 7012 0642 X

Printed in Great Britain by
Cox & Wyman Ltd
Reading, Berkshire

AFTERWORD

Cecil Gray died on Sunday, September 9th, 1951 in a nursing home in Worthing. He was fifty-six years old.

During the following weeks obituaries appeared in various newspapers. *The Times* described him as 'provocative to the point of perversity'; the *Observer* maintained that his writings on music, opinionated though they were, would nevertheless endure 'for their brilliance and truly literary quality'; and the *Manchester Guardian* judged him to be the most unorthodox of music critics:

He was one of the group of young men who, twenty-five years ago, approached music without too much respect for the views of elder critics and composers . . . His *History of Music* contains all that was most attractive in Cecil Gray, his passion for music, his lucidity, and the unpredictable quality of his likes and dislikes.

It was always Cecil's intention to write a sequel to *Musical Chairs*. In Chapter Eleven, when mentioning Clifford Bax and his brother Sir Arnold, Cecil writes that as his relationship with them belongs to the years after 1939 – which was the term he had set to the book – he hoped to 'discant upon them . . . some other time, perhaps'. Indeed, Cecil's private notebooks are full of material appertaining to his life after 1939 that seem only to be waiting for him to transcribe them. Alas, he never did write another volume. In this Afterword, therefore, I hope to give some idea of the later years of this 'perverse', 'unpredictable' and 'brilliant' man who was also my father; the Cecil Gray as seen by those who knew him well. Thus, in a sense, the Afterword is a personal conclusion to *Musical Chairs*.

Cecil Gray was better known as a music critic and writer than as a composer, though he would rather it had been the other way round. Nevertheless, first and foremost, his name will be forever linked with the group of young rebel musicians of the 1920s, such as Peter Warlock and Bernard van Dieren. After that he is remembered as the author of several books, including *A Survey of Contemporary Music* (1924), *The History of Music* (1928) and *Sibelius* (1935). But there were also people who were aware that Cecil composed music as well, and after his death Hubert Foss, the former head of Oxford University Press musical department, the publisher of many of his books, wrote in a special obituary in *The Times*:

Cecil Gray's was a towering mind. He himself refrained, with shy insistence of indomitable force, from appearing in public music in this country . . . Secretly he wrote operas; not even his most intimate friends knew the complete measure of his worth as a composer, though a broadcast of one converted a few.

But Cecil had not only the one performed opera, *The Women of Troy*, to his credit. His first work *Deirdre*, completed in 1937, has never been heard in its entirety, although in 1939 he took some material from the third act and made an orchestral piece from it called *Symphonic Prelude for Orchestra*. As Cecil mentions in *Musical Chairs*, it was performed several times both in England and in the United States. His next work, *The Temptation of St. Anthony*, which he finished also in 1937, is still unperformed. He felt that he had, to a great extent, subjected a theme or progression to every possible form of treatment in this opera; that in its way it was as remarkable an achievement as de Sade's *Cent-Vingt Jours de Sodome*; that he had 'developed it, varied it, given counterpoints to it, augmented it, diminished it, inverted it, possessed it in every conceivable position, as in the *Kama Sutra*'. In 1938, under the pseudonym of Marcus Lestrange, he wrote a work which he called *Syllogism or Thesis, Antithesis and Synthesis for Orchestra and Female Chorus*. Michael Ayrton, in a letter to me in 1966, wrote that he had the impression that Cecil had also written an Overture based on *Roma Nobilis* and another work – a setting of St. Francis's *Canticle to the Sun* – but of these last three compositions nothing is known.

The Women of Troy was finished in 1939 and was eventually broadcast by the BBC from their wartime studios in Bedford. The fact that it was transmitted at all was entirely due to the efforts of William Walton and Constant Lambert, as Cecil notes in *Musical Chairs*. Even so, the programme of excerpts only was a source of painful conscience for him, as he comments in one of his private notebooks:

Trojan Women performance: for the first time in my life I compromised. I underwent operation and suffered amputation. Was I right? It gave my friends pleasure, but me pain . . . I sinned against my motto – everything or nothing. Half a loaf is worse than no bread at all.

The composer Kaikoshru Sorabji wrote a review of the performance for the *New English Weekly* which appeared on April 5th, 1944:

Here without any doubt is *the* outstanding work in operatic form produced in this country during the last forty or so years . . . One looks anxiously for a chance to hear this really great work under happier conditions, that is to say, *not* filleted to make a BBC broadcast.

As to the reasons for Cecil having adopted the pseudonym Marcus Lestrange in 1938, it is surely because of the similar action of Philip Heseltine years before. The name Peter Warlock had come into existence simply as a *nom de plume*; Philip had made himself so heartily disliked in the musical world as a critic that, when he composed his first songs, he thought it advisable to call himself by another name. Indeed the songs were enthusiastically received by the entire musical press, and we find Philip writes gleefully to a friend: 'It gives me great satisfaction to reflect what they would have said about these same compositions had they been signed Philip Heseltine . . .' Cecil had not exactly endeared himself either to those in the musical world. He had no time or patience with the mediocrity which he believed ran rife in the artistic circles of those days, and he said so, loud and clear, many, many times. As Ralph Hill wrote in *The Sackbut* in December 1933: 'He cares not a jot for people or their opinions; and those who do not coincide with his own ideas he sweeps aside with testy cynicism, or maybe with a kick from a heavy boot! . . .' This, of course, did not help him to get his music published and performed. So, no doubt remembering Philip Heseltine/Peter Warlock, Cecil also tried to win recognition as a composer by using a pseudonym.

Testy and cynical he may have been as a music critic, but as a friend he was much loved by a great number of people. During the war, among his closest friends were Constant Lambert and Michael Ayrton. Of Constant, Cecil has written much in *Musical Chairs*, but Michael gets only a passing mention; presumably Cecil intended to write more fully about him one day in his next volume of memoirs.

Michael Ayrton was a talented artist although he was much younger than either Constant or Cecil – he was only nineteen when he first met them. (He once said in a broadcast made in 1974 that he could not understand how they tolerated the brash youth that he then was.) He had an idea that in some way he was a sort of replacement for Philip Heseltine – he actually looked rather like him – and it may have been because of this that he fitted so easily into their lives. In the same broadcast Michael remembered Cecil: '. . . he gave the appearance of being rather a morose character . . . I think this was partly because he was always sucking on a pipe which never seemed to be able to stay alight. He had a sense of humour, and he was vastly erudite . . .' In some ways Michael played the role of disciple to Cecil's prophet, sometimes literally sitting at his feet while Cecil discoursed. Years later, in 1948, Michael wrote to Cecil about their relationship:

. . . it became clear to me that at last we have come to understand one another – or at least I have come to understand certain things about my art and life, and about you. . . You and I have come to a point of complete agreement . . . in the consideration of your music, of your writing and of our many, many hours of conversation together, I have come to recognise in you a man in whom I have indestructible belief, an artist in whom I have complete faith.

For a time during the war Constant lived with Michael in the latter's house in All Soul's Place, London, and it would appear that they (and Cecil too) dabbled in the occult. How seriously they took it is difficult to judge, and certainly the infamous Aleister Crowley remained a continuing joke to them. Cecil's interest in the occult went back to the years around 1918 and the beginning of his friendship with Philip Heseltine. In those days Philip's chief preoccupation, apart from music, had been the study of magic. He believed that if one were to make use of a certain magical formula in order to obtain something otherwise unobtainable, and if one believed in it strongly enough, then the likelihood of success would be increased, provided that it were within the limits of possibility in the first place.

Cecil once told me of an incident which occurred in 1918 or 1919 when he and Philip and some friends pretended to 'offer up' a naked young woman as a sacrifice on the altar of a quiet country church. In the middle of the 'ceremony' a sudden bolt of lightning hit the church tower, sending the participants fleeing in terror. It seems that Cecil's and Philip's preoccupation in these matters waned somewhat after that! But in the early 1940s, while Cecil was writing *Gilles de Rais*, the only play he ever wrote, his interest in the occult was renewed. Gilles de Rais, sometimes known as Bluebeard, was a contemporary of Joan of Arc, and was a notorious practitioner of the Black Arts. Cecil, while writing the play, must have attempted to follow his example, for he wrote to Michael on April 16th, 1943 describing some of the consequences:

At exactly 12.40 in the train, a terrific attack began which lasted half an hour, and then stopped as suddenly as it began. The technique was rather different from that of previous similar onslaughts – much more violent and brutal . . . Looking back, in the state of comparative sanity which I have reached in the last week, I realise that I was very near the border line, and only just pulled out in time. But of course it always was my deliberate intention to steer as near to the verge of the precipice without toppling over . . . I always knew that to get inside the skin of Gilles was a risky business, but it was no use trying to do it without.

In his broadcast mentioned before, Michael talked about their interest in magic and remarked that Constant especially seemed to be able to produce extraordinary happenings:

I remember once coming out of a pub in Albany Street with Constant who said 'I will now produce a Scottish midget on a tricycle', and believe it or not, a midget in full Scottish costume on a tricycle came riding down Albany Street . . . It made him laugh uproariously . . . Cecil, I think had a somewhat deeper feeling for magic than Constant did, or certainly a less hilarious one.

Cecil had 250 copies of *Gilles de Rais* privately printed in London in 1945 with 'Decorations,' as he called them, by Michael Ayrton. After publication he sent a copy to George Bernard Shaw who replied from his flat at 4 Whitehall Court on January 31st, 1946:

I have just read *Gilles de Rais* . . . First, before we come to the play as a work of art, a few vulgar considerations. You must change the name, for nobody will ask for a book if they cannot pronounce its name; you will have to call it *Bluebeard: Friend of St. Joan*. And you have perpetrated the most appalling stage direction ever written. A great flame is to shoot up on the stage, and the curtain to be dropped instantly. The audience would conclude that the theatre was on fire; and the death roll would make the play a horror and a hoodoo for years. You must cut that out, or at least make the bishop stir up the fire with a very large poker first.

Since the play has never been performed, it is not known just what a director would make of this problem.

Michael, again in the broadcast already referred to, when talking about Cecil, had said he was '. . . a rich and varied character who improved as he drank more, which doesn't always happen . . .' It was no secret among Cecil's friends even from the earliest days that he had what is now known as a 'drink problem'. Back in November 1921 he had written to Philip Heseltine who was staying in Paris:

I am rather more than usually grisly these days for a multitude of very good reasons – the best of all perhaps being that I have had to suspend alcoholic excesses for the time being. I went to a heart specialist: after about two or three seconds examination he observed: 'Do you by any chance – er – indulge in alcohol?' I murmured affirmatively. 'Do you drink *very* much?' Another murmur. 'How long since, m'Lord?' Why, methinks it were about five years, etc. I was consequently advised to leave it off for some months at least. You can imagine what life is like without drink, especially in London when one lives alone. Still, I suppose one had better try . . . But I don't expect such virtue will last very long.

And how right he was, for it seems that when Philip returned to London the two of them went out on the town together. Later, Cecil lamented to Philip that it seemed fated that whenever they were together, there was always 'a square-faced bottle' between them.

Cecil always admired Dr. Samuel Johnson's remark that 'there are some sluggish men who are improved by drinking, as there are fruits that are not good until they are rotten.' Cecil felt that though some people are the worse for alcohol, he himself was the better; that although it is popularly supposed to destroy the critical sense, he in fact found it intensified his, 'with a cold, white, destructive, sterile, incandescent light.' He was forever being advised by his doctors to give up drinking; if he did so, he was told, then he had a good chance of living to a comparatively healthy old age. But he made a conscious decision to continue in his usual way. For, as he pointed out, where was the attraction in living for years and years in miserable sobriety? He preferred his life to be short, if necessary, but definitely merry.

One of the favourite lunchtime gathering places during the war for Cecil and his companions was a couple of small and shabby rooms above a pub in Great Portland Street. When the nearby premises of Paganis were bombed during the blitz, the proprietors rescued the cellar-full of wines which had escaped being damaged, and opened up a small restaurant above the pub. Cecil was one of the privileged few who knew about this, and he and others of his circle worked their way systematically through the wine list until nothing was left. Walter Legge, William Walton, Constant Lambert and Michael Ayrton were among those often to be found there, talking and drinking, drinking and talking, well into the afternoon.

Another place that Cecil and his friends would congregate during this period was the Back Bar of the Café Royal, as he describes in *Musical Chairs*. But what the book does not mention was that it was in the Back Bar that he met Gerald Kersh – one of the most colourful characters in the host of amazing friends – who, like Michael Ayrton, would I am sure have been amply commented upon in a later volume of memoirs.

In 1941 Kersh had had a book published called *They Died With Their Boots Clean*, about life in the Coldstream Guards, which had immediately become a bestseller, an event which he was still celebrating in grand style when Cecil first met him, although he was also continuing to write short stories. Kersh was a complete extrovert and this aspect of him seemed to appeal strongly to Cecil who was, in fact, the opposite. Kersh liked to draw attention to himself in bars and restaurants by his outrageous behaviour while Cecil would sit quietly by, watching and chuckling. Kersh always wore a red carnation in his buttonhole, and one of his favourite tricks was to bend a sixpence between his teeth and to give the bent coin to very surprised strangers 'for luck'. Cecil and Kersh amused themselves (and others) by carrying on a running contest in punning. 'His books deserve a Kershery scrutiny,' said Cecil. 'Onyxy is the best policy,' replied Kersh. 'Onyx *soit qui mal y pense*.' 'A Kersh upon our enemies.' Etc, etc.

Of course, with all his many friends, Cecil pondered on the state of friendship in general in one of his notebooks:

To bump off one's friends would seem a natural and normal act, because we are necessarily rivals on account of the affinity which binds us together – we want the same things in fact, we want the same women; we have the same ambitions and ideals and there is not always room for us both. There is an inevitable clash of interest. This is the tragedy of so many, perhaps most, friendships. But to bump off one's enemies – how shortsighted! How foolish! Where would one be without one's enemies? It is they who keep one's steel tempered . . .

Few people are magnanimous enough to forgive a good turn. It is much easier to forgive someone who has played one a dirty trick.

In *Musical Chairs* Cecil made the decision not to write about the women in his life, and except for a brief reference to his first wife, my mother, he kept to it. He did actually marry three times, was divorced twice; he had two legitimte daughters and at least one illegitimate one. In one of his notebooks can be found the following entries:

The world is full of my daughters. It pullulates with them. You can't escape them. They are all over the place. I keep on running into them.

My best works are probably my daughters, some without opus numbers – not officially acknowledged, but none the worse for that.

Exactly how many daughters there are 'without opus numbers' I am not certain, but I do know of one – Perdita, born in 1919, the daughter of H.D., the Imagist poet, wife of Richard Aldington, and friend of D.H. Lawrence. In her autobio-graphical novel *Bid Me To Live*, first published in 1960, H.D. writes of Cecil as 'Vane'; in the 1984 Virago edition Perdita herself writes an Afterword in which she describes how, during her childhood, she came slowly to realise that she was in fact the daughter of Cecil Gray.

By the time *Bid Me To Live* was published, Cecil had been dead for nine years, but in life he had already had the unpleasant experience of being characterised in two, possibly three, books by D.H. Lawrence in such a way as to wound him deeply, as he remarks in *Musical Chairs*. In *Aaron's Rod* (1922), Lawrence portrayed Cecil as an unat-tractive musician called Cyril Scott – 'a fair, pale, fattish young fellow in pince-nez and dark clothes'; then in 1923 he appears briefly as James Sharpe in *Kangaroo* in an account of the visit by the police to the house in Cornwall during World War I; and some people believe that, in the third and final version of *Lady Chatterley's Lover* (1928), Cecil was the character *à clef* of Duncan Forbes – the man who was going to pretend paternity of the yet unborn child of Lady Chatterley and Mellors. But it was not only D.H. Lawrence who put Cecil into books. Aldous Huxley did too in *Antic Hay* (1924), as the comic Mr. Mercaptan, 'a sleek, comfortable young man' with 'a rather gross, snouty look'; and in the same year as *Bid Me To Live* was first published, Anthony Powell wrote of Cecil in *Casanova's Chinese Restaurant* (1960) as the musician Maclintik, a 'solidly built musical type' whose 'minute circular lenses of his gold-rimmed spectacles . . . made one think of caricatures of Thackeray or President Thiers, imposing upon him the air of a bad-tempered doctor'.

But back in 1926 Cecil's real non-fictional life continued, and that year, at a party given by Augustus John in his studio in Mallord Street, Chelsea, he met and fell violently in love with a beautiful Russian woman called Tasha. At the time of their meeting Tasha was still legally married to Val Gielgud, though they had not lived together for some years. Eventually, after her divorce was finalised in 1927, she and Cecil married; I was born two years later in a little house in Hillsleigh Road, Holland Park. When I was three years old Tasha fell deeply in love with a man called Michael Majolier, and after much agonising, left Cecil and me to go and live with her lover and eventually to marry him. I did not see her again until I was fifteen years old. In 1936 Cecil married again, this time to a Scottish ballet dancer whose professional name was Marie Nielson. Their daughter, my half-sister Fabia, was born in 1938. This marriage did not last either and in about 1941 Marie left Cecil, taking their little daughter with her but leaving me, of course, with my father. It could not have been easy for him to have been left twice with a daughter to look after, with all the corresponding problems of clean laundry and outgrown winter coats and shoes. He was a very conscientious man and must have worried when he thought of his daughters. 'How disconcerting it is,' he wrote in a notebook, 'to have a conscience which is not strong enough to prevent one from sinning, and not weak enough to save one from the pangs of remorse . . .'

Before his first, and between each of his marriages, he had innumerable mistresses and was always madly in love. He was forever the willing victim of the *Lorelei*, and our life echoed to the sound of his boat continually crashing against the rocks and sinking to the bottom amid the noises of revelry and the breaking of good intentions. Blondes, brunettes, redheads, he was immune to none and they wreaked havoc in our lives.

It is not difficult to guess what my father meant to me during my motherless childhood. In the ever-changing environment he was always there, however wild and stormy the sea; kind, benevolent and understanding.

Looking back now, I find it amazing to realise that, in spite of the perpetual turmoil in his personal life and the hours that he spent carousing with his friends, he still found the time and energy to write his books and compose his music. He never went anywhere without a notebook and everyone was used to seeing him suddenly take it out of his pocket and jot down an idea as it occurred to him. These notebooks were never thrown away and came to light among his papers after his death. In them he ponders on every subject that interested him, and this means just about everything. Music, musicians, art, artists, critics, politics, philosophy, life, death, and of course, wives and mistresses:

Women who are easy and pleasant to live with are apt to be unfaithful. *Vice versa*, a woman's faithfulness is often in direct ratio to her unpleasantness. My first wife, during the time she was in love with me, treated me abominably. When she was being unfaithful, she behaved very nicely and kindly. I welcomed the change without divining the reason.

For a long time, up till a few days ago, my indifference to women was comprehensive and absolute. Today I desire intensely every single one I see who is at all presentable – a state of chronic intoxicated inflammation, which if continued is bound to lead to trouble. (Later) It has done.

Married life is like the proverbial description of the English summer – two fine days and a thunderstorm – endlessly repeated. Except that often it is just the one fine day and two thunderstorms – sometimes just three thunderstorms . . .

It is not the individual woman, the personality that I love, but woman, of whom she is the embodiment. And women don't like that, and I don't blame them at all. They want to be loved for themselves, as individuals. And the trouble is that sooner or later they find it out, and then trouble begins, the fur flies.

In spite of his previous two experiences of the state of matrimony, Cecil married yet again, for the third and last time, in 1944. She was Margery Livingstone-Herbage, the first wife of Julian Livingstone-Herbage of the BBC. Cecil and Margery compiled an anthology together called *The Bed, or the Clinophile's Vade Mecum*, published in 1946 – again with 'Decorations' by Michael Ayrton – which featured all the references to bed in literature from the very earliest times to the present. It is an amusing work but the general opinion was that it was rather a trivial one for Cecil and that he would have been better employed using his substantial intellect on something more worthwhile. 'I see the alarming possibility,' he wrote in a notebook, 'that I shall end my days as a poet, novelist, playwright, or all three. What a sad end to a promising musical career!'

Cecil and Margery were very happy together but none of Cecil's friends liked her, and she did not like them. It could almost be said that she went out of her way to alienate them. Michael Ayrton and she had a long-running quarrel which escalated one particular evening into a bad row; this made it impossible for Michael and Cecil to meet for a long time. It would seem that she felt that Michael was in some way a bad influence on her husband, indeed as she felt about several of his friends from before their marriage. It was as if she wanted him left alone to get on with his work, and of course she was extremely possessive towards him.

In 1947 Cecil and Margery left England and went to live in Italy, on the Isle of Capri, where they rented a furnished villa overlooking the Faraglioni rocks, near the villa of Compton Mackenzie. Two old friends of Cecil's – Norman Douglas and Kenneth Macpherson – were among the residents of the island, and they used to meet every day and continued the usual way of life of drinking and eating together and talking. One day, that same year, came a visitor to Capri – none other than Perdita, Cecil's daughter by H.D. and now the adopted daughter of Kenneth Macpherson. 'My legal father introduced me to my father,' writes Perdita in the Afterword to *Bid Me To Live*. But neither father nor daughter seemed to want to admit to their relationship and during the following days, when they found themselves in the same group of friends, they 'conversed politely' and discussed books, the opera and the weather. But, writes Perdita, 'I knew that he knew, and he knew that I knew that he knew . . .'

The idyllic existence on that enchanted island came to a sudden end the following year when Margery, who had been in bed for a week with an unspecified illness, was rushed to hospital in Naples where she died the next day from gall-bladder complications. A few days after her death Michael Ayrton and William Walton visited Cecil on Capri to try to cheer him up; naturally, in those sad circumstances the old quarrel which had estranged Cecil and Michael was finally finished, forgiven and forgotten.

From the moment of Margery's death Cecil seemed to give up on life. His health deteriorated steadily and he was more often than not almost insensible from drink. Graham Greene, in a letter to me a few years ago, remembered such an occasion during this period:

One evening I found myself walking around Capri with him after Margery's death and both of us in a state of extreme intoxication. He repeated over and over again that he had come to Capri as to a Paradise and found that it contained the snake. . .

Poor Cecil! Just as the paradise-garden of Cornwall in 1917 had concealed a serpent in the form of D.H. Lawrence, so now too had Capri – but this one's name was Death. There was to be no happiness there or anywhere else for him from then on. Later he wrote in a notebook:

I despise people who 'get over it,' whom 'time heals' etc. Nine months ago Margery died. I have not 'got over it.' I shall never 'get over it.' I don't want to 'get over it.'

Three years and five months was all Cecil lived after Margery's death. His drinking increased until he was so ill he could hardly walk. A friend called Kem remembers meeting Cecil at the airport when he arrived in England for the last time. Kem had almost to carry Cecil he was so weak, and yet, intent as he was on this form of self-destruction, he had brought a bottle of gin with him. He stayed in Kem's flat for a few days, lying in bed all day long, drinking gin. He was eventually taken to a nursing home in Worthing, near to his beloved Windmill, where at last he died from cirrhosis of the liver.

Cecil's notebooks are full of his musings on death:

Everyone is afraid of either life or death. Those of great vitality, who love every moment of life, are generally far more afraid of dying than those of less vitality, who therefore face death much more bravely than their more virile fellows. It is not courage, but comparative indifference or even a positive desire for death; a fear of life. Personally I am afraid of both life and death. I have fought hard to overcome both, and with some success. I think I can honestly claim that, being born with an ignominious cowardly nature, which is not my fault, I have striven hard all my life to correct it.

And finally fear turns to longing:

Behind all the women I have pursued or possessed, there is an archetypal one whom I have never known and never will except in the moment of death when she will be revealed to me, and she will take me in her arms. She probably is Death herself. The enfolding arms I long for so passionately are those of death . . .

Pauline Gray, London 1985

IN MEMORY OF
M. G.

Naples, 16th March, 1948.

Brightness falls from the air;
Queens have died young and fair;
Dust hath closed Helen's eye.

(THOMAS NASHE.)

Foreword

AN autobiography generally conforms to one or other of two main types, being either a self-portrait—a subjective record of things felt and thought by the writer, or memoirs—an objective account or description of personalities encountered or things seen.

My original conception was of the first order, but I abandoned it in favour of the second, which in its turn I discarded with the intention of writing both separately. In the end I decided to attempt the combination of the two in one.

Apart from a few brief incursions over the temporal frontier in pursuit of my quarry, I have set the limit and period of these reminiscences at the year 1939—a highly appropriate dividing line between that which has been and that which will be.

CECIL GRAY

London—Sussex—Capri
1946–7

Chapter One

ONE morning, early in September, 1945, I left my chambers in Albany and proceeded in leisurely but purposeful fashion in the direction of the British Museum.

My intention in visiting the Reading Room that morning was by no means the outcome of a sudden impulse, but of a long-deferred resolution, a *schwer gefasste Entschluss*, to quote the words of Beethoven prefixed to the *finale* of the last of his posthumous string quartets.

For some time past I had been gradually and inescapably forced to the unpalatable conclusion that if I were to make any further progress as a composer I must retrace my steps, start afresh as a student—in fact, go to school again. In the light of this conviction, and with this end in view, I had decided to embark upon an intensive study of the complete works of Bach, from first volume to last of the monumental *Gesellschaft* edition.

In the German language the word "Bach" denotes a stream, and in the language of music the name of Bach has a similar connotation, symbolizing the whole stream of the art throughout the ages. Or it might perhaps be more apt to say that his work constitutes not one stream, but two streams, which flow from a high watershed: a source from which two rivers run— the one flowing back through time towards the Middle Ages, Gregorian Chant, and even further back still, into classical pagan antiquity; the other forward to the art of modern times, and to that which is yet to come.

The whole of musical art is summed up in Bach. To him all

9

things lead, from him all things take their departure. Bach, in a word, is God in the firmament of music, however much one may on occasion vehemently deny it and blaspheme against his ascendancy. In the end one has to come back to him: without him there is no salvation. He is the Alpha and Omega, comprising the past, present and future. Everyone can find in him what he seeks, for all things are contained in him.

It was with such thoughts in my mind that I made my way towards my destination, with the intention of performing the act of total immersion in that sacred stream, and in the hope of emerging from it phoenix-like, purified, revivified, renewed.

On arriving there and passing through the great central Reading Room, which was in the process of being reconditioned and put into service again after having been closed for some years during the war, I reflected, with something of a shock, that it was no less than thirty years since I first began to read under that majestic dome, and that I should soon be qualifying for the rank of the oldest inhabitant—the G.O.M. of the British Museum Reading Room. I felt chilly and grown old.

On reaching the North Library, which alone was actively functioning in these days, I duly made my way towards the music catalogue, situate in the corridor to the right of the entrance, and approached the section devoted to the letter "B". But on seeking the two volumes containing the list of the works of Bach I found, to my consternation, that both of them were absent: there was a gap on the shelf in the place where they should have been. I looked around to see whether possibly some other reader was in the act of consulting them—but no, there was no one else present.

The obvious, natural explanation, of course, was that the volumes had been temporarily removed by the staff for the purpose of making new entries, or for altering the press-marks of the old. The fact remained that my *Entschluss*, so *schwer gefasste*—the execution of which I had sought vainly to evade, to postpone, over which I had procrastinated and temporized during a period of months and even years—had been decisively thwarted by purely external circumstances over which I had no control. *Es muss sein, es muss sein*, I had said to myself resolutely as I crossed the threshold of the Museum: but seemingly it was not to be. The Fates had willed otherwise.

For many years it had been an established custom of mine, when visiting the Reading Room, to arrive shortly before eleven-thirty, fill in my tickets for books, deposit them, and then seek a neighbouring tavern until the books were likely to be forthcoming—generally after about an hour. So I had planned it on this occasion. Glancing at my watch I noted that the magic hour had arrived at which "They" open; consequently, disconcerted, disconsolate, disillusioned, disorientated, I made my way to a tavern in Museum Street which I had long known and assiduously frequented ever since I had been a regular reader, in order to decide upon my future plan of action.

I had not been there for some years, however, and on re-entering it after this considerable lapse of time I experienced another shock: the place was entirely changed, completely unrecognizable. Not merely were the barmaids different: one is used to that. There is no more apt symbol of the transitoriness of all mortal and mundane things than a barmaid, the veritable embodiment of Maya, here to-day and gone to-morrow. Worse than that, the landlord was changed, and the very building itself had been entirely reconstructed; worst of all, there was not a single familiar face among the clientele, and I reflected sadly that most of those with whom I had spent so many pleasant hours there in drinking and talking were dead, and the rest dispersed. Again the sense of age, of the passage of time, afflicted me. I felt like a strayed ghost.

Taking my drink with me to a corner seat I drew from my pocket a Penguin volume I had casually purchased in Charing Cross Road on my way to the Museum, and idly turned over the pages. It chanced to be the autobiography of a philosopher and antiquarian whose name was completely unknown to me— R. G. Collingwood. I discovered from the brief prefatory

editorial note that the book had been written in 1939 when
the author was fifty years of age. I reflected that I also was
precisely that age, and that I had often seriously considered the
project of writing my autobiography, but had always put it
aside, saying to myself that it was too early, and that there was
still plenty of time before it was necessary to entertain the idea
seriously. Reading on further, however, I discovered that the
author had died shortly after completing his book, in his early
fifties. Whereupon the *alter ego*, or *Doppelgänger*, who is my
inseparable, inescapable, and always unwelcome companion,
whispered sibilantly in my ear, saying: "If you really mean to
do it, you had better do it now; perhaps you have not so much
time as you think."

I am not more superstitious than the majority of people—
rather less than most, I should say—but I have always had a
deep unalterable conviction of the existence of what is vaguely
called *destiny*, a belief in a design, purpose, and pattern underlying the outwardly confused and incoherent surface of one's
life, a kind of hidden meaning. The hackneyed Shakespearian
dictum to the effect that "There's a divinity that shapes our
ends, rough-hew them how we will", has always struck me as
being a complete reversal of the true state of affairs, and I
strongly suspect that Shakespeare had intended to say exactly
the opposite: namely, that destiny provides the rough-hewn
cast which we are at liberty to shape and finish in detail, even
to modify considerably, but not fundamentally or radically
alter.

However that may be, I was conscious at the time of a
definite conviction that the concatenation of events described
above was not a mere coincidence, but was in the nature of a
command, an imperious summons, an inner compulsion, to the
effect that the immediate task which lay ahead of me was to
write this book, and that everything else could, and must, wait.
It was, in fine, a categorical imperative which I could only
accept and obey. Whether I liked it or not, I felt I had no
choice.

So that is why, instead of being in the Reading Room of the British Museum studying Bach, as had been my original intention, I find myself sitting at my desk in Albany writing these pages, surrounded by the illustrious shades of the great departed—Byron, Macaulay, Gladstone, Bulwer Lytton—to say nothing of the lesser lights of the living, such as Clifford Bax, Patrick Hamilton, G. B. Stern, Terence Rattigan, J. B. Priestley, and all.

Apart from that, however, the whole episode is deeply symbolic and representative of the life and personality with which the book purports to deal. Always I have been torn in two directions, in an endless tug-of-war between my musical and my literary inclinations, both equally strong and equally balanced. At times the one achieves the ascendancy, at times the other; sometimes there is a complete equipoise.

This division of energy between two activities, either of which separately is more than enough to claim the entire energies and undivided attention of any man, however gifted, has unquestionably been a potential source of weakness and distraction. At the same time it may well prove to have been a source of strength, since in the attempt to resolve this state of perpetual tension between two opposing forces, I have been led to cultivate the forms of expression in which they are to a great extent reconciled—opera or music-drama on the one hand: musical criticism, biography and history on the other.

Before this synthesis was arrived at, the struggle between the two forces was a violent one: each of them, music and literature, fighting fiercely for the ascendancy. And since it has been achieved, I have noticed a tendency in recent years towards a renewed separation between the two faculties, towards autonomy or partition between the two warring elements. My latest productions, for example, have been a purely literary play, and a purely musical work for orchestra—and now this book. I am not at all sure that I approve of this schism; on the contrary I rather hope that in years to come the breach will be healed, the divorce rescinded. For the time being it is only a decree *nisi*, not yet made absolute. A reconciliation is still possible and will no doubt be effected.

If I were to be asked the question which of the two forms of artistic expression preponderated in me—the literary or the musical—I could only answer thus: "Both or neither, not one or the other. I am writer *and* composer, not writer *or* composer —or else I am nothing. Both forms of expression come equally naturally to me (or, more accurately, perhaps, with equal difficulty); both are equally essential to me in the attempt to realize whatever faculties or potentialities I may possess. It is impossible for me to distinguish between them, or to give precedence to the one over the other."

The fact remains, unfortunately, that this duality constitutes a heavy handicap, a formidable weapon put into the hands of one's enemies—or detractors—of whom I have more than a quiverful. Musicians, I have noticed, tend to deliver themselves of ecstatic and hypocritical eulogies of my literary capacities, while writers are wont to treat me patronizingly as a mere musician with no right to intrude upon their own special domain. In short, I am regarded by musicians as a writer, by writers as a musician.

Such, of course, has been the fate of many others who have similarly practised two or more arts, especially in this country where versatility is more profoundly distrusted than anywhere else—notably William Blake, Dante Gabriel Rossetti, and Wyndham Lewis. (I need hardly say, I hope, that I am not necessarily comparing myself in stature to any of the aforenamed artists. I merely wish to suggest that the nature of the problem presented is the same—a duality which is at the same time the necessary and inevitable expression of a fundamental unity of personality.) The particular form of dichotomy in my case is unusual. While many musicians have written extensively, and some of them have written well, there has never been any doubt as to which of their two activities was the more important; no one asks whether Wagner, Schumann, or

Berlioz were primarily composers or writers of books. (Again, no question of comparative measurement.)

In this connexion, incidentally, it is interesting to observe that one of those mentioned above, namely Wyndham Lewis (of whom more anon), has written somewhere that it is a great advantage for an artist to have two entirely separate *media* at his disposal, for he can therefore realize one side of himself completely in the one direction, and the other side of himself in the other, keeping both of them pure and without admixture, as if in water-tight compartments. Theoretically this sounds plausible enough, but in practice it does not work out like that at all. The pictorial art of Blake, Rossetti—and of Lewis himself, whether he knows it or not—is full of literary and poetic implications, while their writing is highly visual and descriptive; and I am certainly no exception to this rule. My music, I freely recognize, has always some literary, philosophic, or otherwise extraneous implications, while my writing tends continually to aspire to the condition of music, in accordance with the Paternal formula.

But, I repeat, I am both musician and writer, or if you prefer it, neither; indivisible or nothing at all, a duality or a nullity. Both activities are inseparable in me, both modes of thought are part of me; I cannot express myself wholly in one direction to the exclusion of the other.

One of the great philosophers of the Taoist school, Chuang-Tzu, describes how one night he fell asleep and dreamt that he was a butterfly, and all his emotions and sensations were those of a butterfly to such an extent that when he woke up he could not decide whether he was a man who had previously been dreaming that he was a butterfly, or whether he was then a butterfly dreaming that he was a man. Similarly, I find it impossible to say whether I am a musician dreaming that I am a writer, or a writer dreaming that I am a musician. Perhaps both are delusions: perhaps I am only the equivalent of an anthropoid ape dreaming he is a butterfly, and a caterpillar dreaming that he is a man. I only know for certain that I have experienced intensely the sensations both of a musician and a writer; moments in.which words and musical notes have come to life and palpitated in the warmth of my hands like those Mexican jumping-beans which one used to buy in toyshops in my early youth.

Chapter Two

THE writer of the article in Grove's *Dictionary of Music and Musicians* (Supplementary Volume), which concerns itself with me, states rightly that I was born on 19th May, 1895, but wrongly that this momentous event occurred in London. Actually, my birthplace was Edinburgh.

The correction is not made in any pedantic spirit, but because it involves an important issue, namely that I am as near to being one hundred per cent. Scottish as it is possible for anyone to be. So far back as I can trace my ancestry on both sides of my family tree there appears to be no trace of other than pure Caledonian descent. No taint of Sassenach blood pollutes my veins, so far as can be ascertained.

In itself, of course, this question of racial origins should not be of the slightest importance. No one could be less of a *doctrinaire* nationalist than I. Indeed, the self-conscious chauvinism which has characterized and disfigured so much art and literature of the 19th and early 20th centuries has always been profoundly distasteful to me, however greatly I may admire some of its products. My deep reverence for the art of Yeats and Synge, of Balakirev, Moussorgsky and Borodin, for example, has always been in despite of their nationalistic ideals, and solely on account of their individual genius.

The fact remains that this *echt* Scottish nationality is strongly characteristic and in high degree determinative of whatever qualities I may possess, both good and bad. It is indeed, I am forced to recognize, of primary importance, and any attempt to write about myself or my work without reference to my racial origins would be doomed to futility.

I am, in short, a typical Scot in all essential respects, but I see no reason to be either proud or ashamed of it. The fact that an artist should think, speak, write, paint, or compose in the language or idiom of his native country does not seem to me to be a matter for either self-congratulation or self-reproach. One should accept the fact of one's nationality as one accepts the fact of one's sex, the colour of one's hair, the length of one's nose, and so on, as things which cannot be changed except artificially, and then always detrimentally.

One's nationality, indeed, is no more important than such things, but, I hasten to add, no less important. It determines one's nature to a very much greater extent than many would-be cosmopolitans and internationalists would care to admit.

Up to about the age of seventeen or so I was a complete and intransigent cosmopolitan. If there was anything I detested it was the conventional Scottish racial idolatry of Sir Walter Scott and Robert Burns. I have never been able to endure either of them. At the same time, I felt no bonds of attachment to the culture which existed on the other side of the River Tweed. "Englishness" as such I have always disliked as much as, if not more than, the bastard culture of Lowland Scotland. English art in the Middle Ages, when it was an integral part of the European heritage, and in the time of the Renaissance, when cultural values were largely continental and predominantly Italian, I could and did wholeheartedly appreciate; but the more characteristically and unmistakably English it became, in the 18th and 19th centuries, the less it meant to me. Even to-day the whole hierarchy of the English novelists from Fielding and Smollett, through Dickens and Thackeray, up to Hardy and Meredith and Trollope, means precisely nothing to me. I simply cannot read them. I have tried hard, I have read several books of each, I have given them all a fair trial, but it is no use. The only English novelists I can read with any pleasure are such as George Moore or Joseph Conrad, an Irishman and a Pole, both influenced by French traditions.

As for the English musical renaissance in modern times of which one heard so much in my youth, the little I knew of it meant less than nothing to me, apart from the equivocal figure of Delius, who, again, was more a Continental than an insular figure.

In short, both in literature and in music my attachments and admirations lay outside these Islands, and were predominantly, overwhelmingly Latin. I have always felt about German music as I do about English literature: the more national it is the less I like it. The universality of a Shakespeare or a Beethoven transcends all national and racial frontiers, but with lesser figures I feel constrained and ill at ease. The Teutonic and Anglo-Saxon worlds, as such, are, and always have been, antipathetic to me.

France and Italy, on the other hand, these are, and always have been, my spiritual homes: French literature and Italian music in particular have meant more to me than anything else in life. In Bach, Beethoven, and Mozart it is the strong Italian substratum of thought that chiefly holds me; it is the comparative absence of that element in Brahms, Schumann, and Bruckner which repels me. And in these instinctive Latin predilections and sympathies I unmistakably reveal my Scottish nationality. Scottish culture in historical times, in so far as it existed, was French and Italian rather than English; and the Old Alliance between France and Scotland, which lasted for so many centuries, was not merely political, but was based as well on many subtle spiritual affinities. Although the alliance has ceased to be a political reality, it still remains an historical and a psychological affinity. France and Scotland are as closely united to-day in the spirit as they ever were. Whenever I have been asked in France, "*Vous êtes anglais, monsieur?*" I have always indignantly denied the imputation and replied: "*Mais non—pas du tout—je suis écossais.*" The distinction is always appreciated, and incidentally the attitude and treatment change, and very perceptibly. The English, as they themselves may no doubt have noticed, are not particularly beloved in France, in spite of their lavish expenditure; whereas the Scots are, in spite of their alleged parsimony (which is a myth).

My strongly Latin bias, then, and my comparatively antipathetic reaction towards the Anglo-Saxon, Teutonic and Scandinavian worlds, are basically Scottish; and the axis around which these predilections and antipathies revolve, in so far as art is concerned, is the sense of form. I cannot do better than quote, in this connexion, a passage from the autobiographical volume entitled *Inland Far* by Clifford Bax:

> "The Latin peoples must be exasperated by our indifference, our blindness to beauty of form, to literary architecture. With the exception of one man I can recall no evidence that any critic in this country is able to perceive where it exists or is conscious of its absence. Our race has always valued vitality and ignored structure. The French are lukewarm about Shakespeare, presumably because he was an indifferent architect. We, in turn, care nothing for Racine because his sense of form was stronger than his vitality. We do not resent a rambling or even a ramshackle design. We have not recognized that architectural beauty can be achieved only by a powerful mind, and that the ability to achieve it is the most masculine attribute of an artist. The man who prefers *Martin Chuzzlewit* to *Phèdre* has but chosen between formless vitality and unvitalized form. If he prefers it also to *The Symposium* he has proclaimed himself as a person more fitted to consort with Caliban than with Prospero . . . Were it not for this defect in our race we should never have heard the ridiculous doctrine that the size of a work has no bearing upon its merit, that a cameo is an achievement as noteworthy as a cathedral."

Mr. Bax is, of course, writing of the specifically English genius and, as an Englishman himself, can surely be unhesitatingly acquitted of bias in the matter. His observations seem to me to be simply in the nature of a statement of incontrovertible fact, and not of opinion. It is difficult indeed to think of a single acknowledged literary masterpiece written by an Englishman, except perhaps Milton's *Paradise Lost*, which is a perfect formal construction from beginning to end, and very few even in which there is any attempt to achieve it, except in miniature forms. The same is even more true of English music. The admittedly beautiful compositions of the great Tudor masters are all on a small formal scale; even when of considerable length they are only strings of exquisite miniatures. Purcell himself had no sense of form on a large scale, and in the whole field of modern English music, with its scores of symphonies, cantatas, operas, and all the rest of the larger forms, it is difficult to point to a single unchallengeable formal masterpiece of big dimensions—anything that in this respect can be compared to parallel achievements in other countries.

This will, I know, be regarded as a mere expression of prejudiced opinion, but if so I, nevertheless, enjoy the support of every intelligent foreign musician I have ever met. With regard to the final passage in Mr. Bax's above-quoted stricture, I must even confess to having uneasy qualms of conscience since, in my book on *Peter Warlock*, I sought to establish the proposition which, I am now compelled to admit, he justly derides, namely, that the material size of a work of art bears no relation to its intrinsic value, and that a small good work is equal in merit to a good large one. But this was a piece of special pleading on my part, in an attempt to show that Peter Warlock's exquisitely achieved miniatures were of more value than the grandiose failures of most of his rivals—a proposition that I still believe to be true. A good small work will always be better than a large bad one; but everything else being equal, the question of size is one of positive importance. The fineness of Peter Warlock's achievement is indeed typically English; he was a superb miniaturist, like his Elizabethan forbears and like most great English artists in other spheres. He realized and accepted the fact of his incapacity to create in the larger forms, and thereby accomplished more work of lasting value than his more ambitious colleagues and rivals were able to do.

Clifford Bax is absolutely right. A complete anæsthesia to formal considerations is the most conspicuous common factor exhibited by English artists in every age and in every medium, and one which is shared by the public for which they create. The greatest of all English artists, possibly the greatest poet and dramatist who has ever lived, is so completely lacking in any sense of form and design that one cannot even say that it is a defect: Shakespeare just blandly ignored all formal considerations whatsoever, and all the problems thereby involved. They simply did not exist for him, and in that fact lies his very greatness and the greatness of many other English artists.

This Anglican indifference to form, in fact, is a positive quality in the hands of a master—it is perhaps the supremest manifestation of genius, this capacity to dispense with form, and simply to move as the spirit moves one, without preconceived destination or *arrière pensée*, living from moment to moment and trusting in a Divine providence, a *deus ex machina*, to bring things to a satisfying conclusion. And it may well be a weakness in the Latin artist that he is too concerned with formal considerations at the expense of other qualities which are possibly more valuable.

The truth probably consists in this: that the very greatest can afford to ignore the principles of formal organization, but in those of lesser stature it is a grave fault. Hence one finds that in English art, as on the English railways (except, significantly, on the Continental routes), there are only two classes—first and third. The great Latin artists tend to travel second class, but how many of them there are in comparison with the few stray, sparse, isolated, unique first-class travellers on the English line!

In short, the English probably possess all the qualities which go to make great art—imagination, power, subtlety, grace, comprehension, style, the gift of laughter and of tears—all save only one: the gift for structural organization and formal perfection.

This characteristic is, moreover, observable in other walks of life. The English genius in all directions consists primarily in the capacity for rapid and imaginative improvization. The very British Empire itself has no recognizable shape or form or Constitution. It simply grew spontaneously, miraculously, and, to the amazement of onlookers, still continues to exist—a unique political institution. Again, compare London with any other capital city in the world. It is utterly shapeless and amorphous, lacking in even the most elementary factors of design—a vital organic growth and nothing more. But in this consists its greatness, its character. If London ever falls into the itching hands of town-planners—which God forbid!—she will lose her soul, her personality. One would not have her other than she is.

Compare London, however, with my native city—Edinburgh, and you will appreciate the fundamental difference between the English character and the Scottish more clearly than in any other way: the one a formless, haphazard conglomeration of inconsistent and contradictory elements, the other the most grandly and logically planned, the most formally perfect city of modern times, with the sole possible exception of Paris; like a symphony or a fugue. In the one, narrow, congested, crooked, winding streets lead in every conceivable direction, save in that of a straight line towards their logical destinations; in the other, broad, majestic, symmetrical thoroughfares pursue a pre-ordained purpose, fulfil a preconceived design, and achieve a perfect, harmonious form. And it is significant to note that where London attempts to belie her nature and to emulate alien models, as in such abortions as Oxford Street, Kingsway and the Strand, she contradicts her innermost nature.

This characteristically Palladian, classic sense of form which one encounters in the Scottish capital, and which is reflected in the national temperament, is primarily, as I have suggested, the outcome of the Old Alliance between Scotland and France, aptly symbolized by the coat-of-arms over the inner gate of Edinburgh Castle, in which the Scottish Lion is sculptured, surrounded by *fleurs de lys*. But there is another side to the national character—equally strong, even possibly stronger— that which is represented by the Old Town, with its precipitous, melodramatic sky-scrapers and picturesque "closes"; but this side, again, is at the opposite pole to the Anglo-Saxon,

Teutonic, or Scandinavian traditions, and is also in spirit Latin, but Italian here rather than French: with the same crude violence and emotional intensity that one finds in early Verdi, or in Donizetti.

I like to think, incidentally, that the legend which ascribes a Scottish ancestry to Donizetti is based upon fact, and that a kind of racial atavism impelled him to the choice of *Lucia di Lammermoor* as the subject of one of his greatest works. However that may be, I have never anywhere encountered anything resembling mediaeval Edinburgh outside Italy. The spirit is recognizably the same.

The Scots, indeed, to sum up, are singularly un-Nordic in their intellectual and æsthetic synthesis, combining the instinct for logic, clarity, and precision of form, derived from French plastic art and literature on the one hand, with the emotional intensity of Italian music on the other. In fact, it would be difficult to find a more complete antithesis than is afforded by a comparison of the English and the Scottish races. They could not be more foreign to each other if they existed at the opposite ends of the globe, instead of being close neighbours; and the age-long conflict between the two countries was not primarily or basically political, but devolved from a psychological and temperamental incompatibility.

And so it is with me. I have absolutely nothing in common with the English character or temperament; and the two poles or extremes between which my personality oscillates are the strongly formal and the violently emotional, both of them basically Latin—French and Italian respectively, by affinity. In a word, I am Celt and Latin.

In other important respects, both in qualities and failings, I am typical of my race. My mental processes are, as a rule, phenomenally slow and laborious, cautious and far-seeing. Physiologically myopic and be-spectacled, I am psychologically long-sighted. In all I do, whether in writing or composing, I see the end in the beginning, the beginning in the end (like Mary, Queen of Scots, though I always forget which way she put it—but they both amount to the same thing). Spontaneity and improvisation are sadly foreign to me in any shape or form. I have to think things out a long way ahead. If I am given sufficient time I generally get them right. If I have to act on the spur of the moment and make rapid decisions, I am nearly always wrong.

Norman Douglas, in *South Wind*, writes of his character Keith—a portrait which, incidentally, is perhaps something of a self-portrait:—

> "Keith could be decidedly fatiguing, especially when dead sober. He had all the Scotchman's passion for dissecting the obvious, discovering new facets in the commonplace, and squeezing the last drop out of a foregone conclusion."

It is this racial characteristic which is largely responsible for the intensive cult for the philosophy of Hegel in the Northern Kingdom, with his inveterate propensity for pursuing an idea remorselessly and relentlessly throughout all possible metamorphoses, ramifications and permutations; and I freely confess to sharing in the national vices so ruthlessly exposed by Norman Douglas. Once my teeth are firmly fixed in an idea I cannot let go of it until I have extracted from it the uttermost final potentialities.

This, of course, is a form of Scottish parsimony. A poor people, living on barren soil, in a vile climate, cannot afford to be prodigal, and no doubt my regrettable tendency to squeeze the last drop out of my ideas is due to poverty of invention and the necessity of making the most of what little goods I possess. And I am by no means immune from the perverse national weakness for Hegel. Indeed, his doctrine, or theory, of the triune principle of thesis, antithesis and synthesis, has always exercised a profound influence upon me, even before I ever became acquainted with it. The formula of stating a theme A, then another B, and then combining them into A + B, had always been the keystone of my mental processes and technique long before I ever heard the name of Hegel.

Incidentally, it is always a danger signal in the eyes of my long-suffering friends when, towards the early hours of the morning, I begin to expatiate upon the Hegelian doctrine of thesis, antithesis and synthesis. Another one is the equally regrettable propensity of intoning Jacobite songs on similar occasions. But I have said above that the national temperament inclines to oscillate between the two extremes of rigid formalism and violent emotionalism, and in such deplorable behaviour I am merely functioning as a microcosm of my race and nation.

Since we are on the subject this would seem to be an appropriate moment at which to state the fact that, like most of my fellow-countrymen, I am fervently addicted to alcoholic beverages. I have a natural aversion from beer, the staple drink of the Teutonic races, while gin, the drink of Englishmen, I only tolerate as an alternative preferable to nothing at all. Port, sherry, madeira and such like artificial products, made chiefly for the English market, leave me comparatively cold; but for the product of my native country on the one hand, and the unspoilt vintages of France and Italy, my taste and capacity are infinite. Here again, in fact, we have another example of the Latin-Caledonian polarity of which I have been speaking.

My national addiction to alcohol, incidentally, is intensified by certain personal physiological characteristics. I am tall and proportionately broad, while my heart and pulse beats are ordinarily lethargic and subnormal. In consequence, I only attain to the normal condition enjoyed by the average man after some degree of artificial stimulation, and I can therefore absorb a quite phenomenal amount of alcohol without any result other than a heightened sense of well-being and an enhanced cerebral activity.

I have noticed, in fact, in connexion with this question of alcohol, that people can be divided up into two definite categories; the subnormal type of which I am an example, and the super-normal, with rapid pulse and heart beat, and high blood pressure. These latter, so far from being stimulated by alcohol tend rather under its influence to become obtuse, somnolent and generally ill-tempered, quarrelsome, and objectionable in every way. Such as they, I maintain, should never be allowed to drink at all, or at least only in the strictest moderation. It is they who are, quite literally "the worse for drink", even when strictly sober. I, and those like me, are always the better for drink, even when not strictly sober.

To sum up and recapitulate: in my work I am a typical Scot in the combination of a vein of emotional intensity with the restraining influence of strict formal discipline. I am, in fact, completely helpless and adrift without a strong frame within which I can contain myself, and it is the very violence and intensity of the emotional content which necessitates a precise formal mould without which, indeed, it would degenerate into mere distasteful incoherence. The Scot without discipline is perhaps the most objectionable specimen on the face of the earth. This is perhaps the explanation and justification of the hold which Calvinism has upon my unfortunate country (in itself, abstractly considered, the most monstrous creed ever formulated by the mind of man), namely, that no doubt it provides a rein and bridle better fitted to curb the turbulent spirit of the race than the comparatively wise and gentle humanism of the Roman Catholic Church, or that of the *Via Media*, the English way.

Similarly, in the field of art, the imperative need for some strict formal discipline accounts for the attraction and influence of Latin, and particularly French, art. Actually, my closest spiritual affinities are with literary rather than musical Latins, such as Flaubert and Baudelaire, in whom intense romantic emotion is embodied in classical forms—the romantic spirit in the classical body, that is the centre of the target at which I aim my arrows of desire. But of all artists who have ever lived it is Dante Alighieri who best exemplifies *in excelsis* all the aspirations and potentialities which I exhibit *in infimis:* with his glorious device of the *terza rima*, the virtue of which consists in the way in which the first line of a *canto* is indissolubly welded to the last, as in a steel chain. And the form of art to which I am least drawn temperamentally is English art, especially as exemplified in such typical artists as Thomas Hardy and Vaughan Williams. I can generally, with a painful effort, succeed in appreciating its qualities objectively. For example, I am perfectly conscious of the element of real greatness in the latter, which distinguishes him from many of his contemporary compatriots—I am well aware of the difference between V.W. and X.Y.Z. But in the case of Thomas Hardy I confess myself baffled, completely at a loss to account for the veneration with which he is regarded in his native land. It is one of my blind spots, I suppose; but I am consoled by the reflection that it is one which I seem to share with writers and readers of every country in the world except England. But as for England herself, I hasten to add, there is no other country in the world in which I prefer to live, and I like her people very much more than I like my compatriots. In nothing am I more typically Scottish.

It only remains to mention in this connexion a more positive aspect of nationalism which has exercised a decisive influence upon me. I have already said that up to my seventeenth year or thereabouts I actively detested every manifestation of conventional Scottish nationalism as exemplified particularly in the cult for Robert Burns, who has always been, and still is, one of my *bêtes noires*. But when I first came across a collection of the *Songs of the Hebrides*, made by Marjory Kennedy Fraser, I experienced an emotion which I can only describe as a "revelation". No music I had ever heard before—with one solitary exception which will be referred to later—had ever made such a deep emotional appeal to me: and this in spite of the deplorably amateurish and inadequate piano accompaniments unnecessarily provided by the editor and collector.

With all the crudity of their presentation and, as I have been told by subsequent students, the highly suspect accuracy of their notation, these songs probably constitute the most important single musical influence in my life, and I owe it to Mrs. Kennedy Fraser. I have noticed that whenever my Pegasus—or Rosinante—sniffs the air, paws the ground, and kicks up his heels, the characteristic whinny he emits is unmistakably that of the *Songs of the Hebrides*.

I do not know the islands well; indeed, I have only visited the inner fringes—Skye, Mull, Staffa, Iona; but that is enough, and more than enough. To tell the truth, I am afraid to venture further for fear that I should never return: that once I had entered into that magic circle I should not be able to escape from the enchantment, a kind of *envoûtement*, which emanates from that mysterious region, as in a story of Arthur Machen or Algernon Blackwood, and most powerfully operates in these songs.

There is, indeed, something about the Hebrides, the Western Isles, that has a quite uncanny and inexplicable appeal to the Scot, and to none more than to me. I have lived most of my life in England and I have travelled far and wide, but the islands are always present in the background of my consciousness.

> From the lone sheiling in the misty island
> Mountains divide us, and a waste of seas;
> But still the blood is strong, the heart is Highland,
> And we in dreams behold the Hebrides.

And so in the world of art; however far afield I travel, whether I am in the desert with Saint Anthony, or on the ruined battlements of the city of Troy, the songs of my native land break through and impose themselves upon me, in spite of myself, against my will.

Chapter Three

SO MUCH for the racial, national, and regional aspects of my gradually emergent personality. It remains to attempt some analysis of such hereditary predispositions and characteristics as may have played some part in its formation.

In most of the crucial issues of life I am resolutely opposed to the dreary *cliché* to the effect that "the truth, as usual, lies between the two extremes". I have, on the contrary, generally found that the truth lies not at the central point between two opposite poles, but at both simultaneously; not in the reconciliation of opposites, but in their antithesis and combination: in the juxtaposition and clash of black and white rather than in their coalescence into a neutral grey: in the struggle between two antagonistic principles or truths rather than in the *via media* which lies between them.

But in the matter of the relation between free-will and predestination, in the question of the extent to which one is the passive and helpless outcome of pre-natal influences latent in the germ plasms and hormones of innumerable generations of ancestors, and to what extent one is a free individual personality, and master of one's fate and soul—in that one matter, in that crucial issue, I am reluctantly forced into an acceptance of the *via media*, the point between two extremes. It seems impossible to deny that one is to a great extent inevitably conditioned by one's ancestry, one's inherited characteristics; but to admit that one was entirely so conditioned, and incapable of any independent action or thought, would amount to a denial of one's individuality which would make life intolerable to any thinking or sentient person.

The problem of free-will *versus* predestination, which is the central issue of all theology and philosophy, is not one which has ever been satisfactorily apprehended or resolved in the medium of words. Just as Albert Schweitzer, himself a theologian, has so admirably observed in his monumental study of Bach, that "the doctrine of the Trinity can be expressed much more clearly and satisfactorily in music than in verbal *formulæ*", so the ultimate comprehension, or rather intuition, of the solution of this most baffling of all metaphysical problems can be more readily approached through the medium of music than of words.

A Bach fugue is the symbolic embodiment of the principle of predestination. Everything in it is latent, pre-ordained; nothing happens, or can happen, that is not contained in embryo within the theme, as the oak is contained in the acorn.

Beethoven, on the other hand, exemplifies the opposite principle of free-will. He is master of his fate, the captain of his soul. There is no element in his work of divine inevitability. The whole plot can be reversed at a moment's notice, and frequently is, as the outcome of pure wilfulness or caprice. The element of the unexpected is paramount. Anything can, and generally does, happen with him.

Bach, in fact, represents the element of fate, the divine, the pre-ordained; Beethoven is Promethean man, the rebel. The reconciliation of the two opposing principles is to be found in the music of Mozart, the mediator between God and Man, half deity, half human. In his work one finds the combination of absolute inevitability, together with unfettered freedom. The developments of the thought seem to be divinely pre-ordained, yet are continually subject to the intervention of the element of the unexpected, the incalculable. In the music of Mozart, in fact, the conflicting principles of free-will and predestination are reconciled and resolved into a harmonious unity as in no philosophic system that has ever been formulated.

And so it is with each individual. The pre-ordained hereditary element in each of us may amount to fifty per cent., possibly to ninety per cent., perhaps even to ninety-nine, but never to a hundred. There always remains the incalculable element, however small, which is nevertheless all-important— the leaven which transmutes the entire inert mass of inherited characteristics: the element of pure, intrinsic personality which makes every human being, every leaf on a tree even, different from every other, and owes nothing to any parents or ancestors, near or remote, or to any combination of external circumstances . . .

On the paternal side of my ancestry I come of middle-class stock, industrious tillers of the soil, well-to-do, reasonably prosperous farmers, with nothing particular to commend them so far as I can discover—with one exception, and that only a remote forbear: namely, one Henry Bell (1767–1830), a notable engineer and one of the pioneers of steam navigation. Born in Linlithgow, where his father was a millwright, he later worked in an engineering firm in London, and later in Glasgow, where he studied mechanics. In 1812, a small vessel, forty feet long, built under his direction and with an engine constructed by himself, was launched on the Clyde, being the first steam vessel in Europe.

It is a curious coincidence that on this side of my family tree the only noteworthy ancestor was an engineer who was the son of a miller, for on the other side, my mother's, the family name was Miller and most members of it were, and are, engineers. I believe, in fact, that the circumstance is more than a coincidence, for long before I became aware of the ancestral origins of Henry Bell, and without attaching any importance to the maternal surname, I had always cherished a deep, passionate, romantic attachment to mills, and especially windmills; to such an extent, indeed, that when, in February, 1938, I was lying in bed one morning reading the daily newspaper and came across an announcement to the effect that an old windmill in Sussex was for sale, I leapt forth from my bed like a sword from its scabbard and, without even pausing to shave, dressed, went down to see it by the first train available and bought it straightway. I still possess it, and indeed these very lines are written there, in an octagonal room looking out over Chanctonbury Ring on the South Downs.

But whether this love of mills is due to some kind of atavism or merely to coincidence, there can be no doubt, and no question of coincidence, where the engineering propensities of my ancestry are concerned, and their strong influence upon me. In my incessant preoccupation with problems of design and construction, of stress, balance, equipoise, and stability, I clearly discern and acknowledge myself to be the descendant of a line of engineers. And, as in the matter of nationality, I am neither proud nor ashamed of the fact: it is equally a source of strength and weakness, responsible for most of my virtues and most of my defects.

The two things, of course, always go together. In any artist, in any human personality whatsoever, virtues and shortcomings are indissolubly inter-connected and inseparable—a truism or platitude which is nevertheless the basis of all sound criticism, but cannot be too often reiterated, since it is so frequently disregarded in practice, even by masters of that difficult art. No artist, however great, is without his faults, and the greater his qualities the greater his corresponding faults will inevitably be. Nothing is easier than to achieve a plausible demolition of the greatest genius; you have merely to dwell on the defects and ignore the virtues in order to establish an irrefutable case, and the major part of what passes for criticism to-day, or yesterday, or any other day, has no other basis.

The artist, moreover, is generally as well aware of his short-comings as any critic, and probably better. He will not always admit them—that is another matter. But if he is wise he accepts their inevitable existence philosophically. If he tries to avoid or eliminate his congenital shortcomings in response to soundly based criticism, whether of others or of himself, he can only achieve it by eliminating his virtues as well: by ceasing to be himself, in fact, through a kind of self-castration.

So far as I personally am concerned, no one could be more

keenly aware of his deficiencies and shortcomings; indeed, I have always suffered from a too severe sense of self-criticism, which has frequently hamstrung my creative faculties, especially in the early years of my development. It is only recently that I have come to accept the inevitability and inescapability of my faults, and there is no critic who can tell me more disagreeable truths about myself than I can. I believe this to be true of most artists, if they are honest with themselves, and I think most artists of any real talent are. They could not be good artists if they were not, for the capacity for self-criticism is one of the most important factors in creation. To expect him to be honest in confessing his failings to the world is perhaps expecting too much, but I am perfectly prepared to do so if only because the world will inevitably detect them, sooner or later, with or without my assistance. So why not admit to them and have done?

With regard to this matter of self-criticism, incidentally, I used to subscribe unthinkingly to the dictum that the artist is the last person in the world to be able to judge his work objectively. I no longer believe this to be true, and now resolutely maintain that the artist's best critic is himself, *always provided*, as I have said, *that he is honest with himself*. After all, he alone knows what he is trying to do—what he set out to do; and no one else, ultimately, can know whether he has succeeded or not. I am not suggesting that his critical sense is infallible, that he is always right. I only suggest that he is more likely to be right than anyone else, *provided that he is honest with himself*. The Greeks said that to know oneself (γνωθι σεαυτον) was the foundation of all wisdom, and they were right; they were also right in suggesting that it is exceedingly difficult to achieve, and that few succeed. But it is easier to know oneself than to know someone else, and I believe myself to be a better critic of my own work than I could be of anyone else's, or than anyone else could be of it.

The truth of the matter would seem to be this. In the process of creation the critical sense is involved from first to last, and only in so far as it has been actively functioning will the product be worth consideration at all. After a work is completed, the critical function is in entire abeyance, and one has no sense of values whatsoever. Just as the recently delivered mother may regard her offspring with utter aversion or infatuation, without good reason for either, so the artist, after the completion of a work, will be entirely unreliable and capricious in his reactions towards it for some time to come. But after a certain period—difficult to specify and varying with different individuals—there comes a time, I maintain, when one is able to judge it objectively and calmly. Some artists, I admit, never seem to arrive at this tertiary stage, and remain forever infatuated with their creations, but they are a minority and are almost invariably mediocrities.

To clinch the matter: an artist may well be wrong in his estimate of the value of his own work, but are critics always right? Are they not, indeed, more often wrong than right; and is the artist not, on the whole, more often right than wrong— *always provided that he is honest with himself?*

Dr. Vaughan Williams very shrewdly placed his finger on the point which is at once the source of my greatest strength and my greatest weakness, the central point and *solar plexus* of my music, when, on the occasion of the performance of my *Women of Troy* he observed, after some kind words of appreciation: "You never attempt anything that you cannot achieve." This is absolutely and entirely true, as much an adverse criticism as a compliment. In other words, I am usually afraid to take risks, to take a chance—in my work, that is: life is a different matter. I tend to play for safety, in fact, and I attribute this characteristic firstly, to the proverbial native caution and canniness of the Scot, but even more to that of the descendant of a race of engineers. I build a work with infinite care and circumspection, as my ancestors would have built a bridge or a mountain railway. Everything has to be carefully planned beforehand, nothing left to chance, as if human lives depended on it. Every bolt and every rivet must be tested and found to be secure: if a flaw is even suspected anywhere, out it must come: if the structure seems insecure here or there, another counterpoint must be thrown in to strengthen it, and so forth.

I only first became consciously aware of this occupational characteristic, racial and ancestral, when I was in Brazil some ten years ago and travelled on the railway which winds its way from the swampy plain of Santos right up to San Paulo in the mountains—surely one of the most majestic and impressive feats of engineering in the world. I was as thrilled by it as by the *Art of Fugue* of Bach or the *Divina Commedia* of Dante. I was at the time engaged in contemplating the construction of my *Temptation of Saint Anthony*, and I felt myself to be in the presence of a kindred spirit. I do not doubt that the engineer who built it was a Scot. I should be surprised to learn that he was not, although I have never tried to discover his name or racial origin.

In short, to sum up my national, regional and ancestral derivations, I am compelled to face the somewhat unpalatable conclusion that I am possibly only a Scottish engineer who has taken the wrong turning—a Kipling MacAndrew who occupies himself with music instead of machinery; and I hasten to announce the possibility before my critics and enemies discover the facts for themselves, thus taking the wind out of their sails. But if I thus willingly reveal the source from which my most characteristic faults spring, I ask in return that it should be recognized also to be the source of whatever good qualities I may possess—the power of construction on a large scale, the ability to carry out a monumental conception with dogged tenacity over a long period of time.

When I had occasion, recently, to revisit the iron-foundry in Edinburgh from which I chiefly derive the modest financial resources which have so far enabled me to write music without the disagreeable concomitant of starvation, I was strangely moved at meeting and shaking hands with many of the tough, loyal old veterans who had worked there since I was a small boy, and to whose exertions I owe the fortunate circumstances under which I have been able to do what I have done—little though that may be. But I like to think that they would be the first to recognize and acknowledge a tenacity of purpose and a solidity of workmanship not altogether unworthy of their own; that if I have taken the fruits of their labour I have, in my different way, given back at least as much as I have taken—that I have, in a word, justified my existence. At least I can honestly say that I have a clear conscience in this respect.

If the debt I owe to the maternal side of my ancestry is large, both material and spiritual, that which I owe to the paternal side is in both respects non-existent, so far as I can discover. Apart from the remote Henry Bell, in fact, there is no trace whatever of any possible hereditary influences on the Gray side of the family. I have already said that it was, and had been for generations, a race of farmers, and I have never had any feeling for the soil or for any of its aspects—rather a positive and lively distaste.

My father was a typical representative of his line and stock. Apart from the traditional national cult for Robert Burns, which I detested, his sole literary predilections were for Rudyard Kipling and an obscure Australian poet named Lindsay Gordon. The visual arts meant precisely nothing to him, and music he positively disliked—he was, I believe, literally tone-deaf. His interests, apart from farming, lay entirely in outdoor activities, chiefly connected with horses, a species from which I have always had a profound aversion. His chief indoor recreation as a young man, I have been told, was dancing, and I have always refused to dance a step from the earliest years of which I have any recollection, save for one memorable occasion in later life to which allusion will be subsequently made.

It would be difficult, in fact, to find, or to imagine, two human beings more completely contrasted, with less in common, than my father and myself. He was a complete Philistine in all that appertained to art; I cared for nothing but art and detested all that he cared for.

In such an antagonistic relationship there were obviously the seeds of disastrous possibilities. If they did not come to fruition, the credit is entirely due to my father. Apart from his complete indifference to intellectual and artistic pursuits he was by no means a fool, and allowed me to go my own way, more or less, without hindrance or interference. For this I shall always be grateful. He was a man of kindly and tolerant disposition, constitutionally incapable of a mean or ignoble action, and unfortunately one only realizes the rarity of such a nature in maturity, and in my case too late, to show my appreciation of it, for he died while I was in my early twenties. He was not only a good man, but a gentle man, which is something more than a gentleman, though he was that as well.

We only once had a serious quarrel: it was during the War (1914–18) and he was fulminating against the entire German race, as was the habit of the time and the custom of the country, declaring that all German males should be castrated, all German women sterilized, and all German children exterminated. I mildly protested, saying that I had found Germans to be no worse and no better than any other race on the face of the earth; whereupon he retorted that he hoped to live to see the day when I should be put up against a wall and shot. He did not mean a word of it, really; as I have said, he was in practice the gentlest and kindliest of men and incapable of hurting a fly. (Shooting game is, of course, a sport, and therefore exempt from stricture according to the code of ethics promulgated by The Race.) Such utterances were merely an unthinking automatic regurgitation of articles he had been reading in the papers and I readily forgave him, with the magnanimity of youth. But the trouble is that since then I have sometimes wondered uneasily whether perhaps he had not been right in his suggested solution of our problems . . .

The whole race of Grays, I have said, were complete Philistines, so far as I can ascertain, with, however, one notable exception; but he was clearly in the nature of what biologists call a "sport"—an eccentric and unaccountable phenomenon. This was Stewart Gray, a cousin who, incidentally, was best man at the wedding of my father and mother.

In early life he was a respectable and prosperous solicitor, practising in Edinburgh, with a wife and family. As years went on, however, he began to grow restive and to show unmistakable signs of eccentricity. It seems that he had been studying the works of Marx and Engels, and had become convinced of the validity of their premises. Since it must be difficult, if not impossible, for a sincere and honest man to continue in the practice of the legal profession once he has come to question the very foundations of the social structure on which the law is based, and which it is intended to buttress and protect, Stewart decided to make a complete break.

The final *dénouement* of the situation, so far as I can discover, must have been of the kind described by G. K. Chesterton in *The Club of Queer Trades*, in which a judge, similarly disillusioned with his calling, broke off suddenly in the middle of a case he was trying and, to the scandal of the court, burst forth into a ribald ditty ending with the refrain:

"Rowty owty, tiddledy owty,
Tiddledy owty ow,"

and then, after bowing to the court, retired into private life.

The exact details are unknown, and at this distance of time are likely to remain so, but some such indecorous scandal undoubtedly occurred in connexion with the abrupt termination of Stewart's legal career, whereupon he deserted his wife and family, and all his worldly goods and possessions, in the manner of Gauguin, and became a social outcast, rebel and political agitator. He travelled about the country, living from hand to mouth, preaching the gospel of a heaven upon earth; and during a period of severe unemployment—it must have been about 1908 or 1909—he organized and set himself at the head of a movement called "The Hunger Marchers", a large body of unemployed, assembled from all parts of the country, whom he led in a pilgrimage on foot to Westminster in order to present their demands to Parliament. After that he became a regular speaker at Marble Arch and in Trafalgar Square, where his picturesque personality and appearance (he looked like a Hebrew prophet, with long beard, hair flowing over his shoulders, and blazing eyes) and his impassioned eloquence, attracted huge crowds and aroused enormous enthusiasm.

At the same time, it is interesting to note that his knowledge of the law was not entirely unemployed. I am not acquainted with the legal technicalities involved, but I understand that, roughly speaking, if the leasehold or tenancy of a building has come to within a few years of its expiry, and the premises remain unoccupied, anyone who is aware of the circumstances can take possession without paying rent and without the possibility of eviction. Anyhow, whatever the actual legal facts may be, Stewart discovered some such house near Regent's Park lying empty in a state of dilapidation, with only a short term to run, and promptly installed himself. There was no water, no heating, no light, no furniture—nothing but the roof and four walls; but it nevertheless became a place of shelter to a whole army of outcasts, unemployed, beggars, thieves, drunks, prostitutes, and penurious artists, to the scandalized fury and resentment of the ultra-respectable neighbourhood. Every effort was made to obtain a summons and have Stewart ejected, but the shrewd erstwhile solicitor knew his law and all efforts were unavailing.

One evening, in this strange establishment, a starving Lascar, in search of something to eat, discovered in one of the cupboards an ancient kipper, which the other inmates, even in the extremity of hunger, had not had the courage to confront, preferring the alternative of death by starvation. But the Lascar was made of sterner stuff, or was unable to resist the temptation, and he ate the kipper, dying the next day of acute ptomaine poisoning. During the following night the ghost of the Lascar presented itself with such vividness to Stewart that, unable to sleep, he felt himself irresistibly impelled to record his vision. He wrenched a wooden panel from one of the doors, made a weird concoction of colours from any and every ingredient he could find in the place and, with the aid of a toothbrush, set to work in a frenzy of inspiration. He had never painted, or even drawn before, but I am told there was an uncanny power in the result, and from that time onward he devoted most of his time to painting, resorting only to public oratory as a means of earning the few shillings a week he needed for bare subsistence—which was all that he asked from life.

After the lease of the Regent's Park house had definitely expired, Stewart led a nomad existence. He was a genuine Communist, not merely in theory, which is easy, but in practice also, which is exceedingly difficult; and according to the strict letter and not only the spirit, which is more difficult still. As he preached so he practised. He would share his last shilling with anyone, and expected everyone to do the same in return. He had no sense of property at all. Whatever he had was yours, with the perfectly reasonable and natural corollary that whatever you had was his; and when I first settled in London in 1916 and had the intention of seeking out the one member of my family for whom I felt an instinctive sympathy, I was warned by all who knew him, with a convincing unanimity born of bitter experience, never to invite Stewart to come and stay with me. Once established anywhere it was impossible to get rid of him. He would simply stay on indefinitely until, with infinite pain and sorrow—for everybody loved him—one had to eject him either by force or through invoking the aid of the police, if you wanted to have a life of your own. He didn't want a life of his own, and could not understand why anyone else should. He was, in fact, one of Nature's Communists—perhaps the only one who has ever lived.

His relations with the police, however, were not always hostile. A friend of mine, who had once hospitably accommodated Stewart for some time, was surprised and alarmed on one occasion when, returning home late one night, he discovered Stewart blissfully asleep in bed with a woman locked in his arms, while, hanging on a peg near by, was a police-woman's helmet . . .

I never saw any of his pictures and I do not know what has become of them since his death; but I do know that at some time in the 'twenties he held an exhibition of his works in a studio in Fitzroy Street, and that Augustus John wrote a few kindly words of introduction in the catalogue. My illustrious friend has since denied that he ever did such a thing, but he must have forgotten because I could not possibly have invented or imagined it. Stewart and he were very well acquainted and when Stewart died, about ten years ago, he bequeathed to the latter his entire worldly goods, which must have been very much like those of the Yonghy-Bonghy-Bo of Edward Lear—"two old chairs and half a candle, one old jug without a handle", contained in a cottage in Canvey Island, where he lived in his last days and which he had decorated with frescoes of his own from top to bottom, as I have been credibly informed. But John tells me that, very negligently, he never troubled to take possession of his legacy and it probably still remains there to this day.

I met the old man on many occasions, but was careful not to enter into close or intimate relations with him. Having a naturally soft heart, I knew only too well that he might easily turn into an Old Man of the Sea with a grip around my neck if I allowed him to establish it, which I would not easily be able to shake off.

Apart from this one phenomenal figure, who certainly in himself more than compensates for the generations of drab and dreary dullards who had begotten him, no ancestors or collaterals on the paternal side of my family tree are to be discovered who display any noteworthy characteristics of any kind, apart from the remote Henry Bell—nothing but an interminable sequence of honest, hardworking, God-fearing farmers, to whom I obviously owe nothing at all, either of worldly or unworldly goods. But before leaving them, it is perhaps of interest to record the fact that my father's sister, aged over eighty-five years, lives, and always has lived, in the same house as that in which she was born—an old farmhouse, named Southfield, in Duddingston, near Edinburgh, which has belonged to the family for generations. I do not doubt that she will complete her century there and long outlive me. Longevity is one of the family failings, which I hope I do not inherit. The average duration of the life of a member of the Gray family is formidable and intimidating, and personally I have a horror of growing old, of the state of decrepitude; and my most sincere and earnest prayer is that I shall be allowed to depart in my prime. For especially have I a fear of madness, which is almost invariably the concomitant of old age, as it is of infancy. All babies are mad, and most old people are mad, according to what we call normal human standards. Maturity, in fact, is only a brief interregnum of sanity between two gulfs of insanity, a precarious balance which even in mature years we preserve with difficulty, and with much swaying backwards and forwards and sideways on the tightrope stretched over the vast abysm of madness. Let me die middle-aged and in full possession of my faculties!

At the same time, I realize that insanity can be an alternative preferable to intolerable suffering—from anguish too great to be borne. I came across an example of this once, about ten years ago, in the village of Calvi in Corsica. I was sitting in the Bar Napoléon one day before lunch, absorbing an *apéritif*, when there entered a woman, aged about thirty, who was obviously a complete lunatic, but so mild and harmless as to be in no need of seclusion or detention. She was given a cup of coffee, after which she departed, laughing and singing, quite happy—but quite mad. After she had left I asked the barman about her and he told me her story. A few years before she had been a young and beautiful woman, happily married to a charming husband, with two adorable children, in prosperous circumstances, without a care in the world. Then Fate, resenting such perfect happiness, struck. First her husband died suddenly; then, one after the other, her children. After a short period of intolerable anguish, she went out of her mind and thereby achieved once more complete peace and serenity. All her unhappiness was mercifully blotted out: she remembered nothing. Was she to be pitied or envied? I only know that personally I would prefer an infinity of pain and torment. But she is the only happy lunatic I have ever known: the others have generally suffered from acute and even suicidal depression.

I speak feelingly on the subject since, in addition to the natural deep-seated repugnance which most people feel towards insanity, I have seen too much of it at close quarters. Both my father and grandfather lapsed into a state of senility or second childhood in their last days, and an uncle of mine to whom I was greatly attached and to whom I owed much, died insane, of melancholia. I shall have occasion to refer to him in the next chapter, but I should like to make it clear that there is no question of hereditary insanity in the family. If I should chance to become what is elegantly termed "cuckoo", it will be my own doing, not that of my ancestors, who seem all to have been all too sane, until old age.

Chapter Four

WHEN Frederick Delius was lying, paralyzed and blind, in his house at Grez-sur-Loing in the last years of his life, I visited him on several occasions; and on one of them he asked me to send him, on my return to England, as many congenial books as I could find, since his sole consolation in the terrible afflictions which had descended upon him was that of being read aloud to for hours on end, and he was always at a loss for enough material to keep pace with the rate of consumption.

I naturally promised to do everything possible and asked him to specify the particular kind of book he preferred above all others. He replied, with his inimitable accent which can only be faintly and approximately described as a broad Yorkshire dialect spoken by a Chinaman who had spent a short course of study at Heidelberg and the Sorbonne: "Me dear feller, I can't tell ye any parteecular kind of book I like; but I can tell ye the kind I don't like. I can read almost anythin' and everythin', but for Heaven's sake don't send me the sort of book which begins with the hero lyin' on his back in his leetle cot, lookin' up at a spot on the ceilin'."

I wholeheartedly share this aversion, and shall therefore mercifully spare my readers the infliction entailed by the reminiscences of my earliest years. Apart from anything else, it would bore me to recount them as much as it would bore them to read. But as it happens, I have singularly few early recollections to record. I have been told that both my mother and myself underwent an appalling ordeal on the occasion of my entrance into the world, and that it was highly problematic whether either of us would survive. Both of us did, but only just, and it is more than likely that this initial struggle to exist left an indelible impression upon me. At any rate, I would seem to have passed the first six or seven years of my life in a kind of prolonged marsupial coma, a post-natal trance of utter exhaustion, from which I only spasmodically awakened as the result of some painful or disagreeable experience. My earliest memory is of an occasion on which I nearly returned to the void from which I had so recently emerged, when I was apparently found toying affectionately with an adder, and my father fortunately came along at the crucial moment and dispatched the reptile. My next recollection is of an occasion when a covey of partridges was being driven in the vicinity of the house, and an enthusiastic, but over-temperamental gunman, intent upon his prey, discharged a volley of shot through the window just past my innocent head while I was sitting at luncheon. My next clear recollection is that of being stung by a wasp. When I add to this sombre narrative the fact that my sleeping hours were distracted by the most abominable nightmares that can ever have troubled a child, the vivid memory of which afflicts me even to this day, in fear of which I would fight against the onset of sleep as if it were the devil, and on emerging from which I suffered from what is, I believe, called "telescopic vision"—the eerie sensation of seeing everything as if from a great distance through the wrong end of an opera-glass—from all this it will be seen that my earliest years were not exactly the happiest of my life: an impression which is amply confirmed by the few photographic reproductions of my diminutive person which have survived, portraying me looking at the world with an expression of mingled apprehension and defiance.

This concatenation of unpleasant recollections, which is practically all that I retain in my memory from early childhood, is perhaps responsible for my somewhat jaundiced and pessimistic attitude towards life, of which my few surviving friends are wont to complain.

While we are dealing with and disposing of this morbid topic of early childhood, it might be as well to ventilate the stuffy cupboard in which the most formidable psychological skeleton of my youth lies concealed, and to exorcize it once and for all.

My parents, at the time of my birth, were on terms of close friendship with an old, rich bachelor without any near heirs. With the only too obvious and blatant intention of diverting his money-bags to themselves on his imminent decease—for he was very old and frail—they had me christened with his preposterous and ludicrous name, as a carefully directed compliment. Alas! as so often in life, the Machiavellian scheme failed to materialize. When he died he left his entire fortune to some charitable institution or other, if I remember rightly, leaving to my parents precisely nothing at all, but to me his grotesque name, which I have been compelled to drag behind me through life—Cecil *William Turpie* Gray. Although I have entirely dispensed with it in the affairs of normal life, I always have been, and still am, compelled to inscribe it in legal documents concerned with such trivial occurrences as birth, marriage, and death, and on passports. It has always weighed upon my subconscious mind, but by here revealing my shameful secret I hope successfully to dispose of the melancholy inhibition.

It is not easy. There is no escaping the fact that names are very important, and the psychological effect that they can exercise, both upon the recipient and on the outer world, can be of primary importance. Parents cannot be too careful in the choice of names for their offspring, whose lives can be made or marred by it. Readers may, for example, remember the sad case of the unfortunate man, some years ago, whose life was made unendurable through the possession of the name of Jolly Death—people would keep ringing him up at all hours of the day and night in order to make facetious observations. It actually killed him, I have been told. And I also recall the case of the man—he is probably still alive—who, in addition to the initial misfortune of inheriting the surname of Shufflebottom, was further victimized through being given by his unkind parents the Christian name of Mozart.

It is true, of course, that a grotesque name can on occasion be a positive asset, but very rarely. It is more than probable, for example, that the gifted humorous writer, Nathaniel Gubbins, owes something of his reputation and success to his odd name; but it is not everyone who wishes to, or could be, a professional humorist. With all the talent in the world I doubt if he could have succeeded in having himself accepted by the world as a writer of poetic tragedies. Even more operative would be the subjective psychological conviction of the formidable handicap entailed in the attempt. Simply to change one's name is not enough: it is a kind of forgery, which when found out, as it always is, can act like a boomerang. When it was learnt that Gabriele d'Annunzio, Principe di Montenevoso —"Gabriel of the Annunciation, Prince of the Snowy Mountain" was born Giuseppe Rapagnetta, the resultant damage to his poetic equipment was greater than if he had remained as he had been christened. And the same holds good of the Levantine, Dikran Kouyoumdjian, who became the glamorous English Michael Arlen.

Still, it is perhaps the final proof of merit to be able to rise superior to such a formidable handicap as an absurd name. Shelley was not diminished by Bysshe; I can only hope that Gray will not be diminished by Turpie, although, God knows, and I know, too, I am no Shelley. On the other hand, I enjoy considerable compensations in my appropriate Christian name. Saint Cecilia is the patron saint not only of music, but of the blind; and though I may be only half a musician, I am at least more than half blind.

In turning from these painful aspects of my early life I now come to the most pleasant and actively formative—and once more associated with a ridiculous and risible name. Indeed, if there is in the British Isles a place more calculated than that of Wigan to excite hilarity—and with more reason, because of its more absurd sound—it is Peebles: a music-hall joke, together with mothers-in-law and sausages. Yet this name of a town, and a shire, which occasions such paroxysms of ribald mirth, is associated with the happiest moments of my childhood— probably of my entire life, and arouses in me emotions and sentiments akin to those glamorous associations conjured up in romantic minds by the names of Baghdad, Damascus, Trebizond, Samarkand, or Ispahan; and with better reason probably, for I am told that the reality of these places does not, by any means, correspond with one's idealized poetic concept of them. Once, when young, I met a traveller from an antique land to whom I expressed my nostalgic envy of his privilege in having experienced the beauties of the rose-gardens and the dancing girls of Ispahan; whereupon my interlocutor, somewhat abashed, murmured dubiously: "M'yes . . . but, you see, the trouble is that although the roses of Ispahan are lovely to look at, they have no scent; whereas the dancing girls are ugly and smell like nothing on earth."

Peebles of the silly name does not disenchant like the fabled cities of the Orient, which resound so sonorously throughout the pages of the poets from Keats to Flecker, with their golden roads which lead from silken Samarkand to cedared Lebanon, and so forth and so on; but it has roses which smell and girls who do not—possibly because they do not dance much, if at all—and that there is a connexion between the two phenomena is amply proven to anyone who pays a visit behind the scenes during a ballet performance—a terrifying experience to those whose olfactory organs are in reasonably good working order.

Peebles has magical associations for me, like all that Border country, the place names of which, moreover, are singularly beautiful and evocative (except for Peebles), as much so as those of the Orient, if not more—Melrose, Roxburgh, Selkirk, Kelso, Yarrow, Abbotsford, Galashiels, and the rest: they are a symphony in words, and also as lovely and gracious to the eye as to the ear. Yet all this may to some extent be mere childish fantasy. I have not revisited these enchanted spots since childhood, and now I prefer not to—I should probably be sadly disillusioned. The only point that matters in this connexion is that my childish fantasy created out of these places a glamour and an ecstasy which I have only recaptured since through works of art. In actuality (but what is actuality?) they are probably only dreary little Scottish provincial towns; but to me they were Paradise. What else matters?

A curious and remarkable feature of the psychological associations with this countryside consists in the fact that, looking back on these places and on these times, the predominant impression is one of perpetual sunshine. In my recollection there is not the memory of a single rainy day—nothing but one long, warm, unending summer. Since such a state of affairs is obviously impossible in that sombre Northern land, the climate of which is unanimously recognized to be the vilest in the world and where a fine day, even at the height of summer, is regarded—and rightly—as an event, it follows that this impression must be wholly ascribed to the state of pure, unalloyed bliss which I enjoyed in these halcyon days of my youth. For the first time I was happy from morning to night, and from night to morning, which is perhaps even more important, for it is through the gates of ivory and horn, perhaps, that our deepest impressions in youth are received—in dreams, and in day-dreams. I lived in a dream world, in fact, perpetually, day and night; but not of the nightmares or, to coin a necessary word—the daymares, of my earlier experience.

I came to know this enchanted realm of childish imagination through the circumstance that my uncle (my mother's brother) had a house in Peebles of the absurd name, in which I and my brother used frequently to spend our holidays. Apart from the purely idyllic aspect of childish happiness which I enjoyed on these occasions, it was there that I experienced my first deep and authentic æsthetic emotion. My uncle possessed an odd, primitive example of a species of automatic player-piano, or pianola, on which he was wont to perform in the evening after I had gone to bed. I used to listen with interest, but without being particularly moved by anything, until one night when he was communing with the Angelus, as the instrument was called, there came, in the middle of a piece he was playing, a passage so moving that I was completely and utterly transported; tears poured in torrents down my cheeks and I lay awake half the night sobbing in an ecstasy of joy. From that moment onwards my whole life was changed: it was a revelation. (I suppose I was about seven at the time.)

The next day I naturally enquired of my uncle the identity of the particular piece he had been playing which had so deeply moved me. After search and trial it was duly discovered that the title inscribed on the box in which the record of predilection was contained was the *Overture to Mignon* of Ambroise Thomas. Thereafter I continually importuned him into playing it to me; but eventually it was discovered that, on some occasion or other, the records had been put into the wrong boxes and that the object of my adoration and ecstatic transport was not the *Overture to Mignon* at all, but the Nocturne in G, Op. 37, No. 2, of Chopin.

My first musical experience, then, my initiation into the magic world of art, was due to Chopin. This fact is of more than personal interest, for I have found this phenomenon to be well-nigh universal. As I have written in *The History of Music:*

"It is probably true to say that a larger number of people owe their first authentic musical thrill in early years to him than to any other composer. Question anyone as to the first piece of music which he remembers to have stirred him deeply in childhood or adolescence, and the chances are as much as ten to one that it will turn out to be some piece of Chopin."

This observation, of course, as will have been seen, is up to a point a piece of unconscious autobiography; but it is much more than that. I remember well an occasion at Grez-sur-Loing, with Frederick Delius and Philip Heseltine, when I mentioned this experience, and was interested to learn that the musical awakening of both my friends had been substantially identical; and I have since encountered so many corroborative instances that I am certain that this trilateral experience is due to something more than coincidence.

Chopin, indeed, speaks more clearly and directly, with greater emotional impact, to the young than any other composer; this is his greatest glory, and of all the gifts that can be offered to an artist by God I can think of none greater, none I would sooner choose, than to appeal thus, with such immediacy and urgency, to the innocent, virginal heart of youth.

At the same time, although something of Chopin's unique glamour and enchantment inevitably wanes with the passing of years and the advent of maturity, it is surprising to discover on occasion what an extraordinary tenacity of hold he still has upon one's emotions, and what a power he possesses of transporting one back, even if only for a moment, into the mood of these long-lost paradisal ecstasies of childhood. This particular Nocturne is a case in point. I am bored by the opening section with its trivial, fussy, tripping thirds, and to tell the truth it never meant anything to me: I would always wait impatiently for the slow middle section to begin, with its exquisite haunting *cantabile* melody, which seems as if it never could, and never should, end; and even to-day this lovely tune can still reduce me to tears.

Incidentally, I can never understand why Chopin should be regarded as a Polish composer. His father was a Frenchman; he lived the whole of his actively creative life in France, and the predominant influence on his work is Italian—the influence chiefly of Bellini. The *Polonaises* and *Mazurkas*, which only constitute a small and unimportant part of his output, are the sole works which reveal Slavonic characteristics; for the rest he is predominantly a Latin composer.

I feel very strongly on this point, if only because my deep, instinctive and immediate reaction to Italian music in later life—and to Bellini in particular—is undoubtedly due, in large part, to this early influence of Chopin, who was so deeply indebted to the Italian master. Indeed, the emotion I experienced on first hearing the Chopin Nocturne in early childhood was identically repeated in early manhood when, in the winter of 1919–20, in Palermo, I first heard a work of

Bellini—*La Sonnambula*. I had never previously even so much as looked at a single note of Bellini and had always accepted, unthinkingly and unquestioningly, all the time-honoured *clichés* about Italian music in general and Bellini in particular, which were, and to this day still are, sedulously inculcated into the minds of music students as a result of the contemptuous verdicts passed upon it by Teutonically-biased historians of music and professors of composition.

I went to the theatre, in fact, having nothing better to do, in the expectation of enjoying a hearty laugh, and at first my expectation was not disappointed. It was a second-rate company: both soloists and chorus were mediocre; the orchestra was as poor as only a provincial Italian orchestra can be: the conductor was incompetent, and the scenery and production in general appalling. After a few numbers, however, I gradually lost my superior, condescending smile. I could not quite understand what was happening to me. Occasional passages struck me as being surprisingly fine, and the number of them steadily increased as the work progressed, until with the scene which begins with the words *d'un pensiero* I was completely transported and reduced to the same condition, as I have already said, as that which I had experienced on first hearing the Nocturne of Chopin. It was more than disconcerting to one who, at that time, was chiefly preoccupied with the most audaciously intellectual "modern" and "advanced" music of the period—Schönberg, Stravinsky, and Bartók. Believing that, in part at least, my reaction was due to the super-excellent bottle of Barbera I had previously consumed, I decided, in the interests both of art and science, to repeat the experience, under strictly non-alcoholic conditions—calm, objective, analytical—but the result was identically the same. After this test I could no longer doubt the evidence of my senses and my sense, which alike told me that this was great art of its kind; and I have never changed my opinion since with relation to it, although I have frequently done so in regard to other music.

In this connexion I have always found that for me the authentic, incontrovertible test of a great work of art lies in its capacity to communicate an initial exquisite shudder that runs down one's spine from the nape of the neck to the coccyx, and culminates in the shedding of tears. But so it is in life: the extremities of both joy and sorrow find equally their expression and outlet in tears. Actually, so far as I personally am concerned, I cry more readily from joy than from sorrow. I am not in the least ashamed of this propensity, though it can, on occasion, be embarrassing in public. All our organs have been given to us for a purpose—physical or psychological, or both—and should be exercised, and the lachrymal glands are no exception. They were given to us to cry with, and the evasion of the exercise of their natural and normal function is in its way as deleterious as sexual chastity. Tears are the orgasm of the soul, and he or she who does not have recourse to them on occasion must inevitably develop a state of aridity, atrophy, desiccation, ossification, vitrification, dehydration, of the spirit; and these tight-lipped, cold-hearted, fish-blooded contemporaries of ours who have never shed tears of either joy or sorrow, and boast about it, are only objects for sympathy, commiseration, pity—in fact, for tears. They have never lived intensely, and it were better if they had never been born. Just as chastity is apt to lead to disease of the prostate gland, so the neglect and non-functioning of the tear-ducts leads to a cognate malady of the soul. I think I may say that I am fairly certain never to suffer from either variety of this dismal complaint.

This Chopin-Italian influence which declared itself so early in my life is still as strong to-day as when I first experienced it, and colours all my work with a deep Tyrian murex dye. I cannot rid myself of it, nor would I if I could. It is very much part of me, and probably the best part of me, in my work; and the worst part of me, probably, in my private life, and a cause of great despondency to my friends in that, possessing no voice at all, I am apt, in the early or even late hours of the morning, to break out into impassioned renderings of Italian operatic arias without the slightest provocation. A memorable example of this failing was recently provided by an occasion during the first winter of the war when, in company with Walter Legge and other blithe spirits, I visited John McCormack (Count of the Holy Roman Empire) at his flat in Dorchester House, and after copious libations of champagne, proceeded to expound to him, with musical illustrations, the true authentic style of Italian *cantabile* in general and of Bellini in particular, concluding with a rendering of the *Casta Diva* from *Norma*.

To this day I still do not understand how I escaped a fate many times worse than death at the hands of this notoriously tetchy and choleric artist, who would certainly have been acquitted on a charge of manslaughter as the result of extreme provocation, or even by pleading self-defence. Shortly after my display, however, he retired to bed, shattered, as the result of my singing or of over-indulgence in the joys of *la dive bouteille*—or from a combination of both, which is most likely.

From Peebles to Palermo is a long journey, but from Chopin to Bellini is a mere stone's throw, and surely permits of what would otherwise be a digression. Let us return to Peebles, the source of my first intense musical experience. It was there, also, that I first made contact with the world of literature.

Next door to my uncle there lived a writer, forgotten to-day, but famous in his time—Samuel Rutherford Crockett, a follower of Barrie and Stevenson, and the author of *The Lilac Sunbonnet* and other best-sellers of the period.

I do not exactly remember at what age I first encountered this portentous figure. The awe and veneration with which I regarded a real living author, a man who actually wrote the books one could buy, hold in one's hands and read, were profound: an impression enhanced by his formidable aspect—for he was well over six feet in height and proportionately broad, a colossal figure of a man. His mode of life, moreover, was fabulous and legendary. He saw little of his wife and numerous

family on the rare occasions when he visited them. He had
built at some distance away from the house in which he lived
a magnificent library, containing some ten thousand volumes
or more, in which he would spend his days; attached to which
there was an observatory, in which he would spend his nights,
with a telescope adjusted in such a way that he could lie on
his back in the truckle-bed which he had installed there and
contemplate the starry firmament until he fell asleep. That
was when he was in residence, which was seldom. For the most
part he travelled alone abroad, particularly in Spain, writing
all the time and, as the years went on, with continually increasing production and continually diminishing success, both artistic
and financial, ending up a career which had begun so brilliantly
by becoming an industrious writer of pot-boilers, for which he
had no real aptitude, always working against the clock, always
harassed by debts. He died in harness at Avignon in 1914.

It was in Peebles again, though slightly later, that I first
became acquainted with "real" literature, as opposed to the
omnivorous, indiscriminate reading of juvenile fiction. It was
a rainy day—the only one of which I have any recollection in
Peebles, though, of course, there must have been hundreds of
them; and having exhausted already the more congenial
fictional resources of my uncle's library, I took down at random
from the shelves *The Life of Frederick the Great*, by Thomas
Carlyle, in ten volumes. A stranger and more unpromising
début into the world of books could hardly be imagined, since
to-day, and for a long time past, I have entertained a violent
aversion from "the hairy old bore of Ecclefechan", as Compton
Mackenzie calls him, and all his works. He is indeed, together
with John Knox, of whom he is in many respects a dreary
reincarnation, my *bête noire*, the embodiment of everything
that is most repellent in the national character. In particular,
his gospel of justification through work seems to me to be the
teaching of the Devil. "To Hell with work. The man who
talks to me about work is my enemy." So writes Norman
Douglas, and so say I, and it is an amusing coincidence that

in an almanac of quotations culled from his writings, one for
every day of the year, published privately some years ago, he
allotted the above aphorism to the date of my birthday—
19th May.

In this connexion it may be observed that the reputation
which the Scot has acquired of being by nature hard-working
and industrious is a pure myth, built up by himself to a great
extent. He is, on the contrary, in my experience, the laziest,
most indolent man in the world by nature, not even excepting
the Neapolitan *lazzarone*—but his *far niente* is far from being
dolce. Wherever you travel you will find that the most
irreclaimably recalcitrant beach-combers and loafers are Scots
—and very unpleasant types they are. The terrific display of
tenacity and application which my fellow countrymen impose
upon a credulous world is largely fictitious and, when real and
achieved, is against the grain and only the result of the pressure
of adverse material circumstances. Owing to the poverty of
his soil and country and its detestable climate, the Scot has
been compelled to work harder than most other people in order
to survive, but that is all. He does not enjoy work for its own
sake, as does the Teuton, for example, but only as a means to an
end, the ultimate attainment of wealth and leisure. The
deification of the principle of hard work for its own sake is a
comparatively recent phenomenon, and due to Thomas Carlyle
more than to any other man—and where in all history will
you find a more consistently unhappy specimen of the human
race? His whole life was a contradiction of his inner nature.

No, my old friend Norman Douglas, and I, are much more
typically and representatively Caledonian than "the hairy old
bore of Ecclefechan".

I suffer from the constitutional indolence of my race. Work
is for me always an effort, especially the initial effort. To sit
down at my desk and start a new book or score is sheer purgatory, which I postpone from day to day so long as I can, and
only achieve with the utmost difficulty, the sternest exercise
of will-power and determination. On the other hand, once the

initial effort has been successfully accomplished, I work with comparative ease and swiftness. *Ce n'est que le premier pas qui coûte*, but it often costs me more than I can afford.

My psychological mechanism, in fact, is like that of a motor-car on a frosty morning: it can only be set going with the utmost difficulty. But once started, once warmed up, the engine roars, and generates a surprising degree of energy and power.

I conceive easily; my gestation is long and painful; but parturition is, as a rule, rapid and easy. I conceived my *Temptation of St. Anthony* in a split second, when reading Flaubert's masterpiece for the first time at the age of about twenty, and it took me about twenty years to mature the conception—but less than twenty months to write the work, from first sketch to full score for soloists, chorus and large orchestra, lasting two and a half hours in performance. A similar length of time was required for the gestation of *The History of Music*, but it was actually written in less than a year.

Even as a child I always exhibited this curious polarity, of lethargy until roused, and a kind of Berserker fury after. Once worked up, I would develop a super-normal intensity, and could tap latent, dormant sources of apparently limitless energy. Quite recently, for example, my brother reminded me of an occasion at Peebles when he, I and a friend were playing football together and I challenged the two of them to play together against me. I would have been about nine years of age at the time, and they were both two years older, which represents a formidable handicap, even in single combat, at that period of life. But working myself up into a demoniacal frenzy, I scored goal after goal against them; they had no chance, although they were genuinely playing their best, and even more than that, because they must have been irritated at this one-handed display of superiority on the part of a junior. I was like a whirlwind and an avalanche combined: I was irresistible. [1]

[1] This is also to a great extent, no doubt, a national trait. The charge of a Scottish regiment in battle is accounted the most terrifying spectacle on earth.

On another occasion, which I remember well, goaded to fury by something or other, I did my very best to kill my brother, and might well have succeeded had he not wisely taken refuge in flight. In such moods and moments I was literally possessed, and disposed of a strength which was not inherent—it came from outside of me and was always accompanied by a blinding sensation of seeing not red, but white—an incandescent light of indescribable intensity, in which I completely lost self-control. In later life I have had to learn to subdue these impulses in social life, and to confine their exercise to my work; otherwise I should, no doubt, have ended up long ago, ignominiously, at the Old Bailey and in the columns of *The News of the World*. The consciousness of the existence and the tremendous power of such impulses has naturally inculcated in me a sentiment of deep sympathy and understanding for these unfortunate people, no worse than the rest of us, who have lost control of themselves in crucial moments of blind passion and rage, and committed some unpremeditated and irreparable injury or crime. "There, but for the grace of God, go I."

Peebles, then, is indelibly associated in my mind with the happiest days of my early life, and with the most important experiences which led to my subsequent development; and the indirect and quite unconscious source of it was my maternal uncle, Robert Ernest Miller, of whose tragic end I have already given a premonitory hint. But before describing it in detail, it will be necessary to step back one generation, for only by doing so can the sombre pattern of his fate be clearly indicated and its almost Æschylean nature apprehended.

On the evening before his wedding, my grandfather, Thomas Miller, the engineer and chief architect of the family fortunes, was sitting in front of the fire before retiring to bed when there came a peremptory knock at the door. On opening it he found on the doorstep his future brother-in-law, who asked to be allowed to enter as he had something of great importance to say with regard to the ceremony which was to take place on the following day. What he said was this:—

"Thomas, you are marrying my sister to-morrow; I am sorry for you. I can only give you a word of advice. If you do not, from the very first day, rule her with a rod of iron, your life will not be worth living. If you feel you cannot do this, have the courage to break it off now; I will stand by you—it is not too late." Whereupon he departed.

But the unfortunate Thomas neither broke off the wedding nor ruled with a rod of iron; and as his brother-in-law had justly surmised, his life was not worth living. Indeed, his home was such a hell on earth that he would leave for the iron foundry as early as possible in the morning and return as late as possible at night, every day except, of course, Sunday, when there was no escape.

So it was, more or less, with the father, so it was with the son; and the repetition of the pattern did not even stop there. In each generation it has been the same story—a kind, gentle, talented man, weak, chivalrous to the verge of quixotry and even beyond, who was the prey of a ruthless, selfish, predatory female. One begins to understand how and why there are so many homosexuals about when one contemplates this little family history, which is assuredly not unique. It is Mr. Somerset Maugham's story, *Of Human Bondage*, extended over generation after generation, and if it had not been so admirably treated by him I should be tempted to try my hand at the theme myself.

A precisely similar pre-nuptial episode took place on the occasion of my uncle's wedding as on that of his father before him, when my father vainly attempted to dissuade his brother-in-law from what everyone felt to be a fatal step. Within about a week, during the honeymoon, he left his bride; but within another week he had returned, and for life—a life sentence.

It is true that for long periods of time he was able to escape as a ticket-of-leave man, but the return to prison after an interlude of liberty and freedom is probably more psychologically devastating than not to escape at all; and he never had the courage to break away completely. He had tried once and failed. He never tried again.

His chief form of escape lay in travel. Although nominally head of the family business after the death of his father, he ingeniously contrived innumerable opportunities for visiting customers, real and potential, and sometimes no doubt entirely imaginary, at the opposite ends of the world. There was no part of the earth's surface to which he did not travel in order to escape from his unhappy fate, but he always returned as a result of his unconquerable guilt-consciousness, on which his wife knew so well how to play with the virtuosity of a Menuhin. The most robust of women, she suffered from a succession of imaginary complaints, which invariably brought him back in an agony of remorse at having been—as she was, of course, careful to point out—the cause of the illness: his callousness, his selfishness, his neglect, his cruelty, and so forth, without end. And the poor man really believed it.

The sad truth of the matter is, I am afraid, only too plain and evident. In marriage there can be no equality; one or the other must dominate, and Nature has decreed that it should be the male. Modern civilization has decreed otherwise, and the male has accepted the situation. He fondly believed that woman only wanted equality, and she may have believed herself that she did; but in practice it has not so worked out. Man, civilized man to-day, genuinely desires equality—he has no wish to dominate, and he has abdicated. Woman, instead of accepting the dominion status offered freely, has established a tyranny, an ascendancy over the male—and nowhere is it more evident than in Anglo-Saxon countries. In the United Kingdom and the United States the relation between the maritally united is, in nine cases out of ten, one of female domination and male subjection; in the one case out of ten it is a male domination—but never equality.

The first premonitory symptoms of the female ascendancy which has since spread like a blight over the entire world, is to be found in Scandinavian literature, and drama particularly, especially in Ibsen and Strindberg, and in Strindberg above all. It is no mere coincidence that my unfortunate uncle's wife was a Scandinavian—an unholy combination of the worst elements in the heroines of both these dramatists—and these are strong words, and are meant to be. She was a devil incarnate, and in the end she drove the poor man mad, literally, certifiably mad, after which he shortly died, mercifully; whereupon she devoted the rest of her life (she outlived him some sixteen years) in trying to get into touch with his tortured ghost through the agency of spiritualists and mediums, and squandered vast sums of money in so doing. Having tormented him into the grave, she could not leave him alone in peace there, but had to pursue him even to the astral plane.

His chief escape from life, apart from travel, was painting. As a young man he had entertained the desire and intention of devoting himself to art, and had succeeded in persuading his reluctant parents into allowing him to study in Paris, before definitely deciding whether or not to adopt the obvious career of following in his father's footsteps and becoming his understudy and ultimate successor in the family business.

I have more than a suspicion that the young man, escaping from the family toils for the first time in his life (and in Scotland, in these sour Calvinistic and Knoxious days they must have been formidable) and finding sanctuary in the Paris of those days where life was even more than usually intoxicating—I do not doubt that he kicked over the traces very thoroughly and had what is called "the time of his life", and for once the *cliché* is also the *mot juste*, for they must have been the happiest days he ever knew. But even this period of escape had its psychological boomerang, as we shall see in the sombre sequel.

After about a year or so of bliss in this earthly paradise, ostensibly studying art at Jullien's, but more probably engaged chiefly in making the acquaintance of the delectable trinity of wine, woman and song, he came to the conclusion—or was forced to it by his parents—that he had not enough talent to make a career for himself as an artist. He took the easy way out: returned home and resigned himself to the pursuit of the family calling.

He was no doubt wise in doing so. If he had made painting his profession he would only have ended up as one of the ninety-nine failures out of a hundred potentialities who encumber the groaning earth with unwanted canvases. His tragedy was that he was a misfit in both worlds: an artist *manqué*, yet not a business man *réussi*, although I understand that in the latter capacity he performed his duties competently and conscientiously. Conscience—that was his trouble. He spent his entire life trying to escape from it and never succeeding. He was a weak man, a compromiser; and the hell of the compromiser, the fate of the man who is neither strong enough to follow his own natural bent or to adapt himself purposefully to the world of hard fact and reality, is a terrible one.

Travel and painting, these were his chief solaces; but they were never more than momentary escapes from the hell of his marital life and the comparatively mild purgatory of his business career. In the end he was forced to the form of escape which I have described earlier in connexion with the Corsican woman; but unlike her, even in this last refuge he failed to find happiness. He suffered from melancholy delusions. Although a rich man he was obstinately convinced that he was ruined and penniless. I used to argue with him for hours on end, trying to convince him of the contrary, but all to no purpose. On one occasion he even went so far as to say that the cause of his insolvency was the enormous amount of super-tax he had to pay; but it was impossible to convince him that if he had a large super-tax he must be, at least, comfortably well off; but he could not see it.

The final, grotesque, and deeply tragic delusion was that he had contracted syphilis and that he had infected the entire family with it. There was not, of course, an atom of substance in the belief, nor could there have been, for I am certain that ever since youth he had led a pathetically chaste existence.

I even doubt whether his marriage had even been consummated—in fact, I am sure it was not. The only fragile basis of the grotesque delusion must have related back to his early days as a student in Paris—a guilt-conscience connected with the only happy days in his life. I find this so terrible that I have physical difficulty in writing these words.

The last time I saw him before he was taken away he said to me, sadly and wistfully, pointing to my *History of Music*, which was lying on the table: "Well, at least *you* have justified your existence."

Chapter Five

S O FAR, in speaking of my early years, I have referred only to the periods of holiday, for it was in them that my personality was formed and I became an individual, rather than at school, where I was, for the most part, merely an ordinary, uninteresting member of a community.

After the usual Kindergarten course at the age of five, I was sent to a preparatory school at seven, where I remained until I was twelve. The only noteworthy feature of my first years there was a quite pathological timidity, nervousness and shyness, amounting, for example, to an inability to summon up the necessary courage, in class hours, to ask permission to leave the room, with sometimes disastrous and humiliating consequences. This psychological condition, naturally and inevitably, led to a certain amount of persecution. I was the ideal prey for the sadistic bully who exists in every school, but at this particular stage of my development the consequences were not such as to have any marked influence upon me. Being physically strong, I was soon able to hold my own in battle, and consequently was, for the most part, left in peace. But there is one particular episode in this connexion which stands out clearly in my recollection and has considerable psychological interest and significance.

One winter evening at sundown I was being bullied and tormented by a powerful little brute several years older than myself, when I suddenly became detached and remote, in the midst of his persecution, and found myself admiring the deep red glow of the sunset illumining the wintry landscape, and even the way in which the hated face of my persecutor was lit up and transfigured into something unreal and ethereal. I became completely indifferent and inaccessible to his blows and insults—only interested in the changing effects of light and shade.

This sense of aloofness and detachment has frequently come to my rescue in later years—in moments of illness or emotional stress and distress; but not normally, when I am more acutely sensitive and responsive to externalities than most people. But in these moments of which I am speaking it is as if I become two entirely separate persons: the one who is suffering intensely, and a spectator, calm and dispassionate, whom nothing on earth can touch. It is unfortunately not a faculty that one can evoke at will, but one which comes only at moments of supreme crisis, physical or mental. This ability to contemplate one's sufferings, in utter detachment, impersonally as it were, is the supreme manifestation of the æsthetic sense. If only one could cultivate it, develop it, assiduously practise it, there is nothing one could not achieve; but one would cease to be human: one would become God.

This first experience of the division into actor and spectator which I have described above made a deep and lasting impression upon me, and led me into oddly precocious paths of philosophical and metaphysical speculations concerned with the nature of personality and the reality—or otherwise—of the external world. I would frequently pinch myself hard in order to convince myself of my objective existence. I lived to such an extent in a dream-world of my own, that in these days of childhood the Descartian formula of *cogito ergo sum* would not have been enough to convince me, if I had known it. "I feel, therefore I am" was the only argument I could understand.

But if I frequently doubted the reality of my objective existence, I was also profoundly sceptical concerning the nature of inanimate objects. I was convinced, indeed, that things are not what they seem to be. Had I not once, on coming quietly and suddenly into a room, distinctly experienced the

curious sensation of being an intruder, of having caught the
furniture unawares in the act of executing a fantastic kind of
ballet, and that it had only just had time to settle down again,
with a perceptible jerk, into its normal position as I crossed the
threshold? For some time thereafter I was in the habit of
coughing, or rattling the door-handle, before entering an
empty room, in order to give the furniture warning of my
approach, and time to subside decorously into its correct
posture.

Before I had entered my teens, then, even, I was well on the
way to becoming a disciple of Bishop Berkeley, for whom I have
always entertained a profound regard. The spirit of enquiry,
and the belief that things are not what they seem to be, has
been with me ever since I can remember thinking at all, and
in this I have never changed. Orthodox religion, on the other
hand, meant precisely nothing at all to me as a child, and still
means nothing to me to-day, although I have deeply religious
feelings which will appear in the course of these pages. Both
Old and New Testaments were equally matters of less than
indifference to me. Scripture lessons and Bible classes, indeed,
occasioned me more acute boredom and active dislike than any
other subject in the school curriculum, apart from the Book
of Kings, and especially Omri and Zimri, to whom I had a
romantic attachment based, presumably, on their strange and
sonorous names. So far as the New Testament was concerned
I felt an uneasy guilt-conscience in having to confess to myself
a complete inability to love Jesus, as one was being continually
exhorted to do. In fact, I was convinced that I must be very
wicked indeed for not being able to do so; but the idea of loving
any male, even a God, was already at that age repulsive to me.
A woman, yes: I could have worshipped the Virgin Mary with
utter devotion, but being nurtured in the bosom of the
orthodox Scottish Presbyterian Church, I was given very
clearly to understand that this, if not actually a sin, was to be
sternly discouraged. Mary, in the Calvinist theology as
taught in my youth, was little more than a necessary evil—

necessary, perhaps, but certainly an evil, and the less said about Her the better.

Already, in fact, the pronouncedly normal, heterosexual nature of my feelings was strongly in evidence, and was no doubt accentuated by the fact, which I have subsequently recognized, but of which I must at the time have been subconsciously and uneasily aware without understanding it, that the tendency of the majority of the masters at the school was different. A habit of favouring one boy more than others, for no apparent reason, of indulging in unnecessarily intimate and affectionate contacts—all this gave me a sense of acute disquiet and physical repulsion, especially when, on one or two occasions, I was myself the unwilling recipient of these equivocal and distasteful attentions. In one particular case the behaviour took the peculiarly objectionable form of treating me alternately as an object of favour and then of disfavour, capriciously and inexplicably—in order, of course, to have an excuse for thrashing me, though I did not understand it at the time. But even in my innocence and mystification I was dimly aware of something wrong.

I hasten to add that the enormous number of thrashings I received at my preparatory school only exceptionally belonged to this category. At least nine out of ten were called for and thoroughly justified. I met one of the erstwhile masters of the school some twenty years after I had left, and he told me that I still held the proud record of having had a larger number of beatings than any other boy who had ever been to the school, before or since.

The chief cause of these troubles was home-work: I simply refused to do it. Once I was outside the school gates I was as free and nonchalant as a bird, taking no heed for the morrow. On the way to school next morning, with an agonized, sinking feeling in the pit of my stomach, I would try to achieve a rudimentary grasp of the lessons I was supposed to have prepared the evening before. Sometimes luck favoured me, sometimes not. If not, then I had to pay the penalty.

But if I certainly asked for it, as the saying is, there were masters only too ready and willing and eager to give it. There was one in particular whom I remember vividly, who was given to violent drinking bouts, and would come into morning class at nine reeking of whisky to such an extent that you could almost smell his presence even before he opened the door, which he entered with an ominous scowl and a strap sticking ostentatiously out of his pocket. He was out for a field-day, and was determined to have it. The whole class would eye each other in an agony of apprehension, knowing full well that before the end of the lesson at least six of them would be casualties. I was nearly always one of them and, I repeat, generally with a certain reason and justification—I simply would not do home-work whatever the consequences. And the consequences were often appalling. I was by no means a stoic— one to whom pain meant nothing; on the contrary, I felt pain acutely, and squealed while it was being administered; but of the two evils I preferred it to home-work.

Castigation was of two kinds. The first consisted in flogging the hands of the culprit, with the palms extended, by means of a leather strap divided at the striking point into five thongs. This was the form of penance imposed for ordinary mis- demeanours; the cane on the backside was reserved for excep- tionally grave offences and was only administered by the head- master himself—no one in a lower order of the hierarchy was permitted to wield a weapon of such authority.

I need hardly say that in addition to the normal form of manual punition, I several times incurred the supreme penalty. I remember only too well the circumstances of the final and culminating occasion. Having more than usually neglected my home-work, in the most flagrant fashion, throughout the week, I had been sentenced to deprivation of the Saturday afternoon holiday and commanded to stay behind at school and perform due penance. As my parents had booked seats for a circus on that afternoon I simply ignored the command and absented myself. I enjoyed the circus, but the rest of the week-end was a nightmare. Better than any murderer in a condemned cell I knew the fate that was waiting for me on the following Monday. The murderer, at least, always hopes for a reprieve up to the last moment, but I had no hopes, no illusions. I knew very well what my fate would be, and that it was unescapable.

It is true that on other, less heinous, occasions of delinquency I had been able to evade the worst consequences of my inveterate neglect of home-work by developing a diplomatic illness, generally on Monday morning. To what extent my mother genuinely believed in the reality of my sudden indisposition, or to what extent she acquiesced in, and secretly sympathized with my shortcomings, I do not know; but it was seldom that my pathetic act failed. Naturally, I was not such a fool as to try it on every Monday: it was a desperate expedient reserved only for the most critical emergencies. But I had succumbed to the temptation of having too frequent recourse to it, so that in my moment of most acute need—when I really did feel ill for the best of all possible reasons, abject panic—my trusted resource of malingering failed me for once. All my entreaties, all my enactments of dangerous symptoms, fell on deaf ears and blind eyes.

In sheer desperation I made matters worse. After being absent from school for a day or more, one was under the obligation of bringing back with one, on return, a note written and signed by a parent testifying to the genuineness of the indisposition. Unable to face my terrible fate I simply played truant, hoping against hope to be able to "get away with it" (as Henry James would say), by means of a renewed indisposition on the following day. But again I failed, and it was a miserable and dejected little object that turned up on the Tuesday morning to face the inexorable penalty of its misdeeds.

At nine o'clock precisely every morning roll-call was held, and as my name came nearer I suffered the agonies of the damned. When my name was called at last, in a menacing voice, the head-master raised his eyes and fixed me with a stony glare.

"Here, sir," I faltered.

"Young man, I have a bone to pick with you—several bones, in fact. You will come to my study immediately after roll-call."

The consequences were, of course, as dire as I had imagined. And though far from suggesting that I did not deserve all I got, and even more, I was distinctly aware, even in the midst of my suffering, of the fact that my castigator was enjoying himself hugely and having the time of his life, in a transport of ecstasy. He could hardly bring himself to stop, and I left his study more dead than alive.[1]

But once it was all over I speedily revived and continued in the same course, as if nothing had happened. The circus had been worth it. This should be of interest and value to the students of infantile delinquency and the merits or demerits of corporal punishment. It will, at least, be admitted that I speak with authority on the subject: that I am, in fact, an expert on it from one important angle. My conclusions are as follows:—

No child who is chastised justly, for having done something which he himself well knows to be wrong, will bear the slightest animosity or resentment. As the criminal says, resignedly, when he is deservedly run in: "It's a fair cop, guv'nor, I'll go quietly." That it serves any real corrective purpose, on the other hand, I do not for a moment believe. As I have said, I suffered abominably, for I am more than usually susceptible to pain (as to pleasure: the two go together), but not all the beatings I received had the slightest effect on my conduct. But lastly, and perhaps most important, the administration of corporal punishment *does* have a very definite effect on the character— not of the passive recipient, but of the active agent: an effect which can corrupt all but the finest characters. The sadistic element is latent in every human being, and only requires an opportunity to develop into a monstrous upas tree. The power to inflict pain is not one which should be given to any man.

[1] It is interesting to note that some years later this pedagogue's scholastic career came to a sticky end. I was not surprised.

We have seen something of it in recent times, God knows, but history is full of it; and sometimes the best men, potentially, are the worst examples, such as Nero and Gilles de Rais . . .

In my view, then, and in the light of my considerable experience, I should say that the balance is emphatically against the use of corporal punishment. It does not make the culprit any better, as one school of thought maintains, or bitter or resentful, as their opponents maintain; but it does make the judge, the executor, worse. The one remains unchanged: the other can, and frequently does, become a fiend.

This salutary train of thought reminds me of a curious, and in retrospect decidedly unpleasing game which my brother and I used to play in early days—if you can call it a game. We would at one time spend all our pocket-money on buying dolls stuffed with sawdust, which we soaked in petrol or methylated spirit; then, tying each leg to a separate twig of the branch of a tree, we would set alight to the body, which was at the same time torn limb from limb, to our intense satisfaction. Looking back on these slightly equivocal recreations of my early youth, I am more than ever aware of the truth of what I have just said, namely that in all of us, even the best, there is a latent streak of cruelty which only needs to be developed, and nothing in the whole of creation can be more cruel than these sweet, innocent little creatures we call children, as I know to my cost and as we shall see in due course.

In spite of my natural indolence and refusal to do homework I was actually ahead of my age-level in scholastic attainments: never brilliant, but above the average. At games I was neither good nor bad, but indifferent: simply because I was indifferent, save on the rare occasions of which I have given an example, when a sudden passionate flare-up of interest would produce astonishing results. One day I would play so brilliantly, at cricket or football, that the refereeing master, with a holy light in his eye, would promote me straightway into the first fifteen or eleven; whereupon I would relapse back into mediocrity and give a deplorable display, to the disappointment of all concerned. It has been the same with every game I have ever played, and I have played most of them at one time or another. Apart from the obligatory school games of football and cricket, I have tried my hand at golf, tennis, rowing, fencing, croquet, billiards, and what-not, but always with the same results. Shooting I have consistently refused to practise from my earliest years: to kill any living thing is to me utterly abhorrent, and always has been. Fishing I only tried once, and was so upset when I had a catch that I have never touched a rod again. At the same time, I can see the enormous attractions of that sport, and appreciate the extent to which it must conduce to the cultivation of a philosophic state of mind. I have even seriously considered the possibility of taking it up in my old age, if I have one, and if I am capable of nothing better; but even so I shall emulate the example of the Old Fisherman of the Mists and Mountains, of Chinese legend, who spent his entire time fishing but used no bait, his object *not* being to catch fish.

In chess, the best of all indoor sports, save one, my record is precisely similar: I either play well when inspired, or abominably when not. I have never troubled to learn the opening gambits, which are merely a question of rule-of-thumb and accurate memorization: while the end game, which as a rule alone interests the adept, bores me to such an extent that I prefer to resign, even with a tactical advantage, to a continuation of such dreary proceedings. But I shall always remember a game of chess I once played as a young man, recalling that game of football I played with my brother and his friend, to which I have alluded above. My opponent was of championship rank, but I played so brilliantly and with so unconventional a technique that I completely routed him. The psychological explanation of the feat is a simple one: I was very much in love with his wife, who was a spectator . . .

To return to my preparatory school before leaving it behind for ever: I have in retrospect no praise too great for the high standard of scholastic efficiency set there—and attained. I do not know the present position, but in these days the great reputation enjoyed by Scottish schools in comparison with their English equivalents was more than justified—in fact, there was no comparison at all. When I went, subsequently, to an English public school, at an unusually early age, I already found myself far in advance of boys very much older; and, I hasten to add, this was not due to individual brilliance on my part, but to the high and exacting general level of the national tradition in matters of education.

But if on the purely scholastic side no praise could be too high, on the cultural and æsthetic side no condemnation could be low enough. It was recognized in theory that such values were of importance, but the approach to them was so prosaic and unimaginative as to exercise an utterly sterilizing effect on the young mind. I went there, as will have been seen, a very responsive subject to artistic impressions, but I left in a state entirely impervious to them: hating Shakespeare, hating the Bible, hating Homer and all the Greeks, hating even music, as a result of the insensitive and unintelligent method of tuition. For example: instead of being taught to play my beloved Chopin, however badly, I was given nothing but scales to play and to practise interminably, with pennies placed on the backs of my hands—the idea being that, if one of them fell off, one was playing badly, and one would be sharply rapped on the knuckles. What a way of teaching the practice of art to a child! Small wonder that, as I have said, I came to dislike music, and this dislike persisted until about my fifteenth year.

It is not surprising, in view of all this, and the frustration of my normal and natural inclinations, that in my last years at my preparatory school I began to develop into a complete hooligan. From being the pathologically timid and sensitive small boy who had arrived there, I became one of the ringleaders of a gang of little horrors, who after sundown would roam the streets of Edinburgh smashing street-lamps with stones, throwing handfuls of liquid mud at the windows of inoffensive citizens, spraying shops and public places with evil-smelling chemical compounds, which I concocted—such as sulphur-etted hydrogen—and generally misconducting ourselves like savage beasts in a purely destructive ecstasy. I was also an inveterate thief, and would steal money from my mother's purse if she left it lying about.

Not at all a nice character, I am afraid. We have come a long way from the sweet little boy who sobbed himself to sleep over a Chopin Nocturne! And yet it was the same little boy. Here, again, is valuable and interesting material for the psychologist. From being a potential artist I had become a potential criminal; and the truth is, I suppose, that the artist and the criminal have much in common and a secret sympathy with each other. Both are at heart anti-social, at war with the established order and the accepted mode of life: the one creatively, the other destructively, and they can very easily change places. An artist *manqué* can very easily turn into a criminal *réussi*. The contrary transformation seldom happens, admittedly, but I have known many artists *réussis* who could give most criminals points in their anti-social behaviour. François Villon, on the other hand, is an example of a great poet who also achieved eminence as a professional cracksman. There is more in common, in fact, between the artist and the criminal than between either of them and ordinary social man. I have myself a great sympathy with criminals, and not merely because without the advantages I have enjoyed I might very easily have become one of them; but also because I so often find them much pleasanter company and much more intelligent individuals than those whose laws they have transgressed. And there are many persons in high and honoured places to-day who stand on a much lower level of human decency than some so-called criminals I have known.

I do not wish these remarks to be construed into a defence or glorification of crime. Least of all do I wish to suggest that every forger, burglar, murderer or violator is a Beethoven *manqué* who has been prevented by a corrupt society from expressing his immortal soul; but it seems to me that the connexion between the frustrated artist and the criminal is too close to be ignored, and that the problems resulting from this kinship have not been properly dealt with by those whose business it is to do so.

I have in front of me as I write an instructive case in point, for the knowledge of which I am indebted to my friend Gerald Kersh—the case of one Alister Jenner Clark, an Australian who, some fifteen years ago, was accused and found guilty of murdering his wife by arsenic poisoning. Suspicion had been aroused by the fact that he married again within a week of her death, and an exhumation was ordered. The death penalty was passed, but the sentence was commuted to one of "imprisonment for the term of his natural life and twenty-four hours thereafter" (a nice touch that!). After an attempt to commit suicide in prison, his whole life was changed by a violin recital given to the convicts in the prison chapel. The governor, obviously a most humane and enlightened man, noticing the effect that the music had upon the poor wretch at the concert, went to his cell the next day and asked him if he would like to study music. He answered that he knew nothing about music but would like to try. By some mysterious means, which reflect the utmost credit on all concerned—and especially the governor of the prison—he was able to receive lessons from two nuns once a week on Sundays, after Roman Catholic service in the prison chapel. He made rapid progress and, eventually, through what must undoubtedly have been most flagrant breaches of all conceivable prison regulations, was enabled to study seriously and eventually became a composer. A trio of his for violin, 'cello and piano lies before me and testifies to his gifts. They do not amount to much, admittedly, but considering the circumstances under which the work was written one can only conjecture sadly what he might have become under more favourable conditions. He had undoubtedly the makings of an artist in him, and while I do not defend the practice of wife-killing, I can understand better than most people the state of mind which leads to it. I shall even go so far as to say that if my grandfather or uncle had done what Alister Clark did, I should have whole-heartedly sympathized. There are some women who positively ask to be murdered, and it requires great strength of mind to resist the temptation to gratify their demand. Alister Clark was a weak man.[1] . . .

My favourite form of reading in these days, it is interesting and psychologically instructive to note, consisted in blood-and-thunder penny-dreadfuls dealing with the gallant exploits of Dick Turpin, Claude Duval, Jack Sheppard, and other similar gentry. In all of these productions, incidentally, the same characteristic is to be observed, namely, that the highwayman is represented as a noble, heroic character and the police as despicable villains. In the modern equivalent thriller, the inversion of values is not quite so blatant: the crook still remains the hero up to a point, but the detective is not a villain. The almost Nietzschean trans-valuation of values effected in these literary products of my early youth, however, finds a parallel in the perverse æsthetic of Arnold Schönberg and his school, in accordance with which discord and concord change places, and their rôles are mechanically inverted.

At the age of twelve I was sent, together with my brother, to a well-known English public school not far from London. For this I was exceptionally young. The normal entrance age was fourteen, but I passed the necessary preliminary examination with such ease that the school authorities were prepared to relax the regulations and make an exception in my favour. As I have said above, this was not due to any outstanding ability on my part, but solely to the higher standard of education prevailing in Scottish preparatory schools as compared to those of England. In no particular direction had I exhibited any exceptional ability save one—a quite phenomenal capacity for handling numbers. I remember one occasion when the

[1]For the details of his strange and arresting career I am indebted to an article in the magazine *Leader*, written by George Ivan Smith, the son of the governor of the prison, which appeared in the issue of 7th April, 1945.

master of the class gave out a long list of figures to be added—a task which I accomplished within about thirty seconds, while the others in the class, and the master himself, were only beginning. Seeing me sitting back doing nothing, he sharply reprimanded me, telling me to get on with the sum. I said, nonchalantly, that I had already done it. He gave me what can only be described as "a nasty look", and as I ostentatiously lolled back at my desk and watched him slowly plodding along in company with the rest of the class, I realized that a very unpleasant ordeal was awaiting me if I should prove to have made a mistake. When at length they had all finished, I was naturally called upon first to read out my result. It was correct, and the master was livid with rage.

This odd faculty was quite unrelated to any other aspect of mathematics. In the higher ranges of arithmetic I had no more than ordinary capacity, while in algebra and geometry I was decidedly below the average. That it was connected with my latent, dormant musical faculty I have now no doubt. Did not the great Leibniz describe music as "the unconscious counting of the soul"?

My scholastic precocity, relative to English public-school standards, had disastrous consequences, as any psychologist could have foretold. In the first place, to put a child of twelve, straight from home, before the age of puberty and knowing nothing of the so-called facts of life, into a boarding-school consisting of some four hundred boys who had all passed that critical age and knew rather too much about its facts, was a very rash experiment, and one which could never take place in these comparatively enlightened days.

Consequently, apart from the normal and natural feeling of home-sickness, from which I suffered more violently than most, there was also an acute sense of being, in some way which I could not fathom, different from my companions. Physically undeveloped, completely innocent, and unaware of the first rudiments of sex, I was surrounded by a horde of young monsters who thought and spoke of practically nothing else.

I was terrified and repelled by this dark, hideous, unknown thing—this communal secret from which I alone, it seemed, was excluded by a barrier of incomprehension.

Even under normal conditions such a sense of isolation and difference would have been a cause of psychological disequilibrium, but in this particular case it was accentuated by the fact that the particular school in question, at the time in question, was a hot, steaming compost of sexual vice. I have been told on credible authority that since these days there has been a great change for the better. But at the time of which I am writing, and of which I can speak from personal knowledge, it is no exaggeration to say that boys there who held themselves aloof from vicious practices—and very few there were—became butts for ridicule and contempt.

My first term I can only describe as one endless unmitigated hell. In accordance with tradition, a new boy was treated as a pariah, an outcast, an untouchable, an object of derision, and any attempt to make friendly approaches to others than those of one's own despised caste was regarded as an insolent affront. In my time, it was the custom to allow the boys to choose their own seats for lunch in Hall, so that friends could have places next to each other—an excellent and very sensible arrangement, provided you had friends. I had no friends, and on the first day in Hall I wandered disconsolately from one vast table to another, looking for a vacant seat. Whenever I saw one I made as if to occupy it, only to be met with a yell of indignation: "Go away, you horrid little new man! You can't sit here. Who asked you here? Get out! we don't want you—GO AWAY!"

After vainly repeating the attempt to find a place some twenty times, and invariably meeting with the same hostile reception, I gave up in despair and left the Hall, unnoticed by any of the presiding masters, and took refuge in the lavatory, where I stayed until the meal was over and classes had begun again, or games, as the case might be. This I did every day rather than endure the ordeal again; and I was too shy and secretive to take my troubles to my house-master. Since lunch, or rather dinner, was, of course, the chief—indeed, the only real solid meal in the day, I was wretchedly underfed, and after a few weeks of this Buchenwald *régime* I collapsed and had to be removed to the sanatorium, where the astonished doctor diagnosed my ailment as being nothing but weakness due to starvation.

The truth was elicited, and naturally the state of affairs was promptly rectified; but the whole experience was one from which I never really recovered, physically or psychologically, during the whole of my three years' stay at the school. It even dictated the very pattern of my life, and the title of this book, for I have never lost the sense of isolation, of being excluded and apart, which derives from the nightmarish experiences of these early days at the school—the result of the combination of being a new boy and of sexual immaturity. From being the tough young gangster of my last days at the preparatory school in Scotland, I became again the pathologically shy and timid small boy of the first days there, but with one important difference. The world of school-life is a microcosm of the social system of the world outside, and the individual boy who does not fit in and adjust himself to the pattern suffers the same fate as does the adult later on in life. I became the equivalent of a criminal in the outside world: in fact, I was treated as a pariah, an outcast—very well, then, I would take my revenge: I became furtive, dishonest, a forger, and a thief. If any boy possessed any object that I particularly coveted, I would have no scruples in taking it if I had the opportunity to do so. Sometimes I was found out, sometimes not; but when I was, I was quite unrepentant—only annoyed and humiliated at failure and discovery, without any change of heart: only determined to do it better next time.

One of the conventions of the system in this particular school was that, if one's conduct in class was more than usually bad, one was given a note from the class-master to take to one's house-master, which one then had to take back to the former, duly signed. Having behaved rather worse than usual on one particular occasion, and having already been the recipient of several of these notes, I knew that the consequences would inevitably be fatal. I had been warned, in fact, that I had been given my last chance. So instead of taking the note to my house-master, I carefully and laboriously forged his signature. I was, of course, a fool not to realize that the whole system was simply that of the *agent provocateur* applied to school-life, and that the two masters would be in touch with each other. Many boys, in such circumstances, would simply not deliver the note and say, when caught out, that they had lost it, or forgotten about it. I had tried that before and, of course, failed. Hence my desperate expedient, the outcome of which can be imagined. I was thrashed twice as much and twice as hard as I would have been if I had presented the note in the ordinary way. I thoroughly deserved it, I know; but I still think the system of deliberately tempting a boy to evade justice was a despicable one.

Psychologically, in fact, it will be seen that I was in a pretty bad way, but physically I was not much better. I became subject to occasional fainting fits, and towards the end of my stay I was exempted from taking part in strenuous games such as football—a deprivation which, while I welcomed it, served to increase my sense of loneliness, isolation, and detachment from my fellows.

The whole process was a vicious circle, beginning with a maladjustment to an unsympathetic environment, leading to a self-protective retaliation of an anti-social character, and so on —all accentuated by the crisis of puberty—in a steady crescendo up to the final and inevitable catastrophe.

It was a Saturday afternoon and consequently a half-holiday. I made my solitary way towards the class-room which would normally have been empty on such an occasion, but on arriving there I discovered, to my horror, that a gang of my most assiduous and relentless persecutors was gathered together there. I tried to make my escape unobserved, but it was too late. I was dragged back in triumph, and they proceeded to enjoy themselves at my expense. There were eight or nine of them taking part in the exquisite pleasure of tormenting one solitary boy in every way that their fertile imaginations could devise. For a time I endured it all stoically and patiently, hoping that they would soon tire of what was surely, after all, rather poor sport, one would have thought. But not at all! The more calm and resigned I became, the fiercer and more intensified became the persecution. They were evidently determined to goad me into some positive reaction—and they succeeded.

All the muscles in my body suddenly became taut and tense, a kind of tremor ran down my spine, my mouth went dry, and that white incandescent light I have described earlier in these pages came down in front of my eyes like a curtain through which I could only dimly discern the features of my tormentors. I leapt at the ringleader and experienced a delirious ecstasy as my fists pounded his face; I turned to the next and served him, similarly, and so on to the fifth, I think—hitting, kicking, scratching, biting. Then everything faded out, and the next thing I knew was an hour later, when I came to my senses in the sanatorium. Next day my parents came with a car and took me away to London, where they were then living. So ended my school career, ironically described by Sir Osbert Sitwell in his Autobiography as the "happiest time of one's life".

I have been greatly struck, incidentally, by the surprising similarity of experience undergone by two personalities so dissimilar in most other respects. Sir Osbert was by nature born left-handed and compelled to use the right; so was I. To this day I perform many important physical functions with my left hand—shaving, for example; and my writing, in consequence of having been forced to use the wrong (that is, the right) hand, is childish and laborious. But what is even more interesting is the fact that both of us are therefore impelled to write our books in script. I used formerly to employ a typewriter, but have in recent years conceived an intense distaste for the instrument and, being mentally incapable of dictation (my mind does not work quickly enough), I am compelled, by some mysterious necessity, to form every word with my inadequate right hand, which, in consequence of its unsuitability to the task, generally develops a condition of cramp after a few pages. The sense of effort and strain involved in the process is apparently a necessary condition of our activities—of Sir Osbert Sitwell and myself.

Another experience in common is that of a severe illness occurring at about the same period of development, which, in my case, supervened as a result of the incidents described above. For the six months following I was an invalid, and strictly confined to bed. Eminent specialists were called in: heart disease was diagnosed, and a formidable consensus of expert opinion, at enormous expense, sadly declared that if I survived I would be an invalid for the rest of my life. But the heart is a mysterious organ and, looking back on it all, I am convinced that my heart disease was in origin psychological, self-induced: that I had deliberately, albeit unconsciously, made myself ill, as the only means I could devise of an escape from the life which had become an unendurable nightmare. The imprisoned spirit had made up its mind to escape, and the gaoler, the body, allowed himself to be bribed into complicity.

Sir Osbert writes revealingly concerning the similar crisis which occurred in his adolescence:

> "This short period was the most important of my whole childhood, because it gave me that which is granted to so few children: time— apparently endless time—in which to think and still more to feel . . . Nor am I the only person by any means to have found a physical crisis of this kind helpful to development."

And Sir Osbert goes on to quote the instance of Sir Edwin Lutyens, who once said to him that:—

> "Any talent I may have was due to a long illness as a boy, which afforded me time to think and to subsequent ill-health, because I was not allowed to play games, and so had to teach myself, for my own enjoyment, to use my eyes instead of my feet."

And so it was with me. I owe everything to this illness—or pseudo-illness. It was the making of me, and changed me back from being the potential criminal into the potential artist.

The first manifestation of the conversion was a passion for history (which has never left me) and, while lying in bed I would assimilate innumerable volumes which I would then regurgitate in works of my own creation. During these months I wrote, in rapid succession, in the following order: histories of Venice, the Byzantine Empire, the Ottoman Empire, Ancient Egypt, the House of Medici and, finally, a history of the Italian Republics, which, owing to the inextricable complexities of the subject remained unfinished—more precisely, perhaps, as an historian it finished me.

None of these productions, I need hardly say, was of the slightest intrinsic value, consisting as they did of mere transcriptions, paraphrases and condensations of the books I had been reading; but no doubt the writing of them loosened my pen and gave me a certain facility of expression which I might not otherwise have attained so early in life, and taught me how to select, marshal and present facts—a training which was to stand me in good stead later in life in the writing of *The History of Music*. I would have been about fifteen at this time.

After having been pronounced well enough to resume a comparatively normal vertical existence under close supervision—for it was some time before I was allowed to go out alone into the street, in case I might have a sudden heart attack—I was taken to a Sunday afternoon orchestral concert at the Queen's Hall, conducted by Sir Henry Wood. It was an all-Wagner programme, and the effect it had upon me was overwhelming in its intensity. It came to me as a complete revelation, comparable only to that which I had experienced as a small child, with the Chopin Nocturne. I there and then made up my mind to be a composer: nothing else and nothing less would satisfy me. During the night following the concert, unable to sleep, I got out of bed and, kneeling down, prayed to God for the first time since I had been a small child, asking Him to make me a composer, in return for which I was prepared to make any and every sacrifice. The young Faust, in fact, dedicated himself to God as the old Faust dedicated himself to the Devil, and has frequently regretted it; for He is a hard taskmaster and stern in reprimand of those who fail Him, as I have cause to know, having failed Him so often and having, therefore, frequently paid the just penalty.

From that moment onwards for many years I cared for nothing, thought of nothing else, but music: from morning to night and night to morning. I induced my parents into allowing me to re-learn the piano, which I had neglected since the age of eight. I bought miniature scores and studied harmony and counterpoint and orchestration; I began to compose innumerable piano pieces and songs, of which the unspeakable badness deals me pangs of retrospective anguish to this day— they even occasionally come back to haunt me in dreams, from which I awake in a cold perspiration.

The violence of my obsession was such that at length, in order to pacify me, my parents allowed me to take up the study of music seriously, and by a remarkable stroke of good fortune engaged for that purpose the services of a first-rate musician who was also a sympathetic personality, and seemed to take an interest in me—Healey Willan, now Principal of the Conservatoire of Music in Toronto. Under his able tuition I learnt the rudiments of musical technique, and he is the only teacher from whom I have ever succeeded in learning anything at all. Apart from him I am almost entirely self-taught.

At first I cared little for any music but that of Wagner: it was like a fever in my blood. I must have been one of the last of the race of Perfect Wagnerites, for I have observed that none of my contemporaries or, *a fortiori*, immediate juniors, have passed through the phase of absolute self-immolation to the wizard of Bayreuth which I underwent. It is a thing of the past and is never likely to return: there will be no triumphant revivalist Wagnerian movement in the future comparable to that which has in recent years taken place with regard to Bach or Handel, Mozart or Haydn, to say nothing of many lesser figures. Apart from anything else, Wagner is the composer *par excellence* of adolescence, of immaturity, as Swinburne is the poet. To admire Wagner, except for certain aspects of his technical accomplishment, after the age of about twenty, is a sure sign of arrested development and unfulfilled sexual experience; for the emotional and spiritual content of his work is that of a substitute for life, the first of the *Ersatz* products in the invention of which his race has shown so much ingenuity; and composers since have far outpaced him in the capacity for stimulating the senses and gratifying the emotions which was the secret of his immense success with the generation which is now extinct, and of whom the last venerable survivor is Mr. Ernest Newman, the last of the dodos.

Wagner lies buried under the ruins of the order of which he was the prime creator: he made it, and he perishes with it. Indeed, the extent to which the National Socialist movement had its source and origin in Wagner is still not yet fully recognized—not merely in the chauvinistic, mystic glorification of the Teutonic race as preached in *Die Meistersinger*, the *Jugend* cult expressed in the conception of *Siegfried*, or the Jew-baiting of his polemic writings; but far more significant and fundamental, in the love-death complex, the ecstasy of self-destruction, the longing for annihilation voiced in *Tristan;* but above all in *Die Götterdämmerung*. In his heart of hearts the Teuton, despite every evidence to the contrary, does not really want to conquer: he wants to go down to a glorious tragic death, and if he can bring everything and everybody else down with him at the same time so much the better, the happier he will be. In that lies his psychological fulfilment, his victory; and it looks as if at last he has achieved it. Wagner, in short, is as certainly the creator of the Nazi Revolution as Voltaire and Rousseau were of the French Revolution; and the suicide of Hitler in the ruins of Berlin is the complete Wagnerian *dénouement*—the last scene of *Die Götterdämmerung*.

The fact remains that during these years of my development —from fifteen to eighteen approximately—I was the complete Wagnerian. I lived entirely in the world of *The Ring*, with its gods, Rhinemaidens, Valkyries, giants, dwarfs, heroes, heroines, and all the rest of these preposterous figures. For me, then, they were not mythology but reality: I believed in their veritable existence and lived in and with them. The rest of the Wagnerian canon meant little to me in comparison with *The Ring*. The early works, apart from *The Flying Dutchman* Overture and the Prelude to *Lohengrin*, bored me profoundly; while the hot-house sensuality of *Tristan* and the Teutonic homespun of *Die Meistersinger*, apart from isolated passages, left me comparatively unmoved. As for *Parsifal*, even in my most Wagnerian days I actively disliked it. To-day it is the only work of Wagner's that interests me, for purely technical reasons: I still dislike it—but there are things that one can learn from it. For the rest, the world of Wagner is to-day entirely dead for me, and I never wish to hear another note of his music so long as I live. But I shall never be able, nor do I wish, to forget all that he meant to me in my youth, or the debt that I owe him for awakening the spirit of music that had been lying dormant in me since early childhood, as Siegfried awoke the sleeping Brünnhilde with a kiss.

How, it may be asked, do I reconcile this period of Teutonic Wagnerian domination with the basically Latin predilections which I have proclaimed in earlier pages? Quite simply. Wagner was the precursor and creator of the Nazi order, and in just the same way that Hitler's hordes overran the whole of Europe like a swarm of locusts, eating up and devastating everything that stood in their path; so, in the realm of the spirit did the art of Wagner dominate that of every other country, including the Latin countries, and every individual artist in them, during the period of his ascendancy, which was finally overthrown by the same combination of the forces of East and West as later, in the political field. And so with me personally. In my youth Wagner overwhelmed me, and I was similarly freed from his domination by the revelation operated by the combined influence of Russian, French and English art —of Borodin and Moussorgsky, Debussy and Ravel, and Delius. The final *coup de grâce* was effected by Italian music.

Chapter Six

IN THE foregoing chapter I have attempted to show the close and intimate symbiosis which exists between the artist and the criminal, how together they constitute the obverse and reverse faces of the same anti-social coin, the one creative and the other destructive, and the way in which, in my particular case, they alternated. With my escape from the spiritual prison of school I experienced a sense of liberation and a corresponding development of the positive and creative aspect of the dichotomy. On the other hand, it is curious and instructive to note that the other side of it was not entirely in abeyance—for a short time, indeed, they existed side by side—and no better illustration could possibly be found of the inter-relation of the two activities than the following incident.

In spite of the fact that music came first with me in these years, between fifteen and eighteen, my appetite for and appreciation of literature did not lag far behind, and much of my time was spent in browsing around bookshops and buying books up to the limits of my financial capacity, which were very narrow at that time. One day, when haphazardly turning over the leaves of various volumes of poetry, I came across one by an author of whom I had never heard, but the very first poem in the volume struck so strong and decisive a chord in me that I was physically shaken by it, as I had never before and seldom since have been by any poetry; it was "The Hosting of the Sidhe" in the volume entitled *The Wind among the Reeds*, by W. B. Yeats. I knew I had to have the book or die: I could not even wait for the next day. In trepidation I looked at the price: it was 8s. 6d. I felt tremblingly in my pocket, knowing quite well that I had nothing approaching that sum, and found no more than 2s. 10d., as I had roughly anticipated. What was I to do? One thing alone was certain: I had to have that book. Since I had not enough money to buy it there was only one solution. Looking furtively around, I noted that the assistants were all engaged, so nonchalantly slipping the book into my pocket, I left the shop. Once outside, I broke out into a cold perspiration and my heart was thumping so loudly that I was afraid the passers-by in the street would hear it. On arriving home I collapsed on my bed, more dead than alive, but soon recovered sufficiently to read the whole volume from beginning to end, in a transport of ecstasy.

To this day I do not know quite whether to be proud or ashamed of this exploit. What I should have done, of course, was to have noted the title and waited until I had saved up enough to buy it in a legitimate way; but this simply did not occur to me. I had to have that book then and there, and I acted on sheer impulse. My need was so great that I was ready and willing to run the risk of discovery, with all the disgrace and humiliation that would have attached to it, rather than to suffer a moment's deprivation of this newly-found source of unutterable joy. In later years, on meeting Yeats, I told him the story; he was deeply touched, and absolved me with his pontifical blessing. The episode may reflect adversely upon me, but what greater tribute could be paid to the poet? Yeats appreciated that.

One final anecdote and I have finished with my criminal career. I am now, and have been for a long time, the most honourable and law-abiding citizen, a model of social virtue. It concerns a premeditated theft which, however, was not carried into execution, to my infinite regret, and exemplifies once more the close relationship existing between artistic idealism and criminal practice.

The last, and in many ways the greatest work of Hector Berlioz is the monumental epic opera in two parts, *Les Troyens*. Since Berlioz died in 1869 the work has long been out of copyright and anyone would be at perfect liberty in law to reprint the full score, provided he could secure a copy of it. But the original French publishers obstinately refuse to allow a single copy to pass from their hands except for a public performance in an opera-house, and subject to the signature by the recipient of a solemn undertaking on no account to allow the score out of his hands or to permit any transcription of it in full or in part. The consequence is that one of the greatest works in the literature of music remains a sealed book to all music-lovers and students, apart from the inadequate vocal score, and seems fated to remain in perpetuity the private property of a purely commercial firm of publishers, instead of belonging, as it should, to the whole world.

Such a state of affairs seemed to me—and surely is—utterly intolerable, and I consequently determined on a scheme to burgle the premises and remove a copy of the score and have it published; being willing, in the event of prosecution, to serve a sentence of imprisonment. With this end in view, I succeeded in making tentative contacts with some promising crooks in Paris, but the project fell through on account of the excessive charges demanded for what would have been a very simple and straightforward job of work. Then the war broke out, and I have abandoned the idea for good. But will some casuist tell me: if the scheme had succeeded, would it have been a crime or a virtuous act on my part? I know what *I* think.[1]

Now, as I say, I have turned over a new leaf and, although like the celebrated fictional amateur cracksman Raffles I live in Albany, I have finally renounced the life of crime for which at one time I seemed destined. I doubt whether I should have been very successful at it, in any case.

At the period of which I am writing (1910–14) the career of a musician seemed as remote a possibility as a life of crime— remoter even, and it was decided that when my health had sufficiently recovered I should take up the study of chemistry with a view to entering ultimately into the metallurgical side

[1]Bernard van Dieren and W. J. Turner were fellow-conspirators.

of the family business, the iron-foundry in Edinburgh. After a few months of study in a laboratory, however, I knew no more about the uncongenial subject than when I started; in fact, in any subject which does not interest me, my capacity for acquiring knowledge is spectacularly subnormal—I am like a village idiot. My parents were mournfully compelled to recognize the fact that it was useless for me to continue—that I should never be anything but an abject failure as either an analytical chemist or a business man. On the other hand, the idea of taking up music as a profession was not even considered seriously. In consequence, it was decided that, pending a definite decision as to my ultimate career, I should temporize and mark time by taking a course at a university.

I was generously offered the choice between Oxford and Cambridge, but with a degree of insight which surprises me to-day I resolutely declined both alternatives, and agreed upon a compromise in the form of study for an Arts degree at Edinburgh University. I suppose I must have been subconsciously aware of the fact that these two venerable institutions, despite the glamorous seductiveness of their reputation, were only a continuation and prolongation of the world from which I had fought so violently to escape—the sequence of public school and university, leading to the finished product of the English gentleman, together constituting the absolute antithesis to the world of art which alone meant anything to me.

I chose more wisely than I knew, for, although it is no doubt possible to point to an occasional artist who has been to one or the other of these establishments and has escaped with his soul intact, such examples are few and far between. I cannot think of a single painter or sculptor and, apart from Vaughan Williams, not a single musician—only a handful of minor poets who might have been major if they had escaped the fate of spending their most formative and impressionable years in one or the other of these mediaeval institutions. I hasten to add that no one has a greater respect and veneration for them than I have, but the time of life to which they are suited is not youth but maturity. No one should be admitted to Oxford or Cambridge before attaining the age of at least forty, for only then is one capable of appreciating and absorbing all they have to give, while avoiding the irreparable injury they almost invariably inflict upon the adolescent mind, especially on that of the potential artist. They act like a blight upon the creative spirit from which the younger, less traditional universities, such as that of Edinburgh, are free. These latter are neither one thing nor the other, negative and therefore comparatively harmless.

In accordance with this compromise I spent the greater part of my sixteenth and seventeenth years with a dreary succession of tutors and professional coaches, filling up the breaches in my general scholastic education which had been occasioned by my illness, in order to pass my matriculation, which I was able to do without much difficulty, and I entered upon a course of study at Edinburgh University in 1913, taking as subjects for the first year history and French literature.

Music, however, continued to be my chief preoccupation in these years, and my knowledge and appreciation of it received an enormously accentuated stimulus through annual visits to Bad Nauheim, near Frankfurt-on-Main, whither I had been ordered for heart treatment, and where there was an excellent orchestra which played three times a day: morning, afternoon and evening, with special symphony concerts once a week, to say nothing of frequent chamber-music recitals, in virtue of which I became acquainted with the entire field of German instrumental music from Haydn to Richard Strauss. In addition, one of the dearest ambitions of my youth was realized, in my first visit to Italy, in 1912, before I went to Edinburgh University. After wintering on the Côte d'Azur with my parents, we reached Rome in early spring, where we stayed for a couple of months, returning by way of Florence, Venice and Munich, *en route* for Bad Nauheim. What nostalgic memories of these wonderful pre-War days these recollections revive!—the last days of the old world, the old order and civilization, destined so soon to disappear and which I was privileged to know, if only for one brief, fleeting moment.

The Edinburgh compromise worked admirably. My knowledge of both history and French literature were far in advance of the standard required and, apart from attending the necessary number of lectures, I was able to devote my entire time to music and literature. Apart from attempts at composition, I formed the habit of writing a short story every day—a practice which I maintained unbroken for over a month. But neither these literary efforts nor the music I wrote gave me any satisfaction: it was all uniformly bad, without any redeeming feature. On the other hand, a certain measure of reassurance, both to my parents and myself, was afforded by my success in winning the Lord Rector's Prize for the year (1914), which was awarded for an essay on the subject of "Carlyle and Michelet compared as historians and men of letters", the adjudicator being no less formidable a scholar and critic than Professor George Saintsbury. The subject was, of course, providentially suited to me, as I already knew most of Carlyle's work and read French well enough to be able to digest the voluminous output of the great historian of the Romantic Movement in France.

I spent the entire proceeds—about twenty pounds, so far as I can remember, the first money I ever earned by my pen—on buying books, including principally an edition of the complete works of Turgeniev: which leads me to the final paramount influence in these early years of development—the Russian. I cannot clearly recollect now which of the two constituted the initial impact of this influence, the literature or the music; but they came so closely together that any distinction between them is immaterial. But the combined effect on me was overwhelming, like that of a disease, a raging fever. The Slav influence ousted the Teutonic, entirely curing me of it, but inculcating a subtle virus of its own. Both, however, were alien influences; neither of them have exercised any permanent influence upon my work, for good or bad. But the

Russian obsession, like the Wagnerian, was, while it lasted, all-powerful and reached its climax when, in the summer of 1914, on my way from Edinburgh to Bad Nauheim for my annual course of treatment, I spent a week in London, during which I had the privilege of enjoying one of the greatest artistic experiences ever known to mortal man—the final pre-War season of the Russian opera and ballet company at Covent Garden. All available seats had, of course, been reserved for weeks ahead, so I had to spend the greater part of each day standing in a queue for the gallery. Not that I grudged a moment of it; on the contrary, one's enjoyment was positively enhanced by the penance one had to undergo in advance. How much pleasanter, incidentally, to make penance first and have the pleasure afterwards!

Among the many memorable experiences of that wonderful season, the ones which stand out most prominently in my recollection were the *Daphnis et Chloë* of Ravel, *Le Rossignol* and *Petrouchka* of Stravinsky, but above all the *Boris Godounov* of Moussorgsky with Chaliapin in the title rôle—an unforgettable revelation of consummate artistry, both vocal and histrionic, displayed in one of the greatest masterpieces of music drama. Small matter that the version one heard was the bowdlerization effected by Rimsky-Korsakov: the effect of the original version could not have been more overwhelming.

I was no longer a Wagnerian. The spell was broken, the Teutonic mists dispersed. Next day I left for Bad Nauheim; it must have been about the 20th July, 1914. On arriving there I was too utterly and blissfully intoxicated with music to pay the slightest attention to the rapidly lowering storm-clouds on the political horizon. Anxious telegrams from my parents, urging me to return, I blandly ignored. Panic-stricken alarmists, I thought; had I not read *The Great Illusion* of Norman Angell, in which the author conclusively proved that war benefits no one, not even the victor? The peoples of Europe are not such fools; besides, next Saturday there is that symphony concert, which I must on no account miss!

But a day came when my doctor, a genial little German Jew named Lilienstein, came to see me, very worried, and entreated me to leave at once. Russia had declared war on Germany, and it was only a matter of days before England would inevitably be involved. I suddenly awoke, aghast, from my blissful musical dreams to a world of harsh political reality, and made arrangements for departure. My reactions were not at all of a tragic nature, of anticipations of world-wide ruin and slaughter, and so forth, but chiefly of annoyance at the interruption of what promised to be a most enjoyable series of concerts.

My chief recollections of my last days in Bad Nauheim were, firstly, a vision of entrancing loveliness in the form of a beautiful girl in a diaphanous rose-coloured frock on the terrace of the Kursaal—I can still see her vividly before me as I write—who came between me and the sinking sun in such a way that her exquisite limbs were outlined to me as if naked, in a kind of X-rays; and secondly, a revelation of utter misery and ugliness when, on saying good-bye to my friend, Dr. Lilienstein, in a café, the orchestra struck up *Deutschland über Alles;* whereupon my little Jewish friend and the conductor of the orchestra, a roaring queen if ever there was one, corseted, with painted face and sporting an obvious wig (a good conductor, none the less), jumped up on a table with brimming tankards and drank to the destruction of the enemies of Germany, and of England principally—the arch-enemy.

The journey home was a nightmare. By good fortune rather than design I had decided to return through Holland rather than Belgium. If I had chosen the latter route I should never have got through, and would have spent the next four years of my life in the internment camp of Rühleben, since German troops were already moving into Belgium and civilian traffic had been entirely suspended. As it was, after a tiring journey from Frankfort to Cologne, I had to spend over twelve hours, without food, drink or sleep, on the platform of the railway station, awaiting what proved to be the last train available for enemy aliens out of Germany, which when it eventually came in and departed, was so crowded that one had to stand all the way to the Dutch frontier. By the time I reached it the frontier officials informed me that it was too late to cross over without a passport or equivalent permit, which I did not possess. But I had a small store of golden sovereigns in my pocket, which in desperation I pressed into the palm of the chief official—whether Dutch or German I do not know—whose attention was thereupon conveniently diverted to another quarter for the space of a few vital seconds, during which I slipped through the barrier unmolested—penniless, but free—arrived back in England after forty-eight hours without food or sleep, and made my way home to Edinburgh.

My feelings about the War were not unnaturally more than a little confused. I had left a self-righteous Chauvinistic Germany proclaiming indignantly to the world that she was being unjustly attacked by neighbours, though desiring nothing but friendship and good-will towards all men; and when I got home I found exactly the same mentality, the same arguments, the same catchwords. The kindly, genial, humanitarian little Jewish doctor I had known, now suddenly transformed, with his face as red as a turkey-cock, standing on the café table and yelling defiance at Germany's enemies, was exactly paralleled in my own home in the person of my father, who seemed to me to have equally become suddenly insane—the mildest, gentlest person in the world, bellowing for German blood.

It seemed to me, in fact, that the whole world had gone mad —as indeed it had—but I was determined to be the one sane person left in it, if possible. I straightway resolved that I would have nothing to do with this *danse macabre*, this sinister St. Vitus dance of destructive fury which had broken loose; at the same time I realized that it was going to be very difficult to keep out of it. My first move was to volunteer immediately for the Army, knowing perfectly well that with my medical record I would be at once rejected. Having thereby placated my bellicose relations I felt at liberty to continue in the path I had mapped out for myself, subject to unavoidable modifications. Shortly before the outbreak of the War I had at last obtained from my parents their reluctant consent to the adoption of a musical career, or at least to a course of study at a continental *conservatoire:* in pursuance whereof I had made arrangements to work at the *Schola Cantorum* under Vincent d'Indy, being as averse to the traditions of the German *conservatoires,* such as Frankfurt and Leipzig as to those of the Royal College and the Royal Academy in London, to say nothing of the Paris Conservatoire. Since the war had put an end to that plan, and my prejudices remained constant, I came to the conclusion that the best solution was to have resort to the one outstanding musical institution in England which was in opposition to the orthodox academic course of training—namely, the Midland Institute at Birmingham, under the direction of Sir (then Mr.) Granville Bantock, to which I duly repaired, in the autumn of 1914.

The experience was acutely disillusioning. The pedantic orthodoxy which in these days prevailed at the College and Academy, and against which I had in anticipation reacted so violently, was replaced in Birmingham by a state of complete anarchy. Bantock's personal tastes and sympathies lay entirely on the side of contemporary developments. Not that the classics were excluded from consideration, by any means; on the contrary, the student was encouraged to study the works of the old masters, but no attempt was made to co-ordinate ancient and modern practice. Even within the new world of modern music everything was equally held up to admiration and approval, and recommended as a model for imitation—Strauss and Debussy, Scriabine and Stravinsky, Ravel and Delius. There was no sense of direction in the methods of tuition employed; one was permitted, and encouraged, to do anything one liked. At one moment I would be studying strict counterpoint and harmony with that highly accomplished musician, Dr. W. H. Harris, and at the next I would be encouraged by the genial Principal to pay no attention to such outworn conventions and to write as the spirit moved me.

The spirit moved me in very strange ways indeed, my first composition submitted for consideration being a setting of a Chinese poem translated by Cranmer Byng, for voice, piano and string quartet, which went so far beyond *Le Rossignol* of Stravinsky in perverse dissonance that even Bantock himself, the arch-priest of modernity, visibly wilted and blenched. But instead of putting it quietly in the waste-paper basket as it deserved, and telling me to go away and write a motet in the style of Palestrina or Byrd, as he should have done, he merely suggested a few minor alterations here and there, and left it at that.

The influence of Bantock was inspiring, invigorating, stimulating; but this was not what I needed, but rather control, discipline, and a sense of direction, and these were not to be had at the Midland Institute. It is probable that, after all, I would have done better to have gone to the College or the Academy in London; it is difficult to say. But just as I should no doubt have reacted violently against the traditions then in vogue at these institutions, and become more wildly experimental than ever, so I reacted against the anarchical methods and outlook of the Midland Institute in favour of a more restrained and conventional style of composition.

In the long run, in fact, the experience possibly did me good, and cured me of my tendency to excess and experimentalism by means of the treatment familiar to modern medical practice, of injecting the patient with a serum prepared from the very germs of the disease from which he is suffering. At the time, however, I felt I was getting nowhere, and I left Birmingham after a term. It was on my return to Edinburgh that I first came across the *Songs of the Hebrides* collected by Marjory Kennedy Fraser, which made upon me the deep impression to which I have alluded at the outset of this book. For the first time I experienced a definite sense of direction: I felt that at last I had found myself. Banished for ever were the Teutonic Wagnerian fogs and the seductive exoticism of the Slavonic world. I reverted to the national polarity—that of the Celt and the Latin, and have never since deserted it.

After spending some months in Edinburgh, working assiduously, I finally obtained permission from my reluctant, long-suffering and always in the end responsive parents, to settle in London, alone, which project was duly realized in September, 1915. I installed myself in a miniature flat at 124, Cheyne Walk, near World's End, where I spent several months composing, writing, reading, and trying—unsuccessfully—to learn to play the piano, hardly ever going out and never seeing anyone—not that there was anyone to see, for I did not know a single soul in London, and I made no effort whatsoever to get to know anyone. I led a completely hermit-like existence.

Not that there was anything new in this. Apart from the incomprehensible friendships of school boyhood, which dissolve so completely at maturity that one would run a mile rather than have to encounter any of the objects of it, if only because one would be unable to find any topic of conversation save the weather, I always led a very lonely, troglodytic existence, in a psychological cave, exclusively nourished on books and music. Human contacts meant little or nothing to me.

To this generalization there was one great exception: a painter, named Eric Robertson, whom I came to know in Edinburgh about 1912, and to whom I owe a very deep debt of gratitude. In the first place it was he who, almost literally, first opened my eyes and introduced me to the world of the visual arts. Théophile Gautier described himself as "one for whom the visible world exists"; I could, in these days, have said that I was one for whom the visible world did not exist at all. I lived in, with, by, and from, the ear almost exclusively, introvert and introspective, in a musical dream-world.

Apart from his service in helping to develop my defective visual sense, Eric Robertson was also a stimulating talker and thinker, who had read widely in many fields. I have known many brilliant men in my time, as will be seen, but none who made a greater impression upon me. This, no doubt, was due in large part to my relative immaturity at the time when I first made his acquaintance—he was about seven years older than I—but not entirely so, for in subsequent years, although we saw each other very seldom, and in latter years hardly at all, I always found his company as stimulating as when it made its first impact upon me.

Above all, however, it was his social sense and genius for human contacts which were of most value to me in these days. It was due to his friendship that I became acquainted with the few intelligent people who lived in Edinburgh—for however lovely a city she may be, and no one admires her more than I, the inhabitants are, for the most part—or were in my youth, at least—the most provincial, puritanical, Philistine community on the face of the earth.

At the time when I first met him, Eric Robertson had already acquired a considerable degree of repute—disrepute would, perhaps, be more accurate, for he was accounted a dangerous and subversive immoralist, and his pictures were a perpetual cause of scandal and indignation in our native city. His particular predilection, his *leif-motif*, was the depiction on large canvases of nude couples, male and female, swooning ecstatically in the moment of exhaustion which succeeds the act of love.

He was unquestionably a fine draughtsman, but as a painter he was too much influenced by the Pre-Raphaelites, Gustave Moreau and William Blake, to appeal to contemporary taste. But if or when the wheel turns full circle, as it generally does sooner or later, it would not entirely surprise me if his art achieved a degree of recognition which it signally failed to achieve in his lifetime. That he had genius no one who ever came into contact with him could possibly doubt. It may well be, however, that he had chosen the wrong medium of expression, and that he was potentially a writer rather than a painter.

To revert: I spent the first few months after my translation to London like a monk in a cell, working hard, going nowhere, seeing no one. I completed the score of a large orchestral work, which I sent to Granville Bantock, and received a letter from him (which I have lost, or mislaid) in which he said many kind and encouraging things, and suggested that I should send it to Sir Dan Godfrey at Bournemouth, who would no doubt be prepared to consider its performance. I never did so, however, not being satisfied with the work. I also embarked on several literary projects mostly connected with music, the chief of which were studies of the Nietzsche-Wagner relationship, and nationalism in art; but I was as dissatisfied with them as with the music I had written.

I had begun to settle down into a state of morbid self-distrust and melancholy impotence when I received a letter from Eric Robertson announcing his proximate arrival in London, and asking me if I could put him up at my place for the duration of his visit. He duly arrived and, recognizing at a glance the symptoms of the disease from which I was suffering, he persuaded me, without much difficulty, to lay my books and music on one side, emerge from my shell, and cultivate Life, with a very large capital L. I was then nearly twenty-one and virtually still a holy innocent in most important respects, but under his able guidance and tuition I soon made up for all the time I had lost, and rather more.

The Café Royal was the chief focus of my initiation into the joys of Life. In these far-off days it was still a café and not the dreary restaurant into which it has since gradually declined: a place, chiefly, where artists foregathered to talk and drink. Within a few days, thanks to Eric, I established contacts which in their turn brought me into touch with others, in an ever-widening series of concentric circles, until within a few weeks I found myself blissfully involved in the vortex of London's artistic and "Bohemian" life. It is more than likely, of course, that this would have happened sooner or later, but the fact remains that the initial impetus, the stone cast into the placid, stagnant waters, came from Eric Robertson. I have always found it difficult to take the first step in any direction: I have generally to be impelled. But once started, I find it equally difficult to stop: I have to be forcibly restrained.

The sudden transformation which took place in my mode of life caused the utmost alarm and despondency at 124, Cheyne Walk. The shy, studious, cloistered young paragon of virtue turned overnight into the precise opposite—a wild, riotous, dissipated youth-about-town, coming home at all hours of the night and making them hideous with revelry in the lowest kind of company, male and female.

If the Café Royal was the centre around which my life vertiginously revolved, the centre around which the Café Royal revolved was an odd character named Rudolph Vesey. A young man of independent means, he was merely a hanger-on to the skirts of the Art world, and did precisely nothing, but on a monumental scale. He lived with an old aunt, exceedingly rich, who was devoted to him; and after he had run through his own private fortune, which he did in a very short time and in spectacular fashion, he proceeded to run through that of his aunt likewise, seemingly with her full consent. His parties, which took place nightly, were Heliogabalian and Sardana-palian in the magnitude and lavishness of his hospitality. He kept open door to all who cared to come; liquor of all kinds flowed in unimaginable profusion, and no restraint of any kind was placed upon the conduct of his guests, which was generally more, and never less, than baroque. At the same time, he was a devout Roman Catholic, and when dawn broke over the orgiastic scene he would invariably repair to Westminster Cathedral for early Mass. He died some years later, as the result of a motor-car accident. I cherish his memory as that of a kindly, gentle, generous fool, whose foolishness, however, was in the grand Petronian, Trimalchian manner.

Waking up early one evening after a more than usually wild orgy at one of Rudolph Vesey's parties, which had continued into the the late hours of the morning, I underwent a sudden revulsion against the crazy existence I had for some time been leading; and, remembering that I had previously seen that Sir Thomas Beecham was to conduct a performance of Berlioz's *Roméo et Juliette* at Queen's Hall that night, I arose, dressed and hastened there. I had already, for a long time, entertained a fanatical devotion to this strange and solitary figure in the history of music (it will be understood that his loneliness and isolation were an important factor in my admiration), but I had never heard this particular work, neither had I ever set eyes on the score.

On taking a seat in the gallery, I found myself sitting next to a person who attracted my attention in a way that I had never experienced before. Immaculately clad in a suit of unusual cut, with delicately moulded Latin features, dark hair and eyes, a complexion with the unearthly pallor of old ivory, and a sardonically twisted mouth, he seemed the very embodiment and reincarnation of some figure from the 1830's, of the period in which Berlioz lived and worked, and wrote the music which I was to hear that evening for the first time; or you might say that he was like an apparition from out of the pages of E. T. A. Hoffmann—inhuman almost, giving forth effortlessly, unconsciously, an hypnotic dæmonic power.

Whether it was due to the music, to the impact of the personality of my mysterious neighbour, or to a combination of both, or merely to a normal psychological reaction, or all three, the fact remains that after the concert was over I went quietly home instead of resorting to the Café Royal and the society of my boon companions, as I would normally have done, and meditated deeply before I retired to bed; coming to the conclusion that it was time I started to work again after the wild, irresponsible, but by no means profitless *intermezzo scherzando* in which I had been indulging; on the contrary, I am sure that it constituted a salutary and much needed corrective to the morbid inclination towards introspection and self-analysis which had been so characteristic of the period of my adolescence.

Such noble resolutions, of course, do not always take effect
immediately, and when they do are liable to subsequent violent
reversal; and I shall not pretend that this experience, with its
combination of the art of Berlioz and the impact of the
personality of the mysterious stranger, was in the nature of a
sudden Pauline Road-to-Damascus conversion: I did not, in
consequence, suddenly turn my back upon the flesh-pots. On
the contrary, I discovered for the first time the interdepen-
dence of the joys of life and of art, and the indissolubility of
the delectable trinity of wine, woman and song, the cult of
which I have, ever since these days, been the most impassioned
advocate and the most consistent practitioner. The artist, in
my view and experience, who does not care for the joys of wine
and the beauty of women, is simply not an artist at all.

I admit, on the other hand, that it is difficult to serve and
placate all three divinities impartially, all the time. The
triple invertible counterpoint is difficult to handle, except in
the years of one's youth, and even then only for a short period.
Work and drink, love and work, love and drink—these three
pairs go together very well, but it is better not to attempt to do
justice to all three simultaneously: the consequence is apt to be
that all alike suffer. In fact, as Abraham Lincoln might have
said, you can do all three part of the time, any two all the time,
but not all three all the time.

Of all the contacts I made in these early formative days the
most important and fruitful was that with Philip Heseltine
("Peter Warlock"), who shared equally with me the cult of the
delectable trinity. I have already described at length and in
detail the circumstances of our meeting and subsequent
friendship, in the book I have devoted to his memory and
surviving reality,[1] so it would be otiose if I were to traverse the
same ground again here.

It is enough to say that, having made myself thoroughly
unpopular in Cheyne Walk by having exchanged "in a trice,
the lilies and languors of virtue for the raptures and roses of

[1] *Peter Warlock.* (Jonathan Cape. 1934.)

vice", it became both desirable and necessary for me to find accommodation elsewhere. The climax came when Eric Robertson found himself impelled by his creative urge, at about four o'clock one morning, to improvise a rhapsody on the piano: his technique consisting chiefly in what are called "chord-clusters" of adjacent tones and semitones, played with the fists and interspersed with meteoric *glissandi* over the whole compass of the keyboard. (I should, perhaps, add that he had previously decorated the walls of the flat with hair-raising frescoes of a kind that would have brought a blush to the cheeks of Toulouse Lautrec.)

On my precipitate and enforced departure from Cheyne Walk, Philip and I set up a joint establishment on the other other side of the river, in Battersea. It was shortly before this that Jacob Epstein, whom we had both come to know in the Café Royal, suggested that we might be interested to meet a musician of his acquaintance, to whom he duly introduced us some few days later. To my astonishment he proved to be none other than the mysterious, enigmatic personality whom I had encountered at the Berlioz concert only a short time before, and who had since haunted my imagination. Such a coincidence was startling and seemed like a direct manifestation of Fate—and such it proved to be in the sequel.

He invited us to his house in Hampstead next day and we duly kept the appointment—Philip rather unwillingly, being in a sceptical and cynical mood at the time. But I remember saying to him that a man of such magnetic personality could not possibly be of other than supreme stature, and my high expectations were amply confirmed. The few fragments of his works which he was able to play—for they were exceedingly difficult, and he was the world's worst pianist—were enough to convince me that I was confronted by one of the most significant musicians of the age.

On returning home that evening I sat down to write a letter to Bernard van Dieren, for such was his name. He saw fit to preserve it, and after his death it was returned to me. If I reproduce it here, in spite of its (to me, at least) distressing naivety, it is because I still unhesitatingly subscribe to its fundamental implications.

9th June, 1916.   124, Cheyne Walk,
                                              Chelsea,
                                                  S.W.

DEAR MR. VAN DIEREN,

I hope you will not think it impertinence on my part to write you after so short an acquaintance; if you do, I hope you will forgive me, but there are so many things I should like to say which are not easily spoken—firstly the effect your work has had upon me. I have seldom been so affected by art before. It is rather difficult to express the exact sensations I experienced, but I might almost say that it came to me not so much as a revelation of undreamt-of possibilities, but rather as a consummation; a fulfilment of an ideal which I have been vaguely formulating for some years—the ideal of an art quite different from anything else that is being done to-day. Wherever I turned, whether to Strauss, Debussy, Ravel, Scriabine, Stravinsky, I was always dissatisfied. At first, of course, in the manner of youth, I endowed them with all the attributes I hoped to find in them, only to be disillusioned in the end. My dream, I need hardly say, was of an art diametrically opposed to that of so-called impressionism, that externality which has so overrun all modern art—an art which would pick up the dropped threads of the so-called classic tradition and weave them together with the rich resource and expressiveness of the ʼ moderns—not indeed as Brahms did it or tried to do it by turning his back upon modern life and by divorcing his art from actuality, by making it spiritually only a feeble echo of his predecessors—but by using this language to express the fundamental emotions of life, by expressing things which could never have been expressed before.

And it seems to me, then, that in your art—what I have heard of it—I have at last found what I have so long been seeking for.

As for myself and my work, the less said the better. I have done nothing. I have spent all the time I might have spent in mastering technical difficulties, etc., in dreaming and in idleness. It is, of course, not too late—I am only 21. But I have one terrible disability, which is indeed largely the reason for my writing you. I so badly need advice and help, and there is no one to whom I can turn. Briefly, it is this.

I think I may say without conceit that I have great ideas and big conceptions for works, but the moment I try to seize anything definite, it all fades away. I can never realise my visions. The music I wish to write defies notation—there is nothing to help me to grasp it. What I want to know then, is this—Is this feeling of impotence an actual thing or is it due merely to insufficient technical mastery? Is the thought inexpressible, or the technical ability inadequate?

Naturally, no one could answer such questions off-hand, but I thought that you yourself might perhaps in your early days have experienced this same feeling. I have tried to evade the problem during the last six months by deliberately setting aside all thoughts of creation, by occupying myself with life instead of art and leaving my artistic development to work subconsciously. But it is no good. I only become miserable and dissatisfied with everything: cynical and disillusioned.

But I do not see what right I have to inflict my difficulties on you. But if you can give me any help or advice I would be eternally grateful. There is no greater hell for an artist than to be haunted by splendid visions and to feel that he can never capture them. But perhaps it is preferable to self-satisfied littleness.

Forgive my presumption in writing to you like this; my admiration of your art is alone responsible for it.

Yours sincerely,
CECIL GRAY.

These thoughts and sentiments, clumsily and inadequately expressed, were written thirty years ago; and if I leave them unaltered it is because, after these many years of vicissitude and stress, including the decisive reversal of many opinions I would have thought immutable, I still think the same of van Dieren's work as I did then. If I were to write that letter to-day I would, I hope, write it better, but that is all: the substance would remain unchanged.

The fact that the majority vote has gone against me, so far as my superlative estimate of the merits of van Dieren's music is concerned, troubles me not at all. I have never had the slightest doubts or misgivings about it since that day in June, 1916, when I first became acquainted with it. There are certain experiences in life which are decisive and this was one of them; not even the opposition of the entire world could shake my faith in that revelation of what the Spanish call *El momento del verdad* (the moment of truth). As it happens, I am by no means alone in my belief. William Walton, Constant Lambert, Arthur Bliss, to mention the names of only three outstanding musicians of our time, all subscribe to my high estimate of van Dieren, and I could easily multiply the number. But even if I were alone it would make no difference: my conviction is absolute.

That his art has faults and shortcomings I would readily admit. I do not know of any art that has not faults equal to and corresponding to its virtues—the two things, as I have said earlier in these pages, go together and condition each other— and no one is better qualified for the rôle of *advocatus diaboli* in the case of van Dieren than I am, simply because I know his work better than anyone else.

The point of crucial importance in this connexion, the reason why I am so sure and unshakable in the rightness of my judgment where van Dieren is concerned, consists in the fact that his music is emphatically not the kind of music I write myself, nor would if I could. Criticism and appreciation, in fact, are of two different kinds: with the first, one admires one's affinities, the things one does oneself or would like to be able to do oneself. This form of appreciation is a form of Narcissism: one is admiring one's own reflection in a mirror. The other form of appreciation consists in the admiration of the qualities one does not possess—of the things one is unable to achieve oneself; and this approach provides a very much more reliable, because more objective, standard of values and judgment than the Narcissist standard.

My profound admiration of the music of van Dieren has always been essentially of the second order—objective and dispassionate rather than subjective and personal, as I shall shortly show. But in any case I do not propose to deal at length with his work here: this is neither the time nor the place. Just as I have devoted a book to the life and work of Peter Warlock in recent years, so I propose in the near future to make a study of van Dieren. It is enough for the moment to say that as the outcome of the deep impression made upon both Philip Heseltine and myself by his work, we both arranged to embark upon a course of tuition with him, with a singularly piquant contrast in results, which bears out the truth of the observations made above. Philip derived great benefit from his course of study with van Dieren and, indeed, found himself to a great extent for the first time as a result of this direct influence. His appreciation of van Dieren was, in fact, of the first kind defined above, what I have called the Narcissist variety, the outcome of a positive affinity. I, on the contrary, in spite of all my admiration for his work, and all his positive and active sympathy for me, was never able to derive any direct benefit from his teaching: my appreciation was of the second order. The highly idiosyncratic nature of his art, and consequently of his method of instruction, proved completely unassimilable and inadaptable to the purposes of my own work. Consequently, after some half a dozen lessons, they were abandoned by mutual consent.

On the other hand, although I derived no direct benefit from the influence of van Dieren so far as my work was concerned, his general cultural, educative influence on me was deep and profound, whereas on Philip it amounted to nothing. To him I owe the greater part of whatever sense of values I possess. I find it difficult to imagine what I should have been, or how I would have developed, if I had never known him.

The direct influence, however, was, as I have said, precisely nil. I might even go further and say that it was positively deleterious in a sense. I was so impressed by his work that I felt I ought to write like him or not at all, and I tried hard and failed dismally.

The consequence was that once more I fell into a condition of utterly despondent sterility. He was well aware of this conflict and genuinely distressed at it, as will be seen from the following extracts from a long letter which he wrote me at this time:—

"I live with you in the mental struggles you are being tormented with, more so perhaps than you imagine, and that because in your reports of them I recognize so well dilemmas and problems on which I too have expended several horse power of energy. I should imagine though that at present you are inclined to let such troubles exercise a power over you they do not deserve. I cannot help thinking you take some of such problems too seriously. Don't you believe that often when one reads a book, one comprehends so well and penetrates into the work so completely, that frequently the very words in it assume a significance they would never possess if they were only seen in relation to the sentence in which they occur? An analogy you find in the biblical studies of mediaeval theologians who from their very penetration into the scriptures become at last even perversely mystical in their interpretation of the period, the sentence, and the single word.

"One can easily reach the same stage with any important work, and from pure comprehension of the whole descend into adoration of the parts down into the mere typographic symbols—an analysis which easily becomes decadent. One then discovers the power of the *mot juste*. Just as this may degenerate into decadence of interpretation, one may reach decadence of création by inverting the mental process. I mean to say that the word would never have the significance it acquires when seen in relation to the whole work and that here lies the danger (by falling into the assumption of the opposite) when creating, of starting from the word. But if you take care of the sentence and the sense, the word will take care of itself. It is the extremely dangerous consciousness of the value of every detail which may drive us into errors then.

"The best way is to trust in one's talent and instinct and to depend anyhow at first on those for the perfection of component detail, and to concentrate one's whole energy on the deliberate shaping of the whole work in its widest proportions—By doing this one will at least get some large works finished and through that become unavoidably conscious of one's own methods, but be past the danger of never getting away from the detail. If the power to follow this line is not thus acquired, the fatal danger is that instead of ever becoming conscious of one's own methods one will only become conscious of other people's methods; a thing which gives wonderful profundity to one's general erudition, but is of very slight, if any, use for assisting one in the creation of original work. Original one is unconsciously—as soon as one endeavours to be original one becomes a swindler. I should think that every talented person is at first somewhat shy and suspicious of his own originality. He is inclined to believe, to fear, that the striking difference between his creations and those of others is the consequence of his technical shortcomings and his insufficient grasp of the medium in, say, music, that serves him as a means of expression. Later, if he has overcome this, he makes the agreeable discovery that what he feared to be his insipid outlook, his clumsy and childish idiom, was nothing else but the manifestation of his individuality.

"Apply all this to musical composition . . .

"If you have for some time forced yourself to achieve works regardless of detail you will become convinced that your technique becomes imperceptibly surer and that—oh miracle—the beauty and perfection of detail is the consequence of unswerving determination never for one moment to lose your grasp of the work as a whole. And also, it naturally follows, that the conscious insistence on perfection of the component parts is always exceedingly dangerous, and unless you have acquired the utmost ease and mastery, almost infallibly absolutely calamitous in so far that it makes the satisfactory achievement of a well shaped and coherent whole impossible . . .

"To become personal for a while, if you would ask me what could be your salvation and your escape from the tyranny, the obsession of the perfect detail, I should say to begin with: try to destroy and exterminate from your mind any tendency to compare either your work or your methods or your personality with that of others, because otherwise I am afraid that your great power of observation and appreciation will become fatal to you as a creator. You would by your sure grasp of others' works and by your capacity for analyzing the roots of their merits become inclined to overrate their conscious power of constant control over the microcosms of their creations at the same time as you would then under-estimate your own power of achieving equivalent results. You are confident of your own talent notwithstanding any disappointments that result from your Hamletish doubts, your hypercritical faculties and your relative over-culture; by all means cultivate this confidence! Then trust your natural talent and it will look after the details while you are concerned with the whole . . ."

From the wisdom and understanding of this letter, of which the foregoing is only a fragment, I derived the utmost benefit. It restored to me a certain measure of self-confidence, which I had completely lost. Unerringly he had placed his finger on the tender, central spot of my malady: my excessive capacity for reverence and admiration of the work of others—of which at the time he was the chief object—coupled with a morbid tendency to self-distrust and self-depreciation.

My enthusiasm for his music led me to organize and present, with the aid of Philip Heseltine, a concert devoted entirely to his work, which constituted my first irruption into the musical

world, and provoked a scandal of the first magnitude. In order
to attract attention to such an obscure artistic event in time of
war, Heseltine and I embarked upon a publicity campaign
which certainly succeeded in its main purpose, for the hall was
filled by a large and fashionable audience.

The credit for this achievement was chiefly due to my
resourceful and fantastic colleague, who had a positive genius
for such things, not even excelled previously by that of the
Futurists or Vorticists, or subsequently by that of the Dadaists
or Surrealists. Using the glamorous pseudonym of Prosdocimus
de Beldamandis—actually the name of a very dull and prosy
musical theorist of the Middle Ages—he issued a flood of
mysterious and sensational manifestos, copies of which were
sent to every artistic and social notability we could think of,
including fashionable society beauties. I, for my part, was
responsible for the programme, the foreword to which excited
even more violent critical hostility than the music itself, which
is saying a great deal.

Altogether, the Press notices evoked by the concert make
surprising reading in these comparatively mild-spoken times,
on account of the degree of invective and animosity they
exhibit, aimed as much at Heseltine and myself as at the
composer, and ending on one memorable occasion in actual
physical hostilities. One evening, shortly after the concert,
Philip and I were sitting talking and drinking, as was our
wont, in the Café Royal, in the company of some friends, when
Edwin Evans, the eminent music critic, complete with frock
coat and silk top-hat, entered the premises and sat down at
another table not far off. Since he had been one of the many
hostile scribes on the occasion, Philip could not resist the
impulse to join him at his table and tell him a few things about
himself. After a short spell of this, Edwin Evans lost his temper
at what was, no doubt, a more than usually offensive observation on the part of my bellicose friend, and struck him in the
face. This was the signal for a general *melée*, including, besides
the principals in the dispute, a number of waiters, members of

the management, and various artists who, without knowing what it was all about, were determined not to be left out of the proceedings. The chief recollection I preserve of the occasion was the spectacle of a little Mexican painter, a friend of mine, named Benjamin Coria, bouncing up and down with an expression of blissful ecstasy, on the stomach of the by then recumbent Edwin Evans.

Such occurrences were by no means uncommon or infrequent in the Café Royal of these days, when artists and critics were prepared to fight for their opinions not merely with pungent pens, but also with formidable fists. Would that these days could come again! Although, on second thoughts, I admit that I am not sure I would care to challenge my friend Ralph Hill (now the successor to Edwin Evans on the *Daily Mail*) to a similar argument, in view of his redoubtable combination of a truculent pen with a reputation as an all-in wrestler, and a height of six and a half feet with a proportionate breadth and muscular development.

The chief cause of the hostilities, it subsequently appeared, lay in the fact that Philip, after a few preliminary insults, had announced our intention of giving a concert devoted to the music of Béla Bartók; in reply to which Edwin Evans retorted that if we dared to attempt to perform the works of an enemy subject in time of war—and which, in any case, were not worth performing—he would personally bring a contingent of drunken Australian soldiers to wreck the hall.

In view of Edwin Evans' subsequent espousal of the cause of internationalism in art, his enthusiastic championship of the merits of Central European composers, and those of Béla Bartók in particular—ending up, indeed, as President of the International Society for Contemporary Music—this reminiscence is of singular piquancy.

In the course of years, however, Edwin mellowed considerably, and I am glad to be able to say that the hostile relations which had formerly existed between us gradually gave place to friendly ones, and that in the end I came to entertain a deep respect for the breadth of erudition and judgment of our former antagonist. He especially won my affection by the very moving and eloquent tribute paid by him to Philip in an obituary notice written on the occasion of the latter's tragic end: an example of the *amende honorable* which I am happy to put on record.

Nevertheless, the fact that such an essentially sound musician and critic could have been led so astray by the prevailing chauvinism of the times, gives the measure of the formidable obstacles with which Philip Heseltine and I, with our completely (and no doubt aggressively) cosmopolitan outlook, had to contend in these days. The Bartók concert, needless to say, never materialized. The obstacles were insurmountable, and I do not doubt that even if we had been able to find a manager sufficiently courageous to lease us a hall for the purpose, and players willing to learn such difficult music and run the risk of losing their lives in playing it as well, the result would have been as Edwin Evans prophesied and threatened. Even the van Dieren concert, devoted to works composed by a neutral, was darkly hinted at as being a sinister form of defeatist, pro-German propaganda, patronized by an audience consisting chiefly of pacifists and conscientious objectors whose sexual morality, in addition, was more than suspect.

Seeing no possibility of making headway with the series of concerts we had planned—a Schönberg concert was to have followed the Bartók—we decided to abandon the scheme until after the War. Sick and tired of London and its hysterical wartime neurosis, I decided to establish myself as far away from it and from the war as I could possibly get; and after having weighed and contrasted the respective merits of John o' Groats and Land's End, decided capriciously in favour of the latter, whither I proceeded in the summer of 1917. There I rented a house for the sum of five pounds per annum, and proceeded to instal myself and my possessions: my nearest, or rather only, civilized neighbour being D. H. Lawrence, who was then living in a cottage near the village of Zennor, only a

few miles away. I had become acquainted with him through
Philip Heseltine, who knew him well, and we soon became very
close friends. But of him more, and much more, in the next
chapter.

At first I was entranced by the magical beauty of Cornwall.
My house at Bosigran Castle, near Gurnard's Head, stood on
the highest summit of the chain of cliffs that stretches unbroken
between St. Ives and Land's End, facing out over the Atlantic
with no land between it and the New World.

This particular summer, 1917, was, so far as Cornwall was
concerned, idyllic; halcyon days succeeded each other without
intermission. The dark blue, almost Mediterranean skies, the
many-tinted rock formations over which great foaming billows
would endlessly surge, the sumptuous carpet of wild flowers
which clothed the cliffs from my house right down to the sea—
campions, wild orchids, gorse and bracken; the unceasing sound
of the waves beating against the cliffs, the poignant, raucous
call of the seagulls, the song of the frogs at sundown, the shrill,
ecstatic screaming of the swallows which darted, flickeringly,
around the desolate, ruined towers of the tin mines in which
they nested, the almost overpowering sweetness of the scent
of the gorse and the wild flowers under a hot sun after a
shower of rain, all combined to create the semblance of a
heaven on earth, a Garden of Eden. I felt I had escaped from
the world of men into a paradisal existence in which the War
and everything connected with it had no place.

For a time, in fact, I was blissfully happy. I lived alone, like
a hermit, cooking and housekeeping for myself with the seagulls
as sole companions, apart from the Lawrences. My primary
intention in thus retiring from the world was to concentrate
upon a period of intensive work; but as many must have found
before me and since, especially in war-time, the little leisure
that remains to one after the diurnal labours of cooking,
shopping and cleaning-up, is more congenially spent in repose
and recreation of the body than in the activity and creation of
the soul. In consequence, I found that once I had finished

with my sordid material preoccupations, the last thing I would contemplate was to sit down at my desk and invoke the coy Muse, whose implacable hatred of domesticity is the only consistent thing about her; and the first thing was to clamber down the cliffs to a cove where I could bathe alone, naked, and unperceived, in the sea and in the sun, for hours on end.

Bathing, incidentally, is a recreation which I cannot endure in company, and have therefore entirely foregone save for this brief period of my life. The ritual of the fashionable *plage*, with its semi-clothed horrors of both sexes and all ages, lewdly displaying their bodies in varying degrees of beige and blisters, is and always has been to me the most repulsive spectacle in the world, not even excepting a butcher's shop, which in fact it resembles. I am not a vegetarian, and I am more than susceptible to the attractions of the female form, but I prefer meat cooked and women clothed, except on certain occasions which need not be specified; the chief reason being purely æsthetic, since only about one per cent—if that—of the human race is tolerable in a state of nudity or semi-nudity.

Any kind of communal bathing, in fact, is to me an utter nausea, and I have consequently never been able to bring myself to partake in the pleasures, no doubt very real, of Turkish, Finnish, or other similar baths in which naked bodies are collected together in close proximity. And I shall never indulge in sea-bathing again unless, or until, that delectable phenomenon, of which I preserve a recollection from early youth, comes back into fashion—the bathing-machine, in which one undressed in purdah-like seclusion and was then drawn by some ancient, superannuated cab-horse some fifty yards into the sea, wherein one could disport oneself alone and unobserved, and to which one again returned in order to dress.

The sea as such, on the other hand, has always exercised upon me a quite hypnotic fascination ever since I was a small child. To this day I can sit for hours on end doing nothing but watch the waves, and listen to them by night. I lose my identity and become merged into the infinite; but it is a dangerous practice and one not to be indulged in too frequently. The attraction, however, is that exercised upon the spectator and the listener, rather than on the participant or actor. In other words, I prefer to contemplate the sea from the shore rather than to be in it, or on it. I am not actually a bad sailor and am seldom, if ever, violently ill, even in bad weather, but I feel uncomfortable, ill at ease, and prefer to pass the time in the bar rather than in tramping around the deck with the salt spray dashing in my face, and bidding defiance to the elements as all sea-dogs are supposed to do, but in practice do not. Indeed, you are much more likely to find the seasoned sea-dog sitting in the bar with you than up aloft, unless he has to be for unavoidable professional reasons. Your hearty, vociferous sea-lover is never a professional sailor, who knows too much about her to love or to trust her one inch. Respect, awe, fascination—the fascination felt by the rabbit for the snake, perhaps—but love, no. I have never met a sailor who said he loved the sea, and if he did I would not believe him.

As for long sea voyages, I have only been on one in my life, when I went to South America and back, and I never want to go on another. I have never been so bored in my life and with an excruciating boredom like that of a dentist's drill. There is, indeed, no worse torment on earth than to be confined for weeks to a ship in which there is not a single person with whom one has a thought in common. I would infinitely prefer to spend the equivalent time in solitary confinement in a cell, alone with my own thoughts.

And so we arrive back from what may have seemed to be a digression at the point from which we started: the essentially solitary nature of my disposition, intensified by experiences early in life. I am, in fact, the least social of beings, in the ordinary accepted sense of the word, as well as the most anti-social in the ethical sense. I dislike company, in fact; I am not, and never have been, what is called "a good mixer", although to-day, by dint of painful experience, I can make a more convincing imitation of being one, when necessary, than I used to be able to do. But I prefer not to. In any congregation of more than six people at a party, whether prandial or merely social, I am acutely unhappy; in the latter category my first instinct is to retire into a corner with a bottle and get drunk as quickly as possible; or better still, to arrive drunk: then, and only then, can I behave in a normally sociable and agreeable fashion.

This propensity to solitariness and detachment, however, does not exclude a considerable gift for friendship; but that is something quite different from the social sense in which I am so completely lacking. I think I can say without exaggeration that few people can ever have had so many close and intimate friends as I have had; unfortunately they are to-day nearly all dead. But even with friends, I have always preferred to be alone with them. Even to be in the company of two equally dear friends is apt, I have always found, to diminish the pleasure of their intercourse; while the conclave of three or more is frequently more painful than agreeable to all concerned.

This is only natural. As in an instrumental *ensemble*, a perfect equilibrium and understanding is more easily achieved by two persons than by three, by three than by four, and so on. Apart from that, it does not by any means follow that because A loves B and C equally, that therefore B will love C. More often than not they detest each other. But the most important element in this connexion consists in the fact that whether consciously or not, whether deliberately or not, one is inevitably a different person with different people. Personally, I am well aware that I present a different aspect or facet of myself to X from that which I present to Y, and that both are equally different from that which I present to Z. With the first, let us say, I talk exclusively on artistic topics; with the second, who is not interested in art, I discuss philosophy; with the third, history and politics; but if all three are gathered together, one can only discuss the weather. This is, of course, a crude and extreme way of putting what seems to me to be an undisputable fact, namely, that no two people know the same Cecil

Gray, and the X Cecil Gray knows is not the X that other people know; and the attempt to adjust oneself simultaneously to several different personalities is to court the fate of the chameleon when placed upon a tartan plaid. No, decidedly: several friends at once constitute a surfeit, an *embarras de richesse;* give me one at a time; only thus can one achieve that supreme felicity of existence, the perfect contact and relationship of two minds, which the presence of a third, however finely attuned to either of the others, or even to both separately, must inevitably disturb or impair. So, at any rate, I have found it.

The fact remains that *au fond* I am essentially a solitary; I would have made a good monk. I am never more happy than when alone—or more unhappy, for that matter, for the two things naturally and inevitably go together. And during the first months of my stay in Cornwall I was as radiantly happy as, during the last, I was supremely miserable. As summer waned and autumn assumed the ascendancy, a change took place which was something much more than the natural outcome of a change of season. The radiant smiling face of the Cornish landscape which I had hitherto known gave place gradually and almost imperceptibly to something very different, something dire and sinister. A growing *malaise* made itself felt: the beauty that had entranced me was only a mask: the paradise-garden concealed a serpent.

It is magical country, but the magic is black. On the south coast around Penzance, only a few miles away to the south, the character and aspect both of Nature and the inhabitants is mild, soft, enervating, agreeable and rather characterless. St. Ives, a few miles to the north, is a picturesque fishing village full of comfortable hotels and old maiden ladies painting watercolours. But the north Atlantic coast, which lies between these two places, with its desolate moors strewn with Druidic monuments and fallen cromlechs and ancient abandoned tin mines going back to the times of the Phoenicians, seems to belong to an entirely different world. In fact, I am sure that it does,

and that it represents a corner of the lost continent of Atlantis
—a conjecture for which there is even a certain measure of
scientific corroboration in the fact that the flora of this strip
of coast, as I have been credibly informed, is separate and
distinct from that found in any other part of England in many
respects.

One does not at once become aware of this quality of
"otherness", as Lawrence would say, largely because of the
engaging initial aspect it presents to you, especially during the
halcyon summer months, when I visited Cornwall for the first
time; and the same applies to the inhabitants, who under a
disarmingly affable exterior conceal a deep hatred of the
intruder, the *foreigner* (as any visitor is regarded by them),
which one only gradually comes to realize after a long time,
during which one often wonders whether, perhaps, one is not
beginning to imagine things.

Altogether, it is like entering the kind of country described
by Algernon Blackwood or Arthur Machen—a land in which
the boundary line between the subjective and the objective
becomes vague and indecisive. You begin to distrust the
evidence of your senses, and to realize uneasily that things are
not always what they seem to be, and this feeling becomes
steadily intensified as you leave St. Ives and—passing Tregerthen Farm and the cottage in which D. H. Lawrence lived
during the years I knew him—approach the village of Zennor,
where the innermost periphery of this spiritual Black Country
begins. From there to Gurnard's Head and Bosigran Castle
(where I lived) the *crescendo* continues, and reaches its climax
beyond in the village of Morvah: a name of which the dark,
sinister sound still strikes a chill into my very marrow.

To pass through that place, in the days of which I am speaking, even in broad daylight and bright sunshine, was always
something of an ordeal, and I cannot believe that it can have
changed: I only breathed freely when I had emerged from it.
The one street of which it consisted was always completely
deserted at any hour, but as I walked down it I was aware of

eyes at every window watching me, peeping at me furtively and with malevolent hostility, from behind curtains. There was a curse on the place, a perpetual black cloud which brooded over it: a spirit of blackness and evil and utter spiritual corruption.

This atmosphere of horror and desolation continues up to, and including, Pendeen, whereafter it gradually begins to lessen and lighten; until by the time you reach St. Just and Sennen it has almost completely evaporated, and at Land's End it no longer exists at all. The evil spell has vanished. (I may say in parenthesis that this impression is not uniquely mine, but has often received corroboration from those acquainted with the strip of country in question: notably and recently from my friend, Sir Arnold Bax, who confesses to having had a precisely similar impression, especially with regard to Morvah. It must have been the centre in ancient times—prehistoric, no doubt—of sacrificial blood-rites and unspeakable abominations, the exhalations of which still unmistakably hover around, poisoning the air.)

Although Morvah constituted the centre of this bad land, Bosigran was sufficiently near it to generate many unpleasant phenomena which were not susceptible of any natural explanation. One particular example of this remains vividly in my memory to this day. I had retired for the night and the weather was calm and serene. Just as I had extinguished my candle preliminary to climbing into bed, there came from the room downstairs, which I had only just left, a terrific crash, like a thunderbolt or an exploding bomb. There could be no question of my having imagined it, or dreamt it, as I had not even had time to get into bed, let alone close my eyes. After a few moments of pardonable apprehension, I relit my candle and proceeded shakily downstairs, not knowing what to expect— but found everything just as I had left it.

This alarming experience occurred twice to me, and after I left Cornwall and let my place, the incoming tenant complained to me of a precisely identical manifestation. (I need hardly say that, being anxious to dispose of my lease, I had not mentioned such possible drawbacks.) It was only some time afterwards that, coming by chance upon a volume dealing with Cornish legends and folk-lore, I found a reference to the activities of malicious, but harmless, elemental sprites called "knockers", which inhabited and emerged from disused tin mines and produced the phenomenon I and my successor had experienced—a kind of Cornish *poltergeist*, in fact. Now, it so happened that my house at Bosigran was surrounded by the shafts and workings of derelict tin-mines, many of which undoubtedly dated back to the days of the ancient Phoenicians. It only remains to be added that such occurrences are, or were, so frequent and familiar in the neighbourhood, that the inhabitants paid no attention to them, knowing them to be completely harmless.

Another curiously disturbing experience, though of a very different order, being a natural and not a supernatural occurrence, took place some short time later. It was a lovely autumn day, with only the faintest possible breath of wind: and with an absolutely clear sky save for one tiny little cloud "no bigger than a man's hand". But that faint, imperceptible breath of wind kept that tiny little cloud just moving in front of the sun throughout the day in such a way that, while the whole surrounding countryside, the entire rest of the world, it seemed, lay blissfully basking in uninterrupted sunshine—that one small strip of land in which I lived remained shrouded in shadow. It seemed to me at the time as if I alone among mortals had been placed under a curse and sentenced to unescapable gloom by a malign fate.

It should be borne in mind that I was only twenty-one at the time and, moreover, completely under the hypnotic spell of the great Romantics, especially Gérard de Nerval, whose sonnet, *El Desdichado* (in the series entitled *Les Chimères*) which I have so often, and so far unsuccessfully, attempted to set to music, was at that time, and for a long time afterwards— perhaps still is—my favourite poem.

Je suis le tenébreux—le veuf—l'inconsolé,
Le prince d'Aquitaine à la tour abolie:
Ma seule *étoile* est morte—et mon luth constellé
Porte le *soleil noir* de la *Mélancolie*.

Dans la nuit du tombeau, toi qui m'as consolé,
Rends-moi le Pausilippe et la mer d'Italie,
La *fleur* qui plaisait tant à mon coeur desolé
Et la treille où le pampre à la rose s'allie.

Suis-je Amour ou Phébus? . . . Lusignan ou Biron?
Mon front est rouge encore du baiser de la reine;
J'ai rêvé dans la grotte où nage la syrène . . .

Et j'ai deux fois vainqueur traversé l'Achéron
Modulant tour à tour sur la lyre d'Orphée
Les soupirs de la sainte et les cris de la fée.

This strange, magically evocative poem continually haunted
my thoughts in these days of my youth and, indeed, still
haunts me; the reason being, no doubt, because it so perfectly
expresses the duality of my nature, the two psychological poles
between which I perpetually oscillate—the first and second
subjects of my symphony—my naturally gloomy and sombre
temperament, as expressed in the first stanza; contrasted with
the glowing invocation to Italy in the second, their working
out and reconciliation in the latter part of the poem, and,
above all, the song of the sirens.

I am seldom, if ever, happy in fact, except when transported
by alcohol, love, or art, by wine, woman, or song; and for me,
ever since I can remember, Italy has always been the symbol
and living source of this divine ecstasy, this liberation from
myself—Italy, the land of wine, song—and woman.   Open
your atlas, reader; look at the map of Italy, and you will see
that her shape is that of the body of a woman. . . .

I have already said that my purpose in moving to Cornwall
was two-fold: firstly, in order to work; and secondly, in order
to escape from the War. The extent to which I failed in the
second objective will be seen in the next chapter, and I have

already indicated the degree of my failure in achieving the first. Of actual, positive, tangible creative work, in fact, little dates from these two years in Cornwall; but it was then and there, none the less, that the seeds were sown of the greater part of anything that I have subsequently achieved, through intensive meditation and a quite formidably extensive quantity of reading, in the course of which I came across, for the first time, the book which has probably exercised a greater influence upon me than any other I have ever read before or since, namely, *La Tentation de Saint Antoine* of Gustave Flaubert—the translation, adaptation and setting to music of which is of all my works the one to which I attach the most importance.

There is, to my mind, looking back upon it, something fateful and providential in the coincidence that led me to become acquainted with this particular book under these particular circumstances; for was I not myself then a little Saint Anthony who had fled to the desert in order to escape from the world and to meditate upon holy things? I have said already that probably I am at heart a monk, and in this book I found the complete counterpart to my own personality, even more than in the poem of Nerval. All my life, in fact, I have been a Saint Anthony, but one who has invariably succumbed to every temptation that has been placed in his path: with such monotonous regularity, in truth, that the Devil himself must have found me very poor sport indeed, and have wished that I would sometimes put up a stiffer fight and give him a better run for his money. A sitting bird cannot possibly interest an expert shot.

However that may be, the fact remains that I recognized in Saint Anthony and his creator—they are, of course, one and the same thing—a kindred spirit. I thereupon resolved to make that book the basis of a gigantic music drama. Nearly twenty years were to elapse before I started to write it, but the conception and the intention had never been absent from my thoughts; once begun, it was finished in about eighteen months, text, full score and all, as I have already said.

In concluding here this attempt at self-portrayal up to the age of twenty-one, I am forcibly struck by the seeming discrepancy which exists between the earlier and the later parts. In the first is presented a child like any other, fundamentally happy, and only unhappy through artificial constraint or repression; in the second, an adolescent, fundamentally unhappy, and only happy as the result of some form of intoxication. Since both terms of the proposition are correctly stated, how are they to be reconciled and explained? Quite simply, and in one way only, as being a form of transformation as complete as that which operates in the change from caterpillar to butterfly in the natural world. And the force that operated that change, and turned the ordinary little boy into the potential artist, was none other than the miseries, sufferings and humiliations undergone at school. Without them he would have been nothing.

Chapter Seven

I HAVE already said that in my troglodytic sojourn in the Cornish Thebaïd my only civilized neighbour was D. H. Lawrence, who was also in flight from a hostile and unsympathetic world. It is hardly surprising under the circumstances that a close friendship should have rapidly developed between us, as between two desert anchorites.

At the very outset of our relationship he particularly endeared himself to me through the extraordinary kindness and helpfulness he showed me in dealing with the practical problems of life: attending sales of furniture on my behalf and buying for me what he deemed necessary, painting the woodwork, and even insisting on scrubbing and polishing the floors for me—he had always, indeed, a strange predilection for such domestic activities, which I was far from sharing, and I was therefore only too glad to leave them to him. In retrospect, however, I am inclined to suspect that in addition to his genuine fondness for such occupations there was also a certain streak of mystical self-abasement involved. But it suited me admirably, and at the time I was not aware of this Dostoievskian element in the situation.

Our friendship ripened quickly, and within a very short time we used to meet virtually every day, either at his place or at mine, over a period of many months. We were, in fact, almost one household: when I was not visiting the Lawrences, they were visiting me.

It was on one such latter occasion that an incident occurred which Lawrence has graphically described in the chapter devoted to the War in his novel *Kangaroo*. The Lawrences

126

were spending the night at my house, and after supper, when it was already dark, we were sitting around the fire amusing ourselves by singing German folk-songs (it must have been a horrible noise) when suddenly there came a peremptory hammering at the front door. I went to open it, but even without waiting for me to do so, the door was flung open and in marched half a dozen or so men with loaded rifles, who proceeded to search the house, saying that lights had been noticed flashing out to sea from my windows. Finding nothing incriminating on the premises, the intruders withdrew, with operatic gestures like a Verdi chorus, and blood-curdling threats to the effect that I would hear more of the matter. Which, indeed, I did: a few days later I received a summons to appear at the local police-court.

Actually, all that had happened was that a strong westerly gale was blowing that night, and one of the drawing-pins fastening the curtains of one of the windows had worked loose and allowed a flicker of light to escape at irregular intervals in such a way as to suggest a signalling code to those suspiciously inclined.

I did not take the matter seriously, however, though I certainly would have done so if I had known the complete and uncomfortable truth, which had unfairly been withheld from me until my appearance and cross-examination in court—namely, that at the very time that my light had been seen shining out to sea, a German submarine had been located in the vicinity. This, coupled with Frieda Lawrence's German nationality and Lawrence's reputation as an immoral and subversive writer, was more than enough to create a thoroughly unpleasant, not to say dangerous, situation for us all. As I subsequently ascertained, the coastguards, police, and the entire local population had been spying on us for a long time past, watching all our movements in the hope of being able to discover something against us, out of what I can only describe as a characteristically Cornish spirit of disinterested malevolence.

As it happened, the immediate outcome was nothing more than a vindictively heavy fine imposed upon me, and we naturally assumed that the matter was at an end, which was far from being the case. It was only very much later, after the War, that I learnt from Frank Dobson, the sculptor, who subsequently stayed for some time in the neighbourhood, that Lawrence, his German wife, and I, were believed to be the ringleaders of an elaborate espionage system: that for some time I went in danger of my life, and that on one occasion an expedition of local worthies, armed with scythes and pitch-forks, set out to march on my house at Bosigran with the intention of murdering me and throwing my body over the cliffs; but that the gallant host, as they drew nearer to their objective, gradually melted away, one by one, until only two of them were left by the time they reached their destination; whereupon they decided to postpone operations until some later and more auspicious occasion. If they had known that I was completely alone, unarmed and defenceless, it might have been a different story. I was only saved, in fact, through the fortunate circumstance that the malevolence of the Cornish was only exceeded by their cowardice.

But the matter did not end there. On the 12th October, 1917, I received a note from Lawrence, which ran as follows:—

"Great trouble in the land—police raiding the house this morning—searching for God knows what—and we must leave the area of Cornwall by Monday and not enter any prohibited area. Come and see us at once. I have not the faintest idea what it is all about—curse them all."

I went over to see the Lawrences immediately and found them in a most difficult position—summarily ejected from their home, without anywhere to go, and completely penniless. Fortunately I was able to supply sufficient funds to pay for their fares to London, where they had decided to go, and I was also able to arrange for them to stay at my mother's flat in Earl's Court. Even there the persecution continued. On visiting them there on one occasion I was intercepted outside the door by a gentleman of the C.I.D. and subjected to a mild form of third-degree examination concerning the Lawrences and my relations with them, which eventually reached such a pitch of impertinence and offensiveness that I told him to clear out or I would throw him out. He went, and nothing more came of it, surprisingly. In that War, unlike the last, there were apparently a few vestiges left of the old doctrine of the liberty of the subject.

In a letter to a friend, Lawrence writes as follows concerning this miserable episode:—

". . . It seems we are never going to have any peace. To-day there has been a man from the Criminal Investigation Department inquiring about us, from Gray. It is quite evident that somebody from Cornwall—somebody we don't know, probably—is writing letters to these various departments—and we are followed everywhere by the persecution. It is just like the Cornish to do such a thing . . ."

How right he was there! The trouble that the Cornish will take, without any question of material or personal advantage, to injure someone who has never done anything to injure them, is quite impressive in its way—the purest form of disinterested, impersonal malevolence that I have ever encountered.

I have to admit, however, that there was just a shred of justification for the distrust and suspicion which Lawrence had aroused in official circles, apart from his German wife, his reputation as a writer of immoral tendencies, and the unfortunate episode in which we had been involved together. He was foolishly lax and indiscreet in speech when in the company of people whom he may sometimes wrongly have supposed to be trustworthy; and at that time he more than once expressed to me—and to others, no doubt—his intention of initiating a disruptive, pacifist and nihilist campaign in the industrial North, with a view to bringing about a speedy end to the War. I remember vividly an occasion in his cottage at Tregerthen before the eviction, when he declared that he had definitely determined on this course of action and asked me whether I would be willing to accompany him: a suggestion to which I agreed unhesitatingly, such was the extent of his influence over me in these days.

That this conversation—and probably others like it—were overheard I have to-day no doubt whatever. One of the less engaging aspects of the Cornish character consists in a mania for spying and listening at keyholes or windows, and on many occasions during my stay in these parts I had a feeling of definite certitude that one was being watched and overheard by eavesdroppers. Needless to say, nothing came of all these fantastic political projects: it was all talk, mere hot air, and as often as not entirely forgotten the next day. But if, as I believe, some of his wilder discourses of this nature had been overheard, it would not be surprising if the local authorities had made a report of them to headquarters; all the more so as, at that time, there was undoubtedly a wave of unrest pervading the country, which only required a leader with a sense of direction to render it formidable, and Lawrence was potentially such a leader. He was, indeed, the stuff of which Hitlers are made, especially at that time when his great gifts were unrecognized and he was on the verge of penury. Unsuccessful and thwarted artists are the most common type of the revolutionary politician; such, it should be remembered, was not only Hitler, but also Goebbels: not only Mussolini, but also Ciano—all of them artists *manqués*. Lawrence was an artist *réussi*, fortunately; otherwise we might well have been saddled with a similar phenomenon here in post-War years as afflicted Russia, Italy and Germany.

Lawrence, in fact, could easily have become a British Hitler. Apart from many striking similarities of doctrine between them, which have become increasingly evident in the passage of the years, there was in Lawrence also the same dark, passionate, fanatical power, the same capacity for casting spells and captivating the sympathies and imagination of the common people, and especially the under-dog. Fortunately he, and we, were saved from this fate by the strength of his artistic genius, in virtue of which his revolutionary impulses received expression in his writings instead of in the field of politics and direct action.

The fact remains that Lawrence was a potential Hitler, and Scotland Yard may well have shown more psychological penetration than appeared at the time, in vaguely apprehending in him a subversive force such as was to emerge in due course elsewhere. The fact that he was also at this time in personal contact with Maxim Litvinov, who had been appointed official representative of the Bolshevik Government in this country, may have helped to accentuate such fears.

However that may be, Lawrence's impulse towards direct political activity died a natural death, and gave place to the opposite but psychologically complementary design of leaving Europe and, instead of destroying the old order, building a new one elsewhere. His conversation and letters of the period were filled with references to this fantastic project. As Mr. Aldous Huxley has written in the preface to *The Letters of D. H. Lawrence:*—

> "He was on the point, so he imagined, of setting off to Florida, where he was going to plant that colony of escape, of which up to the last he never ceased to dream. . . He asked me if I would join the colony, and though I was an intellectually cautious young man, not at all inclined to enthusiasms. . . I answered yes."

This was in 1915. The choice of Florida for the colony of escape was due to Philip Heseltine, who told Lawrence that the orange plantation in which Frederick Delius had lived as a young man still belonged to him, and was therefore at the disposal of anyone inclined to take it over. Philip, indeed, had written to Delius with this idea in view, and had received the following discouraging reply:—

> ". . . My orange grove has been left to itself for twenty years and is no doubt only a wilderness of gigantic weeds and plants. The house itself will also have tumbled down. Even if the house had been habitable I should not have advised Lawrence to live in it . . . I should have loved to be of use to Lawrence whose work I admire, but to let him go to Florida would be sending him to disaster."

By 1917 the *venue* of the colony had shifted to the Andes.

This is an extract from a letter to me written from London:—

"We are a little nearer to definiteness, but not much. These government people are the devil, with their importance, their "expediency"
and their tyranny. But I believe we shall get back to Zennor next
month. I am not anxious to come back just now. One seems to be,
in some queer way, vitally active here. And then, people, one or
two, seem to give a strange response. The Andes become real and
near. . . . I hope this appeals to you as much as it does to me.
I have been expecting to hear from you. You are so queer and
evanescent, one feels one loses you a bit. . . Do write and say how
you are feeling—if you really feel like the Andes. It has become so
concrete and real, the Andes plan, it seems to occupy my heart.
I shall be bitterly disappointed if it doesn't mean much to you."

I am greatly interested to note, incidentally, that in a letter
written to Catherine Carswell about the same time, dealing
with the same topic, Lawrence says that I was prepared to
finance the expedition to the extent of a thousand pounds. In
view of the fact that in these days my sole financial resources
consisted in a modest allowance from my parents of two
hundred pounds a year, I am at a loss to account for this bland
assumption. But let it pass.

So far as the Andes project was concerned Lawrence must
indeed have been "bitterly disappointed", since it meant
literally less than nothing to me; in other words, the prospect
filled me with dismay. My reaction to mountains is the same
as to the sea: I like looking at them from below, but I detest
being on them. I have, in fact, a definite phobia about heights:
I cannot bear looking down over cliffs and precipices. (Freud,
no doubt, has some sinister interpretation of this obsession, but
I prefer not to know it.) I can only say that while the original
conception of a colony of escape in Florida was decidedly congenial, the idea of spending the rest of my life in the Andes in
the company of Lawrence and Frieda, filled me with horror—
the combination of the mountain heights and the psychological
depths was more than I could sanely contemplate. Apart from
anything else, I was already weary and sceptical, sick and tired,
of his dark gods, sensuous underworlds, and all the rest of his
literary "properties". This reaction reached a head with an
exchange of letters, of which one of Lawrence's alone survives;

but I remember well the substance of the letter which gave rise to the following reply. I accused him, in point of fact, of allowing himself to become the object of a kind of esoteric female cult, an Adonis, Atthis, Dionysos religion of which he was the central figure, a Jesus Christ to a regiment of Mary Magdalenes.

44, Mecklenburgh Square, W.C.1.
Wednesday.

You are only half right about the disciples and the alabaster box. If Jesus had paid more attention to Magdalene, and less to his disciples, it would have been better. It was not the ointment-pouring which was so devastating, but the discipleship of the twelve.

As for me and my "women", I know what they are and aren't, and though there is a certain messiness, there is a further reality. Take away the subservience and feet-washing, and the pure understanding between the Magdalene and Jesus went deeper than the understanding between the disciples and Jesus, or Jesus and the Bethany women. But Jesus himself was frightened of the knowledge which subsisted between the Magdalene and him, a knowledge deeper than the knowledge of Christianity and "good", deeper than love anyhow.

And both you and Frieda need to go one world deeper in knowledge. As for spikenard, if I chance to luxuriate in it, it is by the way: not so very Philippically filthy either. Not that it matters.

I don't mind a bit being told where I am wrong—not by you or anybody I respect. Only you don't seem to be going for me in anything where I am really wrong: a bit Pharisaic, both you and Frieda: external.

It seems to me there is a whole world of knowledge to forsake, a new deeper, lower one to *entamer*. And your hatred of me, like Frieda's hatred of me, is your cleavage to a world of knowledge and being which you ought to forsake, which by organic law, you must depart from or die. And my "women" represent, in an impure and unproud, subservient, cringing, bad fashion, I admit—but represent none the less the threshold of a new world, or underworld, of knowledge and being. And the Hebridean songs of the damned: that is, songs of those who inhabit a suggestive underworld which is never revealed or opened, only intimated, only *felt* between the initiated— I won't have it. The old world must burst, the underworld must be open and whole, new world. You want an emotional sensuous underworld, like Frieda and the Hebrideans: my "women" want an ecstatic subtly-intellectual underworld, like the Greeks—Orphicism— like Magdalene at her feet-washing—and there you are.

D. H. Lawrence.

At this distance of time I am more than inclined to suspect that there was a certain element of sour grapes in my denunciation of his acceptance of adoration and homage from a worshipping circle of attractive female disciples, whom Frieda Lawrence had painted for me in glowing and slightly venomous colours, in a letter which I no longer possess. The Cornish Saint Anthony was finding the burden of chastity excessive, and he had no difficulty in finding an excuse for a visit to the metropolis in order to investigate the situation—which he duly did. This violent intrusion of the hair-shirted monk from the Cornish Thebaïd caused a certain disarray and havoc in the ranks of the Orphic mænads before he returned to his hermitage. . . .

The return was of short duration. The situation in Cornwall had become quite untenable after the enforced departure of Lawrence. The enmity of the local population was such that my entire energies were absorbed in resistance to it, which is not a reasonable *modus vivendi*. Indeed, the combination of the hostility of the living inhabitants with that of the malignant ghosts which infested the vicinity was too much for anyone to cope with. As a Chinese sage justly observes: "Of all the thirty-six alternatives, running away is the best." Even the air-raids in London were infinitely preferable to this baleful atmosphere of unceasing hostility, to which must be added the steadily mounting appetite of the military authorities in search of cannon-fodder, the supply of which was beginning to run short. After having volunteered and been rejected for service in 1914, I had been left in peace until the introduction of conscription in 1916, when all forms of exemption were automatically cancelled and revised. Between then and the spring of 1918 I had to submit to no fewer than four medical examinations of the most humiliating kind, having to strip naked and stand in a row with some twenty other prospective victims, and be subjected to the insult of a succession of intimate physical inspections. After three reluctantly-granted exemptions, I was eventually placed in the lowest of all possible military categories—C.3—the principal occupation of which consisted in cleaning out lavatories—a task for which I felt no compelling vocation. Consequently, when called up for service in August, 1918, I merely absented myself. Technically, of course, I was a deserter and as such liable to dire penalties, but no one bothered to do anything about it—the end of the War was so obviously close at hand. I spent the last months of it studying Palestrina and Victoria in the Reading Room of the British Museum. As soon as peace was signed I obtained a passport and went to Italy.

By a strange symbolic coincidence, Lawrence embarked on exactly the same itinerary as I, a few weeks later. Indeed, both of us unaware of it, we dogged each other's footsteps throughout the peninsula, from Florence down to Syracuse, without our paths ever crossing. No doubt it was better so; if we had met we would in all probability have felt it incumbent upon us to attempt to revive the old relationship by means of some form of artificial respiration; but it was already dead beyond recall.

Lawrence himself put it very well in one of the last letters I had from him:—

"I don't know why you and I don't get on very well when we are together. But it seems we don't. It seems we are best apart. You seem to go winding on in some sort of process that just winds me in the other direction. You might just tell me when you think your process is ended, and we'll look at each other again. Meanwhile you dance on in some sort of sensuous dervish dance that winds my brain up like a ticking bomb. God save us, what a business it is even to be acquainted with another creature. But I suppose one day we might hit it off. Be quick and wind yourself to the end. The one thing I don't seem able to stand is the presence of anybody else—barring Frieda, sometimes. Perhaps I shall get over it."

I must confess that to this day I cannot help feeling slightly touched by that little wan tribute to the effect that he could not stand the presence of anybody else but me apart from his wife; but the plain fact of the matter is that, as I have said elsewhere (*Peter Warlock*):

> "Lawrence demanded more from a friend than anyone has the right to demand, or anyone the power to give—a complete surrender of one's personality, which no one with any personality at all could make."

It pleased the late Catherine Carswell in her book on Lawrence, called *The Savage Pilgrimage*, to mention my name as that of one of those who failed to give him the responsive friendship that he craved and deserved; but no woman is in a position to judge the status of friendship between two men, and it so happens that I am better qualified than most people, in that one of my few redeeming features as a human being is a certain gift for friendship. Not many people, indeed, as I have already said, can have had so many and such good friends as I have had; but Lawrence was not one of them, and the fault was not mine.

Let me be perfectly frank. I stood by Lawrence and helped him through a very difficult moment in his life, and the only reward I ever had for it was to be pilloried and caricatured in two of his books. As Norman Douglas says in *Late Harvest*:—

> "Lawrence was one of those mortals to whom one must never show kindness unless one wants to be stabbed in the back afterwards;"

and so it was with me, as with so many, in fact all of his would-be friends. Apart from the chapter alluded to in *Kangaroo*, which is more or less accurate *reportage* and merely represents me as a faintly unpleasant nonentity, I am portrayed in *Aaron's Rod* under the guise of a musician called Cyril Scott. If the eminent composer who bears that name had cared to bring a libel action against the author and publishers, he would certainly have been awarded substantial damages, for a more nauseating specimen of the human race could hardly be imagined.

I hope to be believed, however, if I say that the petty malevolence which animated this vignette entirely failed to hurt me. My only emotion on reading it was of mild wonder at seeing a man of genius, as Lawrence undoubtedly was, going out of his way to depict as an object of aversion and contempt a friend from whom he had received nothing but kindness, loyalty and affection, to say nothing of material aid and support when he needed them badly—the evidence for which is to be found in his own letters. One cannot possibly be hurt by something one cannot understand.

I can now see that the explanation might to some extent be purely æsthetic. Lawrence was incapable, in his full-length novels at least, of creating living characters—only heroes, all of them ludicrously Narcissist self-portraits several times life-size, surrounded by miserable, abject little caricatures of his friends, many times less than life-size, in order to provide foils and contrasts to the dazzling nobility and transcendant greatness of the central figure, himself.

The impression that the innocent reader must receive from his novels and letters is that of a man always seeking desperately for friendship, giving everything, receiving nothing, always being betrayed or disappointed. The truth was quite otherwise. Friendship with Lawrence was essentially a one-way traffic. One was expected to give everything without question. In return you received the scintillations and coruscations of his remarkable mind and sensibility; and for the poor in spirit, those who have little or nothing to give, this exchange was, no doubt, a good bargain, a more than adequate recompense for their wholehearted devotion; but between equals this was not enough—and Lawrence could not brook equals. One had to be a devoted disciple or he had no use for you. And so it was with me. I was clearly cast at one time, like so many others, as can be seen from the letters, for the rôle of the disciple whom Lawrence loved, but I did not feel suited to the rôle. I declined it, and was not forgiven.

I have only so far spoken of Lawrence's relations with men. I am naturally not so well qualified to speak of his relations with women; but from what I do know of them which is not inconsiderable, I am sure that they must have been equally unsatisfactory. Women admired him and cherished him for his genius and fame; they bathed and basked in the radiance of this reflected sunshine like beatific lizards—but for himself as a person they cared very little. He was definitely not attractive to women in himself, as apart from the seductive magic of his pen. His physical personality was puny and insignificant, his vitality low, and his sexual potentialities exclusively cerebral. There can be no possible doubt about that. The man who achieves complete and satisfying sexual experience in life is never obsessed with sex to the extent to which Lawrence was in his writings. Your strong, vital, satisfied male does not rapturously hymn the act of the flesh in his work—very much to the contrary, he is generally very quiet about it. The concupiscent, insatiable Tolstoi preaches austerity and asceticism; it is the Swinburnes and Nietzsches and Lawrences who persistently glorify and magnify the joys they have never really experienced in all their fullness, if at all. It might not be true to say that Lawrence was literally and absolutely impotent— this, I am assured on medical authority, is a very rare physical condition—but I am certain that he was not very far removed from it.

In this connexion it is interesting to observe the ever-recurring obsession in Lawrence's work—beginning with the early *White Peacock* and continuing unbroken until *Lady Chatterley* and other later works—with the *leit-motif* of the virile man of the people (nearly always a gamekeeper), ravishing, against her conscious will, but with her secret subconscious acquiescence, the glamorous, exotic and exquisite feminine aristocrat. In all that has been written about Lawrence by his admirers, nothing has amused or amazed me more than the suggestion that he was intolerant of, or indifferent to, class distinctions. Lawrence—I say it deliberately—was, without qualification, the most class-conscious man I have ever known. Even Catherine Carswell, in her hagiography, rightly permits herself a snigger at the snobbery Lawrence displayed in writing letters to his friends upon coroneted note-paper, with the explanation that "my wife's father was a baron"; and always his allusions to members of the aristocracy with whom he was acquainted were mealy-mouthed and more than nauseating in their class-consciousness. He could not resist the lure of women with titles: he would roll their names around his mouth—Baroness Richthofen, Lady Ottoline Morrell, Lady Cynthia Asquith, The Honourable Dorothy Brett, "daughter of Viscount Esher" (in a smug parenthesis)—they were all potential Ladies Chatterley to his self-imagined all-conquering gamekeeper. All his books are a wish fulfilment of this *leitmotif* which he was unable to realize in life.

Lawrence, in fact, whether to man or woman (or child), and in the rôle of lover or friend or anything else was a lamentable failure, and no apologetics can disguise the fact. I remember one evening during the last war when Norman Douglas and I were comparing notes and exchanging reminiscences concerning him and Norman said: "Do you realize that no one who knew Lawrence well, as we know him, was sorry when he died?" It seemed to me at the time a terrible thing to say, and I was about to repudiate it indignantly, but suddenly became aware of the fact that the statement was absolutely true: that Norman had placed his finger unerringly on the central defect not merely of Lawrence as a person, but as an artist as well—his complete lack of humanity, the absence of any genuine warm response to, by, with, or from any other living being—except, perhaps, his mother.

It is true that many people affected a violent display of sorrow at his death, and wailed and beat their breasts like hired mourners, and very well paid they were, too, for their strenuous literary efforts which appeared in print within a surprisingly (and indecently) short space of time, almost before his corpse was cold. To have known Lawrence, even as a nodding acquaintance, was a highly lucrative asset for a time, and one of the few things in my life of which I am mildly proud is that alone among his so-called friends I refrained from exploiting commercially my memories of him at the time of his death. But of deep human sorrow at the passing of a loved friend there is little trace in these lucrative and quickly written obituaries—

by Huxley, Carswell, Luhan, Brett, Aldington, Murry and—
I forget the rest, except that his wife was one of them.

But there is another side to the picture. His very deficiencies, which I have been at pains to emphasize, were at the same time the source of his greatness as an artist. With fellow human beings, whether in life or in art, he was a failure, and in his sad, thwarted heart he knew it. But where he was at home, where he realized himself completely, was in the world of nature, with *Birds, Beasts and Flowers*, to quote the symbolically significant title of one of his finest works—and with trees. In all literature there is little, if anything, to compare with the extraordinary depth and delicacy of Lawrence's perceptions of Nature in all its forms and manifestations. He was a faun, a child of Pan, a satyr (and he even looked the part). That was the essential Lawrence; there he was truly great.

I conclude my personal experiences and impressions of this strange man with a few final quotations from his letters to me, which illustrate this point:—

> "On some sunny, gentle spring day when celandines are out, I should like to come back to Zennor, to Tregerthen. But it would only be an *Ave atque vale*, I think. I have left Cornwall, as an abiding place, for ever, I am sure. But I shall come back to see it.
>
> "Having been seedy this week, I have sat in bed, my usual style, and looked out of the window in front. There is a field—the thatched roof of a cottage—then trees and other roofs. As evening falls, and it is snowy, there is a clear yellow light, an evening star and a moon. The trees get dark. Those without leaves seem to thrill their twigs above—the firs and pines slant heavy with snow—and I think of looking out of the Tregerthen window at the sea. And I no longer want the sea, the space, the abstraction. There is something living and rather splendid about trees. They stand up so proud, and are alive.
>
> ". . . there are two charming cottages here—one down in a little village, fast asleep for ever; a cottage just under the hill, under the hazel-woods, with its little garden backing to the old churchyard, where the sunny, grey, square-towered church dozes on without rousing: the other on the hill touching the wood. Frieda of course is *dying* for one of these. And when we were down in Hampstead Norris yesterday, I quite shook with panic, lest we should actually go and take the cottage under the hill by the church. A real panic comes over me, when I feel I am on the brink of taking another house.

I truly wish I were a fox or bird—but my ideal now is to have a caravan and a horse, and move on for ever, and never have a neighbour. This is a real after-the-war ideal. There is a gipsy camp near here—and how I envy them—down a sandy lane under some pine trees.

"I find here one is soothed with trees. I never knew how soothing trees are—many trees, and patches of open sunlight, and tree-presences—it is almost like having another being . . . I have come to think that it is enough to lapse along pleasantly with the days. It is very nice. That is why the cottage in the village fills me with such panic. I believe I could go into a soft sort of Hardy-sleep, hearing the church chime from hour to hour, watching the horses at the farm drink at the pond, writing pages that *seemed* beautifully important, and having visits from people who *seemed* all wrong, as coming from the inferior outer world."

It only remains to be added, as a comic postscript, that being a very young man, and more innocent in some respects than my years would warrant, I fondly imagined that the two men of outstanding genius for whom I had a great admiration and affection must inevitably understand and appreciate each other as much as I did both of them. In accordance with this pathetically naïve delusion, I took enormous trouble in effecting an introduction between D. H. Lawrence and Bernard van Dieren, confident in the expectation that they would fall into each other's arms and vow eternal friendship. If I had not been a complete idiot in psychological relationships at that time (I have improved since then, even to the extent of deliberately refraining from establishing contact between two potential congenialities in case of a similarly violent reaction) I would have recognized from the outset that there could have been no other result than that which took place. On the one hand van Dieren, the fastidious, aloof, remote patrician, with his complete self-dedication to orthodox European traditionalism, his instinctive hostility to every form of subversiveness and exoticism, his devout Roman Catholicism and faith in Monarchy and everything which to-day is contemptuously dismissed as "reactionary"; on the other hand Lawrence, a man of the people, a hater of orthodoxy in any shape or form, a born rebel, a sworn foe of tradition, a worshipper of strange and exotic gods—you could not easily find anywhere two individuals, two dispositions, two temperaments more utterly alien and incompatible to each other than these two; and I, like a holy innocent, brought them into contact with each other, believing that they would get on together like the proverbial house on fire. They were both possessed of genius: they must each of them recognize its presence in the other; *ergo* they must inevitably love each other—so I fatuously argued.

To say that the atmosphere they generated between them was heated, oppressive, or electric, would be an abuse of that admirable rhetorical resource called *meiosis;* it was rather arctic; polar, glacial, Siberian. If they had come to blows or spat at each other it would have been a relief. The antipathy between them was almost as much physical as psychological: they could not endure each other's presence. The antagonism, the antithesis, was as intense as that which existed between Michael Angelo and Leonardo da Vinci—masters of mutually exclusive worlds. The parallel, incidentally, is remarkably close, because just as there was a more than superficial resemblance between the physical aspect of Lawrence and Michael Angelo, so there was between van Dieren and Leonardo. The confrontation of the two was one of the most shattering experiences of my life.

Chapter Eight

I
T IS curious and interesting to observe how one tends to repeat the pattern of one's life, quite involuntarily and unconsciously. Just as in September, 1919, after World War No. 1, I instinctively fled to Italy in violent reaction against the spiritual claustrophobia induced by five years of insular confinement, so in September, 1946, after World War No. 2, I found myself irresistibly impelled to execute precisely the same manœuvre and to follow much the same itinerary. *Rends-moi le Pausilippe et la mer d'Italie*, in fact, was on each occasion the categorical imperative of my inner nature, which would not brook denial. No doubt after World War No. 3, for which preparations are already in hand, I shall experience the same impulse—if indeed there is any Italy left to revisit. By the time it breaks out, however, I hope and anticipate that the atomic bomb will have become an obsolete weapon, and given place to bacterial warfare, whereby the human race, with a few chosen exceptions, as in the parallel instance of the Cities of the Plain, will be exterminated, while their redeeming creations, in the form of historical buildings and works of art, will be preserved, like ghostly Chirico cities, through which the few survivors will bat-like flit.

Travel has always been one of the major passions of my life, but always more as an illusion than a reality. As with the rose-gardens and the dancing girls of Ispahan, the ideal is superior to the actual, and in travel I have always found a greater happiness in prospect and retrospect than at the actual time. In other words my pleasures have always been rather those of eager anticipation or recollection in tranquillity than of enjoy-

ment in the moment of experience. In my monastic cell I
yearn for the outside world and long to succumb to its manifold temptations (and generally do): but when I find myself in
the outside world I look forward, as often as not, to the time
when I shall be back again in my little cell, in solitary confinement, like an old lag. But that does not prevent me from
setting out again on my travels at the earliest opportunity, and
on the whole I must confess that the ultimate balance, of
anticipated and recollected pleasure on the one hand, and of
immediate discomfort and disillusionment on the other, has
nearly always been on the credit side of the ledger. The
memory of the latter fades with surprising rapidity; the golden
moments of retrospection steadily increase with the patina of
time.

I have only been out of Europe twice in the course of my
extensive travels—to South America and to North Africa, both
of which I disliked intensely—and I never wish to leave it
again, certainly not for the Western world or the Eastern—for
Uncle Sam or Mother India, or the bawling sons and daughters
of the British Colonies and Dominions. Father Europe, even
ruined and in ruins, is good enough for me; and Europe I know
well, and love, from its topmost extremities in Norway,
Sweden and Finland, to its nethermost parts in Spain and
Sicily. China alone, outside Europe, has lured me nostalgically
in my mature years: but only the Old China, which I am told
no longer exists except as a memory, and has largely been
replaced by a second-hand and shoddy form of Americaniza-
tion. No, I never wish to leave Europe again so long as I live;
I belong to the well-nigh extinct species of the Nietzschean
"good European". To hell with America, Asia, Africa,
Australia—all these dreary A's!

Travel, even under the most favourable conditions, let it be
frankly admitted, is never the unalloyed joy and bliss that one
imagines in anticipation, or recaptures in one's roseate-tinted,
carefully selected recollections. It tends to bring out all that
is worst in human nature, one's own and that of others. Even

the most congenial of companions, male or female, under
normal conditions of life, can become excessively tiresome in
the process of transit, but nothing like so tiresome as one's own
personality when travelling alone. It is the supreme test of
human nature, in both its aspects, social and solitary. Never
have I been so exasperated with my best friends, never so
acutely bored with myself, as when travelling—and the worse
of the two conditions is the latter. There are some places,
incidentally, which no one, however self-reliant and self-
contained, should visit alone unless he is prepared to endure
the uttermost limits of *cafard*, and chief among them is that
loveliest of all cities built by mortal man—Venice. I have
never been so irremediably and irredeemably bored with myself as alone in Venice, and these are strong words, for few
people can have experienced the anguish of the Dark Night of
the Soul more intensely than I have—but never so intensely as
in Venice. (On the other hand, there is no more enchanting
place when in congenial company, as I also know well.)

When I went to Italy in 1919, after World War No. 1, I
travelled alone. I was sick to death of the world and everything
and everybody in it—myself included—and I cherished the
naïve idea that travel was a form of release and escape. And
so far as the first term of the proposition was concerned the
cure worked well enough: one "got away from it all", the
outside world in which one had been forcibly confined throughout the war years as in a straitjacket, but not from oneself, or
rather one's *alter ego*, one's *Doppelgänger*. At home, of course, in
one's natural surroundings, he is always there. You expect to
find him, sitting in your favourite chair, with his feet on the
mantelpiece (your *Doppelgänger* has no manners) when you
come home in the evening, and he always has some facetious
and offensive observations to make. But it is possible to ignore
him, up to a point at least. At home one always has defences,
extraneous resources: friends, lovers, acquaintances, books,
familiar taverns, which help to keep him at bay. But travelling
abroad, alone, you are entirely at his mercy, and the only way

to escape him is to keep moving. On quitting one's normal
environment one leaves him behind on the platform of the
railway station; on arriving in fresh and congenial surroundings
one is blissfully happy for a short time and unaware of his
existence; but the hound of heaven, or rather of hell (or is it
purgatory?) remorselessly tracks one down and inevitably
catches one up. You might say that one travels by fast train,
rapide de luxe; he follows on by slow train, in leisurely fashion
(he is never in a hurry) and arrives a few days later. You find
him sitting waiting for you at the restaurant table one evening
when you come in to dinner, having forgotten all about him;
you then go, if you are wise, to the *bureau* of the hotel and
make arrangements to leave next day. And so it goes on in
each place you visit. Sometimes the period of respite lasts for
longer than usual, but sooner or later he inevitably appears.

Thus I travelled down through the Italian peninsula, from
Venice to Syracuse, with my *Doppelgänger* in close pursuit,
taking in on the way Milan, Florence, Pisa, Siena, San Gimignano, Arezzo, Assisi, Perugia, Orvieto, Rome, Naples, Capri,
Sorrento, Amalfi, Ravello, Palermo, Girgenti, Taormina,
and Catania.

At the best of times there is no drearier city in the world
than Milan, and in the autumn of 1919 it was at its worst. On
arriving there late at night, no room was to be found in any
hotel. Even the waiting-rooms in the station were so full that
I had to sleep on the platform with an overcoat for pillow.
These little physical discomforts, however, were as nothing
compared to the spiritual *malaise* of loneliness in Venice and
the contingent arrival of my enemy the *Doppelgänger*, which
drove me within a few days to Florence, where I remained
unmolested by him for some little time.

While staying there I happened to come across Sacheverell
Sitwell, whom I had got to know slightly in London during the
last year of the war, and his father Sir George, one of the most
singular characters I have ever encountered in the course of a
life by no means poor in this respect. In truth, I rather tend

to go out of my way in order to establish contact with unusual personalities; I am, in fact, something of a collector, with a certain pride in my collection, and taking pleasure in displaying its choicer specimens to fellow-connoisseurs. Sir George Sitwell was a genuine collector's piece, but so obviously a family heirloom that it would not be right for me to trespass on the property which Sir Osbert Sitwell has made so much his own in his Autobiography—a superb piece of portraiture, to which naturally I can add nothing but a few corroborative details. I shall always remember his conversational opening gambit when I was introduced to him for the first time—or it may have been our second meeting:—

"Good morning, Mr. Gray, good morning. What would you say was the average height of garden steps in Italy at the time of the Early Renaissance?" He seemed mildly taken aback, slightly shocked, to discover that I had no definite opinion on the matter. Surely a cultured gentleman would have, at least, *some* idea on such an important and elementary question, he seemed to imply. I was to learn that this was merely a characteristic and not at all exceptional example of the way in which he would take it for granted that his own fantastic and *recherché* erudition was merely part of a gentleman's education. Indeed, I ignominiously failed to pass the test. I subsequently learnt that in speaking of me he observed that "a little more gentlemanliness would not come amiss".

I again met the Sitwells, father and son, in Siena. Since we were staying in the same hotel, I naturally had more opportunity than in Florence of observing and studying his extraordinary personality, surely the last of the long and illustrious line of the great aristocratic English eccentrics, for under present conditions, which seem destined to endure indefinitely, there can be no possible successors.

The clue to the understanding of his curious and arresting character was presented to me one evening when, in the hotel lounge, he established himself in an old-fashioned rocking-chair, in which he dexterously adopted a completely horizontal position, with his pale-red beard pointing towards the ceiling, completely indifferent to the rest of the company, at the same time emitting, nonchalantly, a curious buzzing noise resembling that produced by the rapidly revolving propeller of an aeroplane in the far distance. (It did not give the impression of emanating directly from him, but of being a part of the circumambient atmosphere.)   One had the sense of something curiously remote, suspended, detached; and then I remembered another occasion, when I had visited his castle at Montegufoni, and Sacheverell and I had toiled, painfully panting, behind him up the steep incline which led to it from the high road, while he floated serenely ahead of us, hardly seeming to touch the ground; and another time, in Florence, when I saw him board a rapidly moving tramcar with an aerial leap worthy of Nijinsky himself in the *Spectre de la Rose*, carrying with him an air-cushion which he then proceeded to inflate before majestically placing himself upon it.   There was, in fact, always in everything he did a suggestion of *airiness*, as of a floating and disembodied entity, intangible, detached from the earth; and from what Sir Osbert has so well and revealingly written about him it would appear that this characteristic was reflected in every aspect of his life.   He seemed not quite to belong to this world, but to inhabit a curious universe of his own, of which he was the sole inhabitant.   Another illustration of this was afforded by the circumstance that I occupied a room adjacent to his in the hotel, and that in the middle of the night I was more than once awakened by wild outbursts of almost maniacal laughter, evidently proceeding from his room.   Whether this formidable hilarity was the outcome of waking or of sleeping moments, I naturally cannot say; but whichever the condition that occasioned it, the contrast between this phenomenon and his normally sedate, formal, rather pedantic, and seemingly rather humourless approach to life, was curiously disturbing. Either he regarded life as a colossal joke to which he could only give expression when entirely alone, or else it was his subconscious self finding an outlet in dreams.   Apart from the fact that I cannot bring myself to believe in the Freudian theory of the subconscious, I prefer to accept the former explanation; it is much more in keeping with my conception of this singular and delectable personality.

Then there was an occasion on which we visited together the picture gallery in Siena, when Sir George subjected each painting to such a minute and loving scrutiny that I was considerably impressed by his apparent knowledge and appreciation of the artistic merits of the Sienese school, of which I was an enthusiastic admirer; but on expressing my pleasure to Sacheverell at finding in his father a fellow-lover of Duccio della Buoninsegna, Simone Martini, and the rest of that noble *cortège* of masters, he shook his head sombrely and said:

"You're wrong: it's only forks."

Thinking that I had not heard aright, I made a politely interrogative sound ("?"); whereupon Sacheverell patiently provided the explanation of his enigmatic statement. "He is not really interested in pictures at all on account of their æsthetic qualities: he is engaged on writing a *brochure* on the question of the precise period at which the fork first came into use. When you think he is admiring the beauties of the masters of the Sienese school you are mistaken: he is only looking to see if there are any forks in the particular picture, so that he can establish the date of their introduction more precisely."

While I am on the subject of the Sitwell family it will be as well to say here that although I have never been on terms of close or intimate friendship with any of them, I have also never been on any but the most amicable terms whenever our paths have crossed, which has been seldom; but I am afraid I must be prepared to take the risk of impairing them when I say that the allusions made by Sir Osbert Sitwell in his autobiography to Philip Heseltine ("Peter Warlock") are both malevolent and distorted. But of this more anon . . .

I have already said earlier that my faculty for the appreciation of the visual arts had hitherto always lagged sadly behind that which I entertained for music and literature. In spite of the initiation ceremonies effected by Eric Robertson, and subsequently continued through my intimate contacts with many artists in my Chelsea period during the war and after, I was still comparatively unresponsive and untutored, uncertain of my judgment. While I would never at any stage of my development have hesitated or hedged for a moment in questions of judgment concerning books or music, where pictures were in question I could be easily led and influenced (and probably taken in) by the authoritative and plausible expressions of opinion uttered by those whom, rightly or wrongly, I believed to possess a better claim to their opinions than myself.

In the matter of the visual arts, in fact, I was then, and still largely am, in the position of a member of the public who derives great pleasure from the contemplation of painting, sculpture and architecture, but without possessing any strong convictions as to the validity of his æsthetic reactions or critical judgments. In this field I am no more than an enthusiastic and appreciative amateur, viewing things from the outside; in music and literature I feel myself a professional, a practitioner seeing things from the inside. The difference between the two standpoints is so enormous that I never cease to marvel at the temerity of art critics who have never painted a picture, and of music critics who have never produced a score; neither of them can ever really understand the first thing about the art with which they purport to deal, and of which they so glibly and authoritatively write, or prate.

Having established this clear distinction, I can now go on to say that this, my second visit to Italy, brought about an enormous enhancement of my emotional and intellectual appreciation of the visual arts; and the first and most memorable occasion on which I experienced as authentic, as intense a thrill from painting as I had ever done from music or literature, was while staying in Florence, when I visited Arezzo in order to see there the frescoes in the church of San Francesco by Piero della Francesca.

I had, of course, already seen and admired his Nativity, Baptism, and St. Michael, in the National Gallery, and the Madonna in Christ Church College at Oxford; and it was the feeling of pleasurable anticipation created by these charming, but minor works which induced me to visit Arezzo—one of the dreariest and most uninteresting towns in Italy—but I was totally unprepared for the revelation of splendour that awaited me when I crossed the threshold of the church and saw these frescoes for the first time. I fell into that state of beatific ecstasy which I had so often experienced before in contact with great music and poetry, but never before—or at any rate with anything like the same intensity—with painting. I was literally possessed, and sat there throughout the entire day until the evening, when the light was so dim as to prevent me from seeing any longer; and instead of returning to Florence, as I had intended, I stayed the night without even the customary toothbrush or razor, at a miserable tavern, in order to return the following morning and renew my act of homage and worship at the shrine of the divine Piero della Francesca.

I have frequently attempted to describe and explain to my painting friends, and to art critics of my acquaintance, the unique quality of the emotion aroused in me by the art of Piero, but without success, and meeting generally with blank incomprehension. His greatness is universally admitted, but when Roger Fry (I think it is) speaks somewhere of his cold intellectuality, or words to that effect, I can only confess myself completely baffled; for, as I have said, no painter has ever exercised such a powerful emotional effect upon me as Piero. At the same time, I can see that this overwhelming impact is to a great extent the outcome of his purely formal perfection; but when I first experienced it I was too uncultured and untrained in my visual perceptiveness to appreciate fully this aspect of his art. It was the purely personal quality of his thought and sensibility that moved me so directly, not his unquestionable mastery of the science of perspective, space-relations and all the rest of it. And the essence of his magic, it seems to me, consists in its curious, arrested, trance-like, timeless quality—a monumental, static calm, a condition of ecstasy which hardly belongs to the world of sense; and it was this quality which captured me so irresistibly when I first became acquainted with it. With the more mature appreciation I possess to-day, on the other hand, I recognize that my immediate and whole-hearted response to the art of Piero consists in the combination in it of the two elements so often, and so wrongly, considered to be irreconcilable: deep emotion and formal perfection, romantic feeling and classical structure —just as in Flaubert, in fact. It is this synthesis that I have always sought to attain in my own work, and of which I have found the finest exemplification in the art of these two masters.

Of the life of Piero della Francesca little of importance is known except for the fact that in the last years of his life he became totally blind—dazzled by the splendour and intensity of his inner vision. . . .

During these months in Italy I lived almost entirely in the visual world, which had for the first time been completely opened up to me. Music was laid on one side, and I read nothing but Italian, with a view to acquiring a complete mastery of the language. It is surprising, however, to discover how poor Italy is in great literature in comparison with other countries, or with her own superlative achievement in all other arts. Apart from Dante and Boccaccio in ancient times, and Leopardi and Manzoni in the 19th century, Italian literature is, to me at least, an arid desert. It is true that in my æsthetic youth, during my undergraduate days in Edinburgh, I wallowed rapturously in the novels of d'Annunzio, which are to real literature what *crême de menthe* and *bénédictine* are to wine; but to-day I would find it impossible to read a page of them.

So far as the language was concerned, by the time I left the country after a stay of about six months, I had attained to a fairly complete mastery; but when I revisited Italy last year (1946) after a long absence I discovered, with deep humiliation, that I had forgotten more than half of what I had once known so well. I was forced, indeed, to the sad conclusion which I had long suspected, that I have no real gift for languages; any modest accomplishments I may possess in this direction are due entirely to hard work and nothing else. My French, I should say, is good without being first-rate; German I can read tolerably well, but speak abominably; Spanish I read badly and speak not at all. But notwithstanding the mediocrity of my linguistic attainments, such has been my hopeless and unrequited passion for languages that I have tried my tongue at many others besides those mentioned—Russian, Swedish, Gaelic, and even Arabic, but have failed abjectly in each instance. At one time, inspired by Mr. Arthur Waley, who told me that he had acquired a sound working knowledge of the language after six months of intensive study, I contemplated learning Chinese. What greater felicity could man desire than to read the immortal masterpieces of Tu Fu, Li-Po and Po Chü-i in the originals? But for some reason or another I deferred the enterprise until now, when it is too late to begin—one of my many "unfulfilled desires and vain regrets." . . .

And so I travelled through Italy, feasting my newly widely-opened eyes upon all the treasures which were presented to them: the school of Siena with Duccio della Buoninsegna, the greatest of all so-called Primitives, Simone Martini with his lovely singing melodic line, and innumerable minor, but none the less adorable, masters such as Matteo di Giovanni, Sano di Pietro, Giovanni di Paolo; San Gimignano, where I spent one of the most memorable days of my life, sitting with a bottle of wine in front of me, watching the wagons drawn by white oxen, laden with grapes, lumbering up the main street of the little town with its countless towers, in the blazing autumn sunlight, my mind aflame with the gorgeous tapestry of colours woven by that greatest of little masters, Bennozzo Gozzoli; Orvieto, with the glittering polychromatic façade of its cathedral, which contains the incomparable frescoes of Luca Signorelli, to say nothing of the noble wine to which the town gives its name—one of the noblest wines not merely of Italy, but of the entire world; all these stand out more vividly in my recollection of these days than the more familiar beauties of Rome, Venice, Florence and Naples.

I gradually moved southward as winter drew on and eventually ended up in Sicily, at Palermo, at the Hotel des Palmes, where Wagner had stayed when he visited Sicily in the last years of his life. There is a certain ironically symbolic significance in the fact that it was while living under that roof that the despotic spell which Wagner had cast over me for so long should be decisively broken; for it was then and there that the experience occurred to me which I have described earlier, in the fourth chapter (p. 53), when I heard an opera of Bellini for the first time. The Latin David triumphed over the Teutonic Goliath; I understood for the first time what Nietzsche meant when he asked for "a music which would not die away, nor pale, nor grow dull beside the blue and wanton sea and the clear Mediterranean sky". I also realized that so far as I personally was concerned there was nothing I could learn from Wagner that would be of any use to me in my own work; whereas from the infinitely slighter and comparatively imperfect art of Bellini I could learn a lot: the art of building and shaping a long flowing melodic line, which was what chiefly interested me, then as now, and of which Wagner was always incapable, from first to last.

With this initiation into the hitherto unsuspected beauties of Italian music, which before then I had only experienced indirectly through the medium of Chopin, my musical faculties, dormant for many months, suddenly awoke to life again. I bought a vast quantity of piano and vocal scores of Italian operas and set myself to study them in the bedroom of my hotel, intoning the voice parts on occasion and thereby causing considerable discomfort to my near neighbours, and eliciting complaints from the management. My voice being such as it is, my sympathies, in retrospect, are entirely on the side of the unfortunate victims.

But apart from this sudden revelation and the consequent re-awakening of my musical impulses, there was little in Sicily by way of visual counter-attraction, apart from the mosaics of the Cappella Palatina and Monreale, and of Cefalú—later fated to achieve notoriety as the headquarters of the famous mage, Aleister Crowley.[1]

The passing of the phase of infidelity to music, in favour of the seductive charms of the visual arts, which had even progressed so far as to induce me for a while seriously to consider the possibility of adopting art-criticism as a career (I did not dare to aspire so high as to contemplate creative activity in this direction), was aptly symbolized by an experience which happened to me at the time—nothing in itself, but of a curious psychological import. One evening as dusk was falling I returned to Palermo from Monreale in a tramcar, which stopped opposite a block of shops and flats before entering the centre of the city, and saw in one of the windows the face of a girl which struck me as being the most beautiful I had ever seen, almost a replica of that of the Virgin of the Annunciation of Piero della Francesca in the frescoes of Arezzo. Our eyes met for what can only have been one brief moment but seemed to me like eternity. Time stood still. As the tramcar jolted once more into motion I came out of my trance and, leaping to my feet, jumped off as it was gathering speed and made my way back to the stopping place, but was unable to identify the building and had, in any case, omitted to note the particular floor on which the apparition had manifested itself. Since even in Italy, where such things are understood, it is useless to inquire as to the whereabouts of a girl looking like a Piero della

[1]There must surely be something in the air in Sicily, and especially in the neighbourhood of Palermo, that breeds and attracts magicians. Was not Giuseppe Balsamo, better known as Cagliostro, a native of Palermo? The tradition, moreover, goes back as far as Frederick II, King of Sicily and Jerusalem, (Stupor Mundi), who maintained at his court in Palermo a number of magicians and astrologers, among them the famous Michael Scott; and to this day in the streets of the poorer quarters in Palermo you will find an exceptional number of professional soothsayers and practitioners of the black arts.

Francesca, there was clearly nothing to be done. Abandoning the quest I returned disconsolately to the hotel.

Next day, and for several days after, I repaired to the charmed spot in the hope of a fortunate chance encounter, but in vain. In any case, it was probably a hallucination, a creation of my own fantasy. (Strange tricks of vision can take place in that magic hour between light and darkness.) But whether real or not, whether living flesh and blood or only an idea in my own mind, that face continued to haunt me for years; and even now, after the lapse of a quarter of a century, it still recurs in my dreams, sleeping and waking, and has become the symbolic embodiment of the Muse of painting who cast her eyes upon me then for the first and last time—for if ever I had been able to paint, my master would assuredly have been Piero, and it is that face that I should have spent my life endeavouring to recapture on canvas.

Staying at the same hotel as myself in Palermo was a fellow-countryman who exemplified all that is most detestable in the Scottish race: raw-boned, uncouth, illiterate, uncultured, arrogant, aggressive, ill-mannered, offensive, he appeared to possess no redeeming feature whatsoever and I did my utmost to avoid him, but in vain—he was one of Nature's unavoidables and seemed to have an uncanny kind of sixth sense which enabled him to track one down to the hidden lair in which one was seeking refuge from him; and once he had a grip of his prey there was no hope of escape, any more than from the Ancient Mariner. His lack of sensibility and common decency was such that on one occasion he went so far as to browbeat the hotel orchestra into taking part with him in what he euphemistically called a "sing-song"—a ghastly ritual which he insisted on holding in the hotel lounge, in which he bawled *Annie Laurie, Comin' Through the Rye* and other such Caledonian ditties in an unbelievably hideous, raucous voice to the unwillingly improvised accompaniment of the orchestra.

That is the kind of man he was, and if I seem to labour the point it is with good reason, for it constitutes the essence of the instructive story I am about to relate. When I was in Rome I had bought detailed reproductions on a large scale of the entire Sistine Chapel ceiling of Michael Angelo, in some twenty sections or so, and used often to piece them together on the floor of my bedroom in order to study the work as a whole— the only way, in fact, in which this can properly be done, seeing that the original is practically invisible. It is a curious sensation, all the same, that of looking at a ceiling lying under your feet, and one which, apart from the nature of the work itself, is conducive to vertigo.

One evening before dinner, as I was thus engaged in rapt contemplation of the *magnum opus*, there came a knock at my door and, characteristically, without waiting for a permissive answer, my unescapable compatriot stalked in, and stood rooted to the ground in surprise at the unusual spectacle which confronted him.

"Guid Gawd, mon! what on earth's that ye've got there?"

I explained to him, patiently, that it was a depiction of the story of Genesis from the Creation to the Flood, painted on the ceiling of the Sistine Chapel in the Vatican by one Michael Angelo, and that it had taken him about four and a half years to paint, lying on his back on a scaffolding from morning to night.

In the course of this explanation my irritation at his ill-considered intrusion gave way to interested surprise when I observed the extraordinary and quite unexpected effect that was produced on my unwelcome guest by the gigantic panorama spread before his feet. His jaw dropped, his eyes goggled, and I seriously thought for a moment that he was about to have a stroke. "Gosh, mon!" he gasped incoherently, "ye dinna mean to tell me that aw that was done by one mon—why, it's a whole wurrld; Gawd Himsel' . . ." He stopped abruptly and then, in a changed tone and with a voice strangely different from that which I had hitherto known, he said quietly: "Somethin' queer's happened to me. I'll never be the same mon again. From this moment on me whole life's changed—and it's this that's done it," he said, pointing to the floor, which was a ceiling.

And indeed he was a changed man. This coarse-grained, uneducated, insensitive Philistine had undergone a miraculous conversion, effected by the sudden revelation of a great work of art. This curious experience made a deep and lasting impression upon me, confirming as it did my belief in the divinity of art and its power to enter into the most unlikely vessels, and fill them with the breath of Godhead. During the last war, and continuing since, we have seen the same phenomenon repeated on a vast scale, in the form of an awakening of interest in all aspects of art, especially music, evinced by countless thousands who had never before shown the slightest interest in such things. It constitutes the only bright spot in the picture of contemporary conditions.

For there are three ways of apprehending God: through the channels of the Good, the True, and the Beautiful, represented respectively by Religion, Science, and Art. For some time past religion has failed us; to-day science has betrayed us; the only hope for the future, it would seem, lies in art. It is the last chance we have; everything else has gone. As, in Greek legend, Orpheus with his lyre tamed the savage beasts of the forest, so to-day it may be that art will achieve the infinitely harder task of softening and taming the hearts of men. As I say, it is the only hope left and, personally, I am not without that hope. If I were without it I would not find life worth living. I believe in the possibility of the salvation of humanity through the medium of art. That is my one and only Credo, which nothing can shake—not even the atomic bomb.

By the time I came to leave Sicily I had accumulated a vast quantity of scores and photographic reproductions of pictures which I confided to the care of my compatriot, who had kindly undertaken to have them packed and despatched to London. They duly arrived there, and on unpacking them I found everything there intact save one item only: my set of Michael Angelo reproductions was missing . . .

Among the more interesting minor *trouvailles* of my extensive collection of human oddities was one which I made at this time: Baron Levien, a Danish nobleman who was staying at the Timeo Hotel in Taormina at the same time as I. Elderly, very tall, lean and scrawny, he gave the impression of having strayed into real life from the pages of E. T. A. Hoffmann. Apart from his phenomenal and macabre appearance, he attracted my attention by the fact that every evening after dinner he would settle himself in an armchair with a full orchestral score in which he remained buried until it was time to retire for the night. By dint of cunning manoeuvres I was able to catch a glimpse of the score over his shoulder on several occasions, and on each of them I was able to ascertain that the object of his devotions was some work or other of Berlioz—never anything else.

Since I had been a fanatical idolater of Berlioz from the first moment I heard a note of his, this naturally provided a convenient opening gambit to an introduction, which I duly effected. He was unquestionably the most singular music-lover I have ever encountered. The admirers of Berlioz, we know, tend to be a race apart to a great extent, for the very good reason that Berlioz himself stands apart from all other composers, owing little to any predecessors and giving nothing to any successors: but the practitioners of the cult nevertheless generally find it possible to worship other gods besides him. But not Baron Levien: he was the most consequential and uncompromising of Berliozians, the most logical in his fanaticism. You might say that he concurred in the scholastic orthodox view of Berlioz, as inculcated in elementary histories and text-books written by or under the influence of Teutonic pedants, and simply inverted it. The conventional attitude may be briefly stated as follows: Berlioz has no predecessors or successors: he stands outside the genealogical tradition, *ergo* he cannot be a great composer. Baron Levien would have agreed to the first term of the proposition, but came to the opposite conclusion, namely, that the whole orthodox musical tradition must be wrong and that Berlioz was the one and only great composer of modern times.

While appreciating this fanaticism to the full, I nevertheless tried to convert the Baron to a less exclusive point of view by gently and tactfully bringing to his notice the full scores of Verdi's *Falstaff* and *Otello*, which I had with me. But it was no use: he was not interested. There was only one composer and Baron Levien was his prophet. He wrote music himself in what he fondly believed to be in the style of the master, and I was greatly favoured in being allowed to inspect the products— vast programmatical symphonic poems full of the strangest instrumental experiments which could never possibly have come off in performance.

During my stay in Sicily I had enjoyed complete immunity from the unwelcome attentions of my *Doppelgänger;* indeed, I fondly imagined that I had rid myself of him once and for all. Our last encounter had been in Naples, since when he had left me in peace. But the respite proved to be illusory. Being within near reach of the African continent I had come to the conclusion that it would be foolish not to take advantage of the opportunity of crossing over from Palermo to Tunis for a short visit, and in accordance with this decision I set forth in an aged and decrepit tub called the *Cagliari;* but in the course of the voyage a terrific storm blew up, and we were forced to take refuge in Trapani, the home town of the authoress of the Odyssey, according to Samuel Butler, where we were weather-bound for twenty-four hours; and this gave my enemy his chance, which he was not slow to take. While sitting disconsolately in the one and only café in that miserable little village, wondering why I had left Palermo and wishing I were back, I perceived, to my horror, that I was not alone and that my enemy was seated by my side. There was no escape, and the following dialogue took place between us. (I remember it only too well, in every detail, in spite of the lapse of time.)

DOPPELGÄNGER: Well, well, here we are again! Fancy meeting you here, of all places! What a small world it is, to be sure. Let me see, now, where was it we met last? In Naples, was it not, in the Galleria? And next morning, when I was looking forward to seeing you again, you suddenly left. Too bad, too bad; but still, as I say, here we are again.

SELF: I wish you knew how unspeakably boring you can be, especially when you are heavily facetious as at present.

DOPPELGÄNGER: You are not such very exhilarating company yourself, you know, if I might be allowed a *tu quoque*. As a disciple of the *joie de vivre* and the *dolce far niente*, as the troubadour of the delectable trinity of wine, women and song (your own phrase, I think, if you will permit me to say so), you present a singularly unconvincing appearance. I have never seen anyone look so miserable. I wish you had a mirror so that you could just see yourself as others see you.

SELF: It is only when you plague me with your unwanted company that I am miserable.

DOPPELGÄNGER: That is untrue; you know perfectly well that it is only when you are alone and miserable that I am able to enter into your company. So long as you are enjoying yourself I am powerless to come near you. But here in Trapani there is no one to speak to; there is no music, no painting, sculpture, or architecture—and it was surely very short-sighted or absent-minded on your part to omit to bring any books with you except Dante; and one cannot always be reading Dante, can one? So you will just have to put up with me; you cannot escape. We are going to have a little talk together, you and I; and long overdue it is.

SELF: I have already told you a hundred times that I have absolutely nothing to say to you, deplorable creature that you are: the enemy of all the joys of life, the apostle of the dreary doctrine of justification by works, the embodiment of the bad conscience of my unfortunate race, of the spirit of John Knox, Thomas Carlyle, and all the rest of the pestilential Calvinistic brood who have poisoned the air of my native land for centuries.

DOPPELGÄNGER: You do me an injustice. I am not the outcome of the bad conscience of your unspeakable race, but rather the good conscience of an individual—yourself. I am, in fact, your better self. I am Cecil Gray; *you* are the *alter ego*, the pale simulacrum, the ineffective phantom.

SELF: Have it your own way: it comes to the same thing in the end. Whether you are the outcome of centuries of Scottish Calvinism, or the embodiment of Kant's categorical imperative and moral law, your idea is that I should give up enjoying myself and work for work's sake.

DOPPELGÄNGER: You persist in misunderstanding me. In the first place I do not object to you enjoying yourself. What I object to is you *not* enjoying yourself. I like to see you happy; that is not wasting time. It is when you are miserable, as you are at present, that I feel you are wasting time and would be happier working.

SELF: I agree with Norman Douglas when he says: "To hell with work. The man who talks to me about work is my enemy." He, also, is the product of generations of Scottish Calvinism, and he seems to me to have overcome this disability with spectacular success.

DOPPELGÄNGER: I agree; more than spectacular. Just as Roman Catholic converts become more Catholic than anyone who is bred and brought up in the faith, so Norman Douglas is more pagan than any born pagan could possibly be. I sometimes think that a genuine old-world pagan might be conceivably shocked at the excessive zeal with which he lives up to the tenets of his faith.

SELF: Maybe. The Italians, moreover, have a proverb:

> "*Inglese italianizzato,*
> *Diavolo incarnato*"—

substitute *Scozzese* for *Inglese*, and you get a powerful reinforcement of the pungency of the epigram. But still, you will admit that the paganism of Norman Douglas is a very real thing, and that his distaste for work has led him to happiness and not self-dissatisfaction.

DOPPELGÄNGER: True enough, but Norman Douglas is Norman Douglas; he is unique. You, my friend, are not Norman Douglas.

SELF: Give me time!

DOPPELGÄNGER: Besides, do not forget that Norman Douglas has produced a quantity of fine work. In this his inconsistency reminds me of that epigram of the Chinese poet Po Chü-i, concerning the philosopher Lao-Tzü:

> "Those who speak know nothing;
> Those who know are silent.
> Those words, I am told,
> Were spoken by Lao-Tzü.
> If we are to believe that Lao-Tzü
>   Was himself one who knew,
> How comes it that he wrote a book
>   Of five thousand words?"

How comes it that if *dolce far niente* and *carpe diem* and "to Hell with work" are the rules of life, that Norman Douglas has written so much and so well?—And it did not come easily, either—one can see that.

SELF: One can, indeed. But the explanation is a simple one: much simpler than you suppose. There is no inconsistency. He set out to enjoy life, and did enjoy life. In the process he became financially embarrassed. In order to make a living he wrote books. I doubt whether he would ever have written a line except under the spur of dire necessity. Besides, remember that his first book, *Siren Land*, was not published until he was about forty years of age.

DOPPELGÄNGER: I see. You think you ought to be allowed to enjoy yourself while you are young, and then harvest the fruits in old age or middle age. Let us see now—how old are we?

SELF: Twenty-four.

DOPPELGÄNGER: And what have we achieved?

SELF: Need you ask? You know the answer. Precisely nothing at all.

DOPPELGÄNGER: Precisely.

SELF: Well, what about it?

DOPPELGÄNGER: Do you remember—surely you cannot have forgotten? —a young boy, aged about sixteen, who once prayed on his knees for half the night, asking whatever gods (if any) there be, that he might be allowed to be a composer?

SELF: Yes, I remember the young fool quite well.

DOPPELGÄNGER: I am he.

SELF: I know that—you do not need to tell me.

DOPPELGÄNGER: Then why have you done nothing about it?

SELF: Listen. I have put up with a great deal of abuse from you; *I* propose to tell *you* some home-truths for a change. You like to imagine you are a budding Bach, Mozart and Beethoven, all in one. The world is, and always has been, full of people like you. It is one of the more distressing disorders of puberty. Sometimes it is prolonged into maturity and then it becomes a tragedy, or a comedy, according to the way in which you choose to look at it. Take up a volume of Grove's *Dictionary of Music and Musicians* and turn over the pages; you will find the names of hundreds, of thousands of composers, each one of whom, no doubt, imagined himself to be a great master. Yet how many of them are anything more than names, if even that? A bare handful. Look back for a moment at your own short personal experience of such matters, at your year of study in Birmingham. Look at Granville Bantock, his colossal ambitions, his tremendous vitality, his fabulous output. What of it remains to-day? Very little, and in a few years' time nothing at all of it will survive. Then you will probably remember that brilliant student there who was regarded by all of us, from Bantock downwards, to be the coming genius of our time. Every week nearly he would bring a new Symphonic Poem, fully scored, which we all saluted reverently as a masterpiece. Yet what has happened to him? Nothing: he has just faded away. He is not even dead, poor devil, so far as I know. He looked rather like Schubert. It is always fatal to look like Schubert and to be as prolific as Schubert.

Ivor Gurney was another of them. He also faded away, but ended his days in a madhouse, poor devil—poor devils all, with their pathetic belief in their own genius! Even the lack of recognition in their lifetimes will not quench their pathetic faith in their possession of the divine flame. Just as the Christian, who has suffered pain and poverty and every humiliation and affliction on earth, puts his trust in another and better world where the balance will be rectified and justice done, so the unsuccessful genius believes in posterity. Posterity my—posterior! Posterity is quite as ruthless, and no doubt as unjust as contemporaneity—for I am far from suggesting that the verdict of one's contemporaries is necessarily right, but I am equally sceptical with regard to the verdict of posterity. But that is neither here nor there: we digress. All I am at pains to point out is that your pathetic conviction to the effect that you are a heaven-sent genius has probably no more foundation than the similar conviction entertained by thousands before you, who were probably just as good as you are, and possibly better. And where are they now? In the pages of Grove's *Dictionary*—nowhere else; and not always that, even. But the best example of the point at issue is afforded by the life and death of Benjamin Haydon, the painter.

DOPPELGÄNGER: Do not mention that name!

SELF: Aha! I thought that might upset you. But let me continue. He spent his entire life in the naïve belief that he was one of the greatest painters the world had ever known, and all his energies in painting vast canvases on a scale worthy of Michael Angelo (you have a distinct leaning towards the grandiose and monumental yourself, have you not? Don't squirm!). But there came a moment when the truth dawned upon him, and he blew his brains out.

DOPPELGÄNGER: At least he left behind him a fine book—his Autobiography.

SELF: Yes, indeed; and so much finer than any of his paintings. Perhaps we shall write our autobiography some day; and perhaps it will be better than our music.

DOPPELGÄNGER: I have listened to you patiently, and I confess that there is much truth in what you say. Do you imagine that I never have doubts or misgivings? But that is surely a saving grace. He who never doubts himself is lost, utterly and hopelessly. But you spoil your good case by exaggeration. Never in my wildest moments did I ever imagine myself to be of the stature you sarcastically suggested at the beginning of your onslaught.

SELF: Let it pass: it was only a debating point. But the substance of the accusation remains, and you know my motto: I think it is yours also. *Aut Caesar aut nihil;* everything or nothing. If one cannot achieve the highest, better to remain silent; there is enough bad and second-rate art in the world already—why add to it? How much better just to enjoy life.

DOPPELGÄNGER: All right, but you don't: we keep coming back to that indisputable point. You are as unhappy as I am, fundamentally. We are both of us thwarted, frustrated. But I think we are beginning to understand each other better as a result of this conversation. The fact of the matter is that we need each other; we cannot do without each other: we are bound to each other like the Siamese twins. You despise my frail, tender, creative potentiality; I resent your overbearing, uncompromising, ruthless criticality. But without you I am nothing; without me you are doomed to sterile negation. There is nothing in the world more pathetic than a critical intelligence entirely divorced from the creative faculty.

SELF: Except possibly a creative faculty without any critical, selective sense.

DOPPELGÄNGER: I admit and accept that: once more we agree. But there is one final issue that we must determine before we can arrive at a final understanding. You suggested that unless one is potentially equal to the greatest masters of all time, it were better to hold one's peace. I am more than sympathetic to the ruthless idealism which dictates such an attitude; indeed, I share it, but with certain qualifications. We know well, everyone knows, the names of those who are above criticism, in all essential respects. An occasional imbecile will say that Bach is boring, Mozart trivial, Beethoven pompous, and so on; even composers of great talent will occasionally give vent to such splenetic utterances in justification of their own diametrically opposed activities, and such irresponsible *boutades* are readily forgivable. But everyone in his heart of hearts knows that in talking thus he is talking nonsense. It is sometimes salutary to talk nonsense. *Dolce est disipere in loco.* Well, you know, just as I do, that we can never aspire to membership of that august company which is above criticism. At the same time, we equally decline to accept membership in the ranks of the facile mediocrities. As you justly observe, better to remain silent. But between these two extremes of the unattainable and the contemptible there is an infinite range of possibilities. Take, for example, Gustave Flaubert, for whom we both entertain, I think, an equal love and veneration: I, the aspiring creator, on account of a certain psychological affinity, and you, the critic, on account of his integrity and flawless utterance. Yet we can both of us surely see his great limitations. No one has ever achieved greatness with so little natural endowment. The creative flame was there, but it was small compared with that of many who have achieved much less. How was his achievement effected? You know the answer: through sheer hard work, self-mastery, unremitting devotion to the ideal he had set himself to attain. He is assuredly not one of the great masters of all time, but in the course of a life of arduous striving he produced a small handful of fine works. The greatest, admittedly, are those of vast and possibly unequal output—Shakespeare, Michael Angelo, Beethoven, and so on; but those of the second rank, like Flaubert, Baudelaire, Catullus, and many others, achieve perfection through concentration on limited objectives. This should be the ideal, even if unattainable, of such as we, who are incapable of the highest flights, and yet despise the level plains of mediocrity and facile success.

SELF: Well spoken! Once more we seem to agree. But before we part (I am sure you must be going and I should hate to detain you) let us have a final disagreement. We find ourselves back where we started—at the proposition that the solution of all our troubles lies in hard work. Between a highly problematical and possibly non-existent talent on the one hand, and a very definite tendency towards indolence and love of the good things of life on the other, we are evidently in for a gay time! Besides, when you speak of a temperamental affinity with Flaubert, you forget one important difference. We are both of us monks up to a point; but whereas Flaubert was only really happy in his cell, to which he returned from the outer world, and especially from the arms of Louise Colet (what a ghastly cow that woman must have been!) with an evident sigh of relief; we, on the other hand, sit in our cell, yearning for the outside world, and hating our self-imposed solitude and austerity. Flaubert himself, remember, once confessed that *j'ai peur de la vie;* and while it is quite possible that, deep down, we also are afraid of life, our reaction has been very different—an attempt to overcome that fear by dint of sheer recklessness and acceptance of everything that life has to offer. And that is the better way.

DOPPELGÄNGER: You are right; that is the better way. With your customary critical acumen . . .

SELF: Thank you.

DOPPELGÄNGER: Don't mention it. As I was saying, with your customary critical acumen you have laid your finger on the Achilles heel of that otherwise invulnerable artist, Gustave Flaubert. I do not believe, any more than you do, that saintliness, asceticism, self-denial, austerity, old Uncle John Calvin and all, and all, are the stuff of which the greatest art is made. The artist and the saint stand at opposite poles to each other, and there is just a little too much of the saint about Flaubert.

SELF: A reproach and criticism which I am not likely to incur.

DOPPELGÄNGER: I never had any fears or doubts on that score. And so far from discouraging the fullest acceptance of everything that life has to offer, I would rather advocate it. The best solution of the problem is alternation. Live fully, excessively if need be; then retire into your cell, emerge again, and so on. In this way you can make the best of both worlds. Well, I must be leaving you now. But in pursuance of my argument, you have, no doubt, observed the charming young female on board the *Cagliari?*

SELF: Yes; with fair hair, dazzling white skin, and dark violet eyes—a Circassian; but just a little too plump, would you not agree?

DOPPELGÄNGER: Like a slightly too full-blown rose, perhaps, but none the less acutely desirable.

SELF: The trouble is, of course, that she is travelling with her husband.

DOPPELGÄNGER: I know; but it will be a rough crossing to Tunis, and he is a bad sailor.

SELF: You think . . .?

DOPPELGÄNGER: I do. Well, good-bye. Enjoy yourself; have a good time. But may I take it for granted that you will soon return to London, and that we might possibly collaborate in a little work together?

SELF: All right, damn you! You win.

DOPPELGÄNGER: I knew I should. But I shall not pester you any more for the present. I shall wait for you in London. Till then, good-bye. Till then, as I say, enjoy yourself.

SELF: *Au revoir.*

DOPPELGÄNGER: And do not forget the Circassian.

SELF: As if I should!

Next day the sea had abated sufficiently to permit the resumption of the interrupted voyage to Tunis, and never in my life (and these are designedly strong words) have I been so bored as I was there. To begin with, I dislike intensely everything connected with Mohammed. That there is one God I am prepared to believe; but that Mohammed is His prophet I refuse even to consider. I have taken the trouble to read the Koran, and of all the flatulent collections of platitudinous balderdash that have ever been put together in the form of a book, the Koran is the supreme example. There is not a memorable sentence or phrase or line or word in it from beginning to end—nothing but a desert waste like the land from which it springs; and wherever Mohammedanism has gone it has created a desert. The only time when it ever succeeded in achieving anything positive was in those days when it reacted against itself, in a phase analogous to the Renaissance in Christian Europe: when the arts were cultivated, and the joys of wine were appreciated—both of which were sternly proscribed by the Prophet. In fact, if there is any more pernicious and objectionable figure in world history than Calvin or John Knox, it is surely Mohammed; and the combination of this Mohammedan background with a dingy colonial, provincial French foreground was more than I could stand. I hated it violently and fled back to Sicily by the first boat I could find.

I have always, indeed, been singularly impervious to the "exotic glamour of the Orient" and all its concomitants, with the exception, as I have already said, of China. Everything about that fabulous land and its culture has a direct appeal to me, only exceeded, if at all, by that of Latin Europe.

To begin with, the people. Never having been to China I can only speak of them by the specimens I have encountered abroad. One is always told that one should never judge a nation by those members of it whom one meets outside the country to which they belong, and of all generalizations I should say, from personal experience, that it is one of the soundest and least questionable. I always shudder and seek to escape as quickly as possible whenever I come into contact with my fellow-countrymen abroad, and I have always found that every nationality displays its worst characteristics when uprooted from its native soil. If, then, the Chinese one meets with outside their own country are inferior to those who remain at home, as it is natural to suppose, I can only say that they must be the most admirable and lovable people on the face of the earth; for every Chinaman I have ever met has struck me as being head and shoulders above his Western equivalent in everything that matters most—intelligence, general culture, fine manners, and everything that goes to make that elusive product, a gentleman. The Chinaman is a natural, effortless, born gentleman; we only achieve this ideal with the utmost difficulty and self-discipline—and not always then. With us it is apt to break under the stress of circumstances; never with the Chinaman, whose imperturbable sense of dignity and style is always unimpaired.

So with their art, than which there is none greater in the whole gamut of civilization—in painting, sculpture and, perhaps above all in their poetry, which, even in translation, seems to me to be the equal of any ever written. Their music alone is to me a complete mystery, apart from such things as the simple and charming folk-song which Puccini so justly stole in order to make the lovely "Song of Liu" in *Turandot*. I have studied classical Chinese music earnestly, but with ever-growing perplexity, and a complete inability to derive any æsthetic satisfaction whatever from it. I find it utterly meaningless.

My love of things Chinese—except their music—is not by any means confined to the things of the spirit. I am, and always have been, a devoted addict to their food and cooking, which are in my opinion the finest in the world, except, perhaps, the very best French *cuisine*, which to-day is practically non-existent though it may possibly revive again. At one period of my life, indeed, I used to dine practically every night at the Chinese Restaurant in Piccadilly Circus, and in later years I extended my patronage to include the most remote establishments in the heart of China Town. Actually, however, the best Chinese restaurants are in the West End, and there is no need for the enthusiast to travel to such distant fields as Pennyfields, or Limehouse Causeway.

Another cognate interest for me in things Chinese is the enormous rôle played in the life of poets, painters and scholars by wine. They all, without exception, seem to have been in a state of permanent and blissful intoxication without any apparent ill effects, save perhaps in the case of Li-Po, their greatest poet, who died through drowning while attempting, when drunk, to embrace the reflection of the moon in the Yellow River. This characteristic trait was exceedingly sympathetic to me and, eager to discover their secret, I and two other ardent Sinophilists went to the trouble of importing a vast quantity of Chinese wine from Tientsin. The liquor was contained in elegant earthenware flagons, and was of two kinds: one rose-pink, the other colourless, called respectively *Wu Chia Pi* and *Me Kwe Liu*. The potency was so terrific and the after-effects so much more so even, that I am completely unable to understand how Chinese artists were ever capable of producing any work at all, either during or after their potations. The only plausible explanation is, that the wine of which Li-Po and Po Chü-i so exultantly sing contained a lower alcoholic percentage than that of to-day; or, alternatively, that they were supermen, which is perhaps even more likely.

My greatest debt to China, however, greater even than that to her poetry, painting and sculpture, is that which I owe to her philosophy, to the thinkers of the Taoist school of which Lao Tzu was the first and most important. For me, in fact, the highest point to which human wisdom has attained, whether in religion, philosophy, ethics, or politics is not to be found in Palestine or in Greece; neither in the Germany of Kant, Hegel, Schopenhauer, Nietzsche, nor in the France of Descartes, Voltaire and the Encyclopædists; neither in the England of Hobbes, Locke, Hume, Berkeley, nor the Holland of Baruch Spinoza—but in the Taoist school of Ancient China, who wrote at a time when the rest of the world was sunk in the uttermost depths of barbarism.

In applying for a passport to visit certain countries I am told it is necessary to state one's religious denomination in the application form. In conforming with such a request my entry, if I were to be scrupulously honest, could only be "Taoist". I am, in fact, a professing and practising Taoist. The few shreds of sense that I have succeeded in acquiring during my sojourn on earth are from this source. Listen to wisdom.

"The more restrictive the laws, the poorer the people. The more machinery used, the more trouble in the kingdom. The more clever and skilful the people, the more do they make artificial things. The more the laws are in evidence, the more do robbers and thieves abound."

"Govern a great state as you would cook a small fish."

"If there is righteousness in the heart, there will be beauty in the character. If there is beauty in the character there will be harmony in the home; if there is harmony in the home there will be order in the nation; if there is order in the nation, there will be peace in the world."

"In life, man is soft and tender; in death he is rigid and hard. In life, plants and trees are soft and pliant; in death they are withered and tough. Thus rigidity and hardness are companions of death; softness and tenderness are companions of life. That is why the soldier who trusts only in strength does not conquer; the tree that relies on its strength invites the axe. Great strength dwells below; softness and tenderness dwell above."

Something of my affinity and devotion to the Chinese way of life must have unconsciously influenced my general bearing, because shortly before the war, in 1938, when crossing the Channel to St. Malo by the night boat, which was overcrowded and supremely uncomfortable, I sat in a corner of the lounge, drinking a bottle of wine all by myself and meditating, as is my wont, on the nature of the universe. There were two men standing at the bar near by, and in the midst of one of these inexplicable silences which sometimes occur suddenly in the course of an infernal hubbub, one of them said to his companion in a low voice which nevertheless reached my ears: "Look at that man sitting there in the corner behind you, by himself, drinking a bottle of wine. Doesn't he look like a Chinaman?" I take that as the greatest compliment I have ever received in my life, because there is nothing in my physical appearance even remotely suggestive of a Chinaman. I must have made my attitude towards life felt through my highly incongruous fleshly envelope.

The essence of the Chinese genius, whether expressed in their philosophy, poetry, painting or sculpture, is a kind of static, arrested, timeless, trance-like ecstasy; this quality is the common factor underlying all my oddly assorted and contrasted affinities, or predilections—Hebridean folk-song, the arias of Bellini, the poetry of Gérard de Nerval, the prose of Flaubert, the painting of Piero della Francesca.

Chapter Nine

I RETURNED to England with several projects which I was determined to realize: the writing, both text and music, of three music dramas—*Deirdre*, *The Women of Troy* and *The Temptation of Saint Anthony;* and the *History of Music*, past, present and future, in three volumes. In the course of the years all have been accomplished.

The first of these, *Deirdre*, was the outcome of a dual insemination by the poetry of Yeats, and the music of the Hebrides—the latter greatly predominating. Indeed, despite my fanatical admiration of the poetry of Yeats in my youth, nothing could be less akin in mood to *The Wind Among the Reeds*, and the Celtic Twilight, than my *Deirdre*. Celtic it is, undoubtedly, but the light is that of broad noontide. Whatever its faults or virtues, it is full of the superabundant vitality and vigour of youth.

Like everything I have written, words or music or both, it was the outcome of a long period of gestation followed by a rapid parturition. The short score sketch of all three acts was completed in as many months, but the conception had been in my mind for ten years. (Oh, my elephantine pregnancies! How I envy and yet despise the quick, slick rabbit litters of the facile mediocrities!)

In accordance with the unalterable conditions of my nature I put all my early eggs in one basket. All my youth, from fifteen to twenty-five, is contained and concentrated in that work. I made several half-hearted attempts from time to time at having it performed, and just before the last war, in 1939, on the insistent recommendation of Leslie Heward, it was being seriously considered by the Vic-Wells organization. Naturally the outbreak of the war put an end to any such projects, and I was not unduly disappointed. It belonged to a mode of thought and feeling which I had long outgrown. As a basket of eggs—my first—it has, perhaps, grown slightly addled in the course of years. There is good material in it, enough to make half a dozen good orchestral works, and some day, no doubt, when I have nothing better to do, I shall take the task in hand. As a matter of fact, I have already made one such work out of some of the material contained in the third act, which was duly performed by Leslie Heward in Birmingham. The score subsequently crossed the Atlantic and has been played several times in the United States, but it is still there; I have not troubled to recover it. Apart from this, I have used the old work as a quarry from which to hew material which I have used in other works; consequently it is unlikely, and probably undesirable, that it should ever see the light in its original form, for the time being at least.

The fact is it was born too late. It was an after-birth of a very vital movement. Ten years earlier it would have stood a chance of survival. If it is permissable to mix metaphors, I would say that it missed the tide by a very small margin, and will therefore have to wait until it turns again—which the tide always does.

The tragic tale of *Deirdre* is one to which all the most gifted poets and dramatists of the Irish literary movement were irresistibly attracted—Yeats, Synge, AE, James Stephens, and no doubt many others besides. Actually, the first treatment of the story which I came across was by none of these, but in a poem by Herbert Trench, called "Deirdre Wedded", which instantly captivated me. (This would have been before I first encountered, and stole a volume of the poetry of Yeats, as narrated earlier in these pages.) But, so far as I am aware, no composer before me ever tried his hand at this story of the Celtic Helen—a strange omission, seeing that the subject lends itself so well to musico-dramatic treatment. My friend, Sir

Arnold Bax, tells me that he wrote a five-act libretto on the subject, which he intended setting to music; but for some reason or another the project never materialized.

Quite apart from the question of the merits or demerits of the work, the method of construction which I followed in its composition may perhaps be of sufficient interest for others concerned in such problems to warrant a brief analysis and description.

The initial phase was, of course, the impregnation of my musical faculty by the poetic and dramatic subject. This gave rise to thematic ideas without any definite verbal or dramatic associations. The next stage lay in the construction of the dramatic skeleton, but still without any literary text. The fourth stage consisted in the mapping out of the musical material in more intimate correspondence with the succession of acts and scenes. Then, and only then, did I devote myself to the writing of the text, which, in its turn, was conditioned by the musical exigencies. So the two elements grew up side by side, each alternately modifying and influencing the other. The outcome was an intimate, indissoluble unity of drama, music and text—the three elements gradually evolving in that order, more or less, but subject to a considerable amount of overlapping.

A further point of interest in connexion with this work, quite apart from the question of its merits or the reverse considered simply as music, is the solution of the formal problem involved in the writing of music-drama, or opera, which is here, I think, satisfactorily achieved. The pre-19th-century opera, however great the merits of individual scenes and numbers, seldom conveys any sense of the formal structure and unity of the whole. The fault of the Wagnerian and post-Wagnerian opera consists in the fact that there is too great a formal unity, with the same thematic material running and recurring throughout all numbers, scenes and acts. In this opera I set myself to achieve a fusion, or reconciliation between the two opposed principles. Each scene in each act possesses its own thematic material, which it does not share with any other; but the last scene in the last act constitutes a kind of *coda* in which the entire thematic substance of the work is passed in review and recapitulated—a formal conception which coincides felicitously with the dramatic action, for in this last *scena* Deirdre recapitulates and re-lives her whole life.

Finally, the work is of some technical interest in the matter of the form taken by the text, which is neither verse nor prose, strictly speaking, not yet even free verse: rather, I should say, fettered prose—prose with a subtle but none the less pronounced rhythmical articulation—a medium which I have adopted in subsequent music dramas and have also experimented with in my non-musical drama, *Gilles de Rais*.

As I have said, the short score of all three acts was completed with great rapidity, but before I could start on the full orchestral score an event took place which caused me to lay the work on one side for a considerable period. This was the initiation of a project for a musical journal, of which the editor was Philip Heseltine. It was called *The Sackbut*, and the first number appeared in May, 1920. For some time my entire energies were devoted to its advancement, and to the writing of contributions to its pages.

It is one of the many grave defects of my psychological disposition that, despite the pronounced duality of musician and writer which characterizes it, I am unable to concentrate on both at the same time. (I do not regard the writing of librettos directed to musical purposes as constituting literary activity.) Indeed, changing over from the one medium to the other, from music to literature, from notes to words, has always been a torment to me which does not at all lessen with the passing of the years—if anything it becomes intensified. I do not believe, however, that this is a purely personal equation, but that it applies to everyone who has attempted to practise the two dissimilar and antagonistic arts of music and literature. The fact that they are so frequently forced into close relationship does not lessen, but rather increases, the mutual hostility that they manifest—like that of the sexes. They may hate each other, but they cannot do without each other—on occasions, at least.

The cogency of these observations is surely reinforced by the evidence of facts. Whereas the combination of pictorial and literary talent in one personality is so familiar as almost to be a commonplace, the union of writer and musician is exceedingly rare. Actually, so far as I am aware, no poet in modern times has also been a composer, with the exception of Thomas Campion, whose music, however, is deplorably inferior to his verse. As for Wagner, his poetic achievement is *nil* apart from his music, and his prose is completely unreadable except, no doubt, to Mr. Ernest Newman. The only composer of genius in history who has also been a writer of the first rank is Hector Berlioz, whose Memoirs are by universal consent recognized as a literary masterpiece, like those of Benvenuto Cellini. The writings of Schumann, *et hoc genus omne*, are not literature, but merely well-written music criticism.

Turn to the sister art of painting, on the other hand, and what an imposing array of literary talent suddenly displays itself; from Michael Angelo, with his superb sonnets, and Leonardo da Vinci with his *Trattato della Pittura* and his Notebooks, up to Benjamin Haydon, Joshua Reynolds, William Blake, Dante Gabriel Rossetti, Eugène Delacroix (whose *Journal* alone would earn him immortality even if he had never painted a single picture), up to modern times—in illustration of which one need only mention the names of Gauguin, Van Gogh, Wyndham Lewis, Sickert, Augustus John, Epstein, Dali, Picasso, as a few examples of artists of genius who have wielded the pen almost as successfully as the brush or chisel; there is no end to the list. From which it is only reasonable to assume that there is less difficulty in combining the practice of literature with the graphic and pictorial arts than with music. The reason for this I am unable even to guess, but there can be no flying in the face of the evidence. Musicians, whenever they try to write, generally write abominably; painters generally very well indeed.

My own experience in attempting to practise both arts bears out this general conclusion: I have to alternate between the two. While I am composing music I find it utterly impossible to write tolerably well, and *vice versa;* and every time I feel impelled to switch over from one to the other, I have to go to school again, as it were, and re-learn painfully the technique of whichever of the two crafts is involved, *ab initio* and *ab ovo*— and a very painful process it is, as I have said. One has to change one's æsthetic sex, so to speak, like Tiresias of old, of whom it is said that in his youth he came across two serpents in the act of copulation and when, on striking them with a stick in order to separate them (why?) he suddenly found himself changed into a girl. Some years after, on finding serpents so conjoined once more, he again struck them with his wand and recovered his original sex. As a result of his dual experience, of being alternately man and woman, Tiresias was consulted by the gods and goddesses in order to decide a vital dispute which had arisen between them, namely, as to which of the two sexes derived the greater pleasure from the act of copulation. Tiresias unhesitatingly declared that his pleasure as a female had been ten times greater than that which he had experienced as a male. Hera, infuriated by his verdict (why?), punished him by depriving him of his eyesight.

Unlike Tiresias, I should find it very difficult to decide were I asked, whether I derived greater satisfaction from writing or composing, for I do not enjoy either activity, but suffer equally in both. So far as I am concerned, there is little to choose between the two. In both one experiences marvellous moments, no doubt, but more *mauvais quarts d'heures:* on the balance, the pain outweighs the pleasure.

What is the explanation of this itching sore one has to scratch: why is one cursed by this speck of grit which prevents one from being a reasonable normal oyster, and converts one into a reluctant producer of probably inferior pearls? The answer is that the creative impulse is always a torment except to the facile self-contented mediocrities, with their rabbit-like fertility. To them, I have said, one refuses to belong—even if one could, even if one had the choice, which one has not, in any case. But if one had, would anyone willingly become any-one else, or any different from what he is? I only know that I would not choose to be anyone else than myself, however prosperous, honoured, contented, he might be. Yet I am no Narcissist; I do not love myself. But neither am I a masochist: I do not enjoy self-laceration, physical or mental.

To return to the point of departure. Being unable to devote myself to both composing and writing simultaneously, I laid *Deirdre* on one side and concentrated on the enterprise which Heseltine and I had jointly undertaken—for although he was the nominal editor I was the chief contributor, and he had expressly refused to embark on the project without the assurance of my wholehearted co-operation. I have already told the story of the brevity and vicissitudes of this venture in *Peter Warlock*, so I shall not recapitulate it here. It is enough to say that *The Sackbut* caused a considerable disturbance in the musical world during the short course of its life under our dual direction. (It eventually changed hands and survived for a few dreary years under a different proprietor and editor.) Complete sets of it are exceedingly rare, I have been told, and are eagerly sought after by collectors—God knows why. I do not myself possess a copy of each number, but so far as I am concerned, all the material of any value that I contributed to its pages was subsequently re-written and incorporated in later writing, firstly and chiefly in my *Survey of Contemporary Music*, published by the Oxford University Press in 1924, although completed some time before.

This, my first published book, still sells steadily to-day, a quarter of a century since it was written, which is not unre-markable, seeing that any contemporary survey of any activity is inevitably bound to date from the moment it appears. But apart from a slightly cock-eyed perspective here and there, such as the inadequate attention paid to Alban Berg, Webern, Prokoviev, and William Walton, whose most important works appeared after the publication of my book, it has weathered the storm of years more successfully than might have been expected. Some recently emergent figures are naturally not mentioned at all, as they did not exist creatively at the time of writing, but since few of them are of the slightest importance the omission hardly affects the general picture.

At the time of publication the essays which aroused the most lively controversy were not so much the denigrations of the fashionable gods of the day, such as Stravinsky and Scriabine, but rather the enthusiastic eulogies of Sibelius, Bartók and van Dieren, all of whom were practically unknown at the time of writing except for a few unimportant minor works by the first-named.

Sibelius was recognized, yesterday, by a large section of the musical world, as being the greatest composer of his generation; Bartók is to-day almost universally recognized as being the first of his. I do not doubt, and never have doubted, that to-morrow—if there is any to-morrow, which sometimes appears problematical—my estimate of the value of van Dieren's work will be similar endorsed.

My critics and opponents, in fact, try to represent me as *laudator temporis acti*, one out of touch with the present; it is true, in so far as I am always a few steps ahead of them, and look for my sense of values and guidance to the great masters of former days. I am always simultaneously ahead of and behind my time; I live more in the past and the future than in the present—in the eternal, in fact. Hence, in part, my isolation. I am not grumbling; as I say, I would not have it otherwise—except at moments when the spirit falters, and the flesh is weak. (But they do not last long, these moments!)

The essay on Bartók, incidentally, which first appeared in its original form in the pages of *The Sackbut* in 1920, was translated into German and published in the *Musikblätter des Anbruch*, creating a considerable sensation, since Bartók was then almost as completely unknown and unheard of in Central Europe as elsewhere. I seem to have lost, or temporarily mislaid, the touching letter which the composer wrote, thanking me for the article, and inviting me to visit him in Budapest, which I duly did a few months later. But I still preserve the characteristic note he wrote to me (in English) shortly before my visit, of which the following is an extract:—

DEAR MR. GRAY,

. . . Please let me know exactly by a telegram the time of your arrival. I shall expect you at the station and guide you to Mr. Kodály. Here I send a more recent photograph of mine to you: you must try to address me on your arrival—I am very thin, have grey hairs, and am wearing spectacles. Besides, I shall have with me a copy of *The Sackbut* in order to make for you easier to find me.

Yours very sincerely,

BÉLÁ BARTÓK.

All these secret code instructions proved unnecessary. He was charmingly unaware of the fact that, even in the vast surging crowd which confronted me on my arrival at the central station in Budapest, without the necessity of sending me a recent photograph or of carrying ostentatiously a copy of *The Sackbut*, even with my more than myopic eyes, I would be able to identify at a glance the personality whom I had immediately recognized, from a mere glance at his works, to be one of the most outstanding masters of contemporary music.

And so, of course, it happened. As soon as I set eyes on him in the railway station there was no possibility of doubting his identity: he stood out in almost melodramatic relief against the dim, circumambient, neutral mass of negligible humanity, like a lighthouse in the midst of a stormy sea.

Béla Bartók, of all the great men I have known, was at once the simplest and most elusive, the easiest and the most difficult to describe. He was, to a greater extent than anyone since Mozart, the complete musician, to the exclusion of every other interest in life. He had no feeling for literature, painting, or any other form of art whatever. I remember well an occasion, some years later, when he visited me at my place in London where I had a studio, the walls of which were lined with several thousand books. He looked at them in helpless, child-like amazement and said: "You are a musician, and yet you seem to have nothing but books, books, books!"—He could not understand it. He was married at least twice, to my knowledge, and possibly oftener, but even if he had been married a hundred times I should never be able to believe that he was interested in women as such, or in any aspect of sex. He was, moreover, completely indifferent to the pleasures of the table, whether of food or wine. He was, in fact, a complete ascetic, but with the important distinction that, whereas ascetics are generally tormented by desire for the things which they deny themselves, Bartók was indifferent to all joys save one alone—music: nothing else existed for him. I should say that the only real human relationship in his life consisted in his friendship for Zoltán Kodály, to whom he was devoted; but even this, I suspect, on his side at least, was rather the comradeship of fellow-artists and fellow-workers than of warm human feeling.

Béla Bartók, in short, was completely inhuman. He hardly existed as a personality, but his impersonality was tremendous —he was the living incarnation and embodiment of the spirit of music. He was pure spirit, in fact, and his frail, intense and delicate physique gave the impression of something ethereal and disembodied, like a flame burning in oxygen. No need to inquire, no need to know, the cause of his death: he consumed himself, burnt himself entirely away in the fire of his genius and of his selfless devotion to his art.

He was one of the saints and fanatics of music, and it is just that which makes him and his art intolerable to the *homme moyen sensuel*—that, and a strain of harsh asceticism which in some of his works amounts to almost physical cruelty: whether to himself or his audience, whether masochistic or sadistic—or both (for the two things, so far from being incompatible often, and perhaps generally, go together), it would be difficult to determine. But the flagellatory aspect of his art is very decided-

ly in evidence, particularly in his middle period, and was in
the process of development at the time of my visit to him in
Budapest. The art of Bartók which I had hitherto known, on
which my enthusiastic transports of admiration had been based
—the early volumes of piano pieces, the String Quartet No. 1,
the orchestral *Images* and *Portraits*—had given place to something very different; and I found the change highly disconcerting.

I remember only too well the occasion when I was first
introduced to the recently completed music of the ballet, *The
Marvellous Mandarin*. It was a day of scorching heat in August
(in Budapest), in a street in the centre of the town where the
din of the traffic was intolerable; and Bartók played to me the
piano score on an inferior instrument which was also decidedly
out of tune. Even in orchestral performance this work is a
severe strain on the nervous system, to say nothing of one's
æsthetic sensibilities; consequently my sufferings under the
aggravated circumstances of the performance can perhaps be
estimated, without much exercise of imagination. I have seldom suffered so much from music. It was even too much for
the composer himself. About three-quarters' way through the
work he suddenly stopped playing, saying that he did not feel
in the right mood. I searched my brains desperately for some
complimentary and appreciative words which would not
sound too insincere, but failed. I could find nothing to say.
But later, when walking back with Kodály, with whom I was
staying, to his flat, I confessed my misgivings and disillusionment, and was comforted to learn that my feelings were to
some extent shared, and at any rate completely understood.
"This harmonically exacerbated style," said Kodály, "is a
phase through which Bartók has to pass. He will emerge from
it, you will see." How prophetically right he was is shown by
the last works which, purged from all violence and perversity,
reach back to the early Bartók. But the intervening period
lasted so long that I gave up all hope of any such miraculous
transformation. The quality of sheer musicianship remains
unimpaired and unquestionable throughout all his works, and I

never ceased wholeheartedly to admire it; but much, if not most of his middle-period music, has always been personally antipathetic to me, in marked contrast to my feelings with regard to the early and late works.

In this respect it is perhaps of interest to observe that my reactions to his great contemporary, Arnold Schönberg, are precisely the opposite. In Schönberg I dislike the early and the late, and greatly admire the middle period—the period of the Three Pieces for piano, Op. 11, the *Buch der hängenden Garten*, the Second String Quartet, *Pierrot Lunaire*, and the Five Orchestral Pieces. The early and late Bartók, the middle-period Schónberg, these represent for me in their very different and even antagonistic ways the greatest summits to which the art of music attained during the years in which the respective works were written—*i.e.*, by both composers between the years of 1908 and 1914, and by Bartók in the last years of his life in the 'forties.

I have said that there was a strong element of laceration in the music of Bartók, a pleasure in the infliction of pain on himself or his audience or on both, which became intensified during his middle period; but in his personal relations he was the most courteous and kindly of men. Indeed, his hospitality, and that of Kodály, during my stay in Budapest was more than a little embarrassing in view of the conditions then prevailing. Apart from the fact that neither of them was in prosperous circumstances at the best of times, Hungary was then (1921) undergoing a severe bout of inflation and economic crisis; and I was keenly conscious of the heavy financial burden that I must have been to my friends, who would not permit me even to pay for a tram fare if they could possibly prevent me, such being the quixotically excessive nature of Hungarian hospitality, which one is compelled to accept at the risk of causing mortal offence. The irony of the situation consisted in the fact that with the advantages of the exchange I was in a very much better position to play the part of host than they were, and that I also yearned to make the acquaintance of the night life of Budapest, which even then was the most glamorous in Europe. But I had to forego these beckoning allurements, which I could have well afforded under the circumstances, in order to be a burden on my good friends. Since then I have frequently been inclined to regard excessive hospitality as a vice rather than a virtue. Apart from that, it lays the recipient under an obligation which he is not allowed to repay. It is unfair, but in saying so I hope it will be understood how deeply I appreciate the spontaneous kindliness and generosity which prompts such excesses.

The visitor to Hungary, incidentally—in those days at least—was more at the tender mercies of his hosts than in any other country in the world, seeing that not a word in the language bears the slightest resemblance to a word in any other language in the world except, I have been told, Finnish. But even in Finland, names of streets and so forth have alternative Swedish equivalents, which are to some extent intelligible even to those completely unacquainted with that language: but not in Hungary at the time when I was there. In consequence, the lonely stranger was as completely lost and as helplessly dependent on assistance as if he were a blind man in the moon.

A particularly poignant instance of this is afforded by an experience which occurred to me when walking alone in Budapest. Being afflicted by a sudden and imperious call of nature, I saw, near by, to my inexpressible relief, what was obviously a public convenience with the usual two separate divisions, over which, however, were inscribed respectively the two enigmatic words *Ferfiak* and *Nok*. I waited for a short time in order to observe the entrance or exit of someone from either of the two sections of the building, which would have revealed to me my longed-for destination; but as luck would have it there was none. Since the situation called for urgent measures, I had to decide to take a chance and, concluding that *Nok* was a more masculine-sounding word than the more graceful and romantic alternative *Ferfiak*, I precipitated myself down the steps of the *Nok* staircase, at the foot of which I was met with screams and yells by a stalwart old virago armed with a large broom with which she proceeded vigorously to be-labour me . . .

With all my enthusiastic admiration for Bartók, however, his work had no more direct influence on me than that of van Dieren. In both cases my homage was the outcome of the recognition of great qualities to which I myself could not aspire, the virtues of opposites rather than of affinities—a distinction which I have already sought to establish, and to which I shall return again shortly, for it is as crucial in its importance as it is infinite in its ramifications. With Frederick Delius, whose music attracted me equally in its very different way—indeed, it would be difficult to think of two artists more sharply opposed to each other than Delius and Bartók in almost every respect—there was a certain psychological affinity, but, even so, still no direct influence.

My first acquaintance with the music of Delius dates back to 1912, when I heard what was announced as the first per-formance of a new work entitled *In a Summer Garden*, given by the Scottish Orchestra in Edinburgh under a Polish con-ductor named Emil Mlynarski. I was considerably mystified, and in retrospect I am not at all surprised, having since heard many mystifying performances of the music of Delius under conductors and with orchestras much better qualified to interpret it. Nevertheless, enough of the composer's mentality filtered through what must undoubtedly have been an abominable performance to give me the sense of contact with something rare and unusual.

My next experience of his art was a performance of *Sea Drift*, given by Sir Thomas Beecham, which must have taken place in 1915 or 1916, in Queen's Hall, London. On this occasion any doubts or uncertainties I may have entertained concerning *In a Summer Garden* were completely dispelled. I was profoundly moved by the experience, and when, shortly later, under circumstances I have described elsewhere[1] I came

[1] *Peter Warlock*. (Jonathan Cape. 1934.)

by chance to know Philip Heseltine, who was then Delius's *aide-de-camp* and standard-bearer, I became one of the most devoted adherents to his cause. At the same time, I was never such a wholehearted worshipper at the shrine as Philip was. His excessive reliance on cloying and over-luscious harmonic mannerisms, particularly his fondness for interminable series of chromatically descending sevenths, which he had learnt and taken over from Grieg, together with his complete formal invertebracy, especially in works written on a large scale, repelled me as much as the quality of latent feeling and emotion attracted me.

I only came to know Delius personally in the last year of the war (1918), when he visited England; but from then onwards until his death we were in close contact whenever he was in England or I in France, and on several occasions I stayed with him and his wife, Jelka, at his house in Grez-sur-Loing, near Fontainebleau.

Even at the time when I most admired his work I cannot honestly say that I enjoyed these visits, and I always used to heave a sigh of relief on my departure. There was something indescribably sinister about the household—and I am by no means the only one to have felt it—even before the onset of the terrible illness from which he increasingly suffered for so many years, and eventually died. Mr. Eric Fenby[1] has already described these latter years at length, and so vividly that I am glad to be absolved, on the plea of redundance, from any necessity for traversing the same ground again. I can only say that I am amazed at Mr. Fenby's fortitude in enduring, for several years, experiences that nearly drove me insane after only a few days.

Delius, it must be frankly admitted, was not a lovable man at the best of times, and his character was not of the kind that improves or mellows with illness and the passing of the years. Heroic courage and endurance in the face of his afflictions he certainly displayed, but once that has been said there is nothing

[1]*Delius as I Knew Him.* (Bell. 1936.)

else left to say in his favour as a human being. Always a pitiless egotist, interested in no person but himself, in nothing on earth but music, but ultimately in no other music than his own, except that of Chopin and Grieg, and that only because he had taken so much from them: he became, in the terrible last years, an absolute tyrant, dominating the entire lives of those who surrounded him and draining their vitality like a vampire. These may seem strong words, and too melodramatic, but no one who came within that orbit, I am sure, will question their truth.

Nothing about Delius was more extraordinary than the contrast between his art and his personality; the former characterized chiefly by an almost overpowering sweetness, gentleness and tenderness: the latter by hardness, cruelty and callousness. It is interesting to compare him in this respect with Béla Bartók who, as I have said already, was the absolute antithesis of Delius in every respect. One thing, and one only, they possessed in common: a complete devotion to art, and an equally complete indifference to any art other than their own. But while Delius in his work chiefly aimed at, and achieved, a sense of pity and tenderness, the perfect expression of the Virgilian *lacrimae rerum*, and was in life, in his relationships with fellow-mortals cold, hard and ruthless; Bartók, on the contrary, displayed in his art, especially in his middle period, an almost sadistic violence and brutality, but as a man was kindly, shy, diffident, gentle and wholly lovable.

This paradoxical dichotomy is less uncommon than might be supposed; in fact, it may even be the rule rather than the exception. The artist whose life and work are all of a piece is a rare phenomenon: more often than not it will be found that in his work he aspires towards his opposite.

"When I think of any great poetical writer of the past," (says Yeats), "I comprehend, if I know the lineaments of his life, that the work is the man's flight from his entire horoscope, his blind struggle in the network of the stars."

Yeats himself, so he sometimes said, would sooner have been

a man of action than a poet. Similarly, General Wolfe would rather have written Gray's Elegy than won great battles. The over-sexed Tolstoi continually preached asceticism; the under-sexed D. H. Lawrence was obsessed by the sexual act almost to the exclusion of everything else in human life. Nietzsche, who continually exhorted his disciples to be hard, strong and callous, was himself the mildest and gentlest of mortals, incapable of hurting a fly; and it was this inner contradiction which ultimately destroyed him. It is, in fact, recorded that one fateful day in Turin, after having penned a masterly chapter of his *Will to Power*, decrying the Christian virtues of meekness, gentleness and pity, and glorifying the pagan virtues of pride, strength and ruthlessness, Nietzsche went out into the street and saw there an Italian cab-driver unmercifully beating his horse; whereupon the eloquent apostle of the manly pagan virtues burst into tears, threw his arms around the neck of the astonished and, no doubt, slightly embarrassed quadruped, kissed it on the nose, and was then led quietly away to the lunatic asylum from which he never again emerged except to be taken to another kindred establishment.

This brings us back to Delius, whose most ambitious work is undoubtedly the *Mass of Life*, from the *Also sprach Zarathustra* of Nietzsche. But such is the strange complexity of the nature of the heart of man, that although Delius in his personal life was a very much better Nietzschean than Nietzsche himself, and consistently behaved in the manner approved of by the master, the music of the *Mass of Life* frequently belies the intention of glorifying the pagan values and breathes a spirit of tender melancholy and wistful resignation which are exceedingly difficult to reconcile with the ideal expressed in Nietzsche's famous injunction: "Be hard, my brethren!" Sadness, in fact, keeps breaking in, and the pages in which it does so are generally more convincing than the triumphant hymns in praise of the joys of life.

This curious and inexplicable contradiction is characteristic of everything about Delius. A violent, bigoted, doctrinaire atheist, he spent his last years surrounded and cosseted by representatives of every variety of Christian faith, from Roman Catholic to Moravian Brother, to say nothing of the occasional intrusion of a Buddhist mystic or a theosophist; he professed to despise England and everything English, and lived his entire life abroad; yet, in the last days of his life it was his expressed desire to be laid to rest in an English churchyard. This is, to say the least, disconcerting. If there had been a dramatic last-minute deathbed conversion to the faith against which he had rebelled all his life, *that* one could have understood.

But there was nothing of the kind. Up to the end he remained an unrepentant old pagan. Why this Christian burial in England? Why this combination in the end, of the two things he had always disdained above everything else? Perhaps, after all, the explanation is simpler than it might appear to be. The quintessential spirit of his best work has always seemed to me to be fundamentally Christian, and essentially English. As I have written elsewhere:—

"How magically do the first few pages of *Brigg Fair* evoke the atmosphere of an early summer morning in the English countryside, with its suggestion of a faint mist veiling the horizon, and the fragrant scent of the dawn in the air! What art could be more fitly described as "simple, sensuous, and passionate?" . . . It is as well to bear in mind that this very sweetness and sensuousness is perhaps the most noteworthy characteristic of English art . . . It is the very quintessence of the English spirit."

So, also, is his characteristic indifference to problems of formal construction. I can imagine how the old man would have writhed if I had told him to his face that he was at heart a Christian and an Englishman—I would never have had the courage! But I believe it is the ultimate truth, none the less, and that his last expressed wish clearly shows it. Yet in the end one has to come back again to the question: which is the fundamental Delius—the ruthless egotist that he was in his life, or the tender, wistful idealist that he was in his best work? In short, is Yeats right when he suggests that in his art man aspires towards his opposite? And if so, which is the intrinsic, ultimate reality—the man or the work?

So far as I am personally concerned, I have already indicated the presence of a very decided dichotomy in my nature which corresponds in a sense with that postulated by Yeats: represented by the composer and the critic, the musician and the writer. But without entering again into the question as to whether I am both, alternatively one or other, or neither, I am conscious of being completely consistent within the terms of each separate aspect of my duality. In neither the music nor the words I write am I "in flight from my entire horoscope". As a critic, it is true that I am attracted to my opposite, as I have already abundantly shown, but the kind of prose I write is by no means that which I most admire, or would choose to write if I had any choice in the matter. And so in music, as I have said, my critical admiration for the work of others has never enabled me to assimilate anything from them, however much I have wished to or tried. I cannot escape from my horoscope, in fact, with the best will in the world. The network of the stars holds me as a spider's web holds a fly. I am chained to my affinities like a prisoner to the walls of his cell. If I had my will and my way, I would write prose like Walter Savage Landor, but I know I cannot; and I would infinitely prefer to write music like that of van Dieren, or Bartók, or Sibelius, if only I could, rather than that which I do.—Not Delius, observe. I would not choose to write like Delius; perhaps because he is a partial affinity, too close in some respects, too far apart in others.

I have already spoken of his lack of formal sense, and his complete indifference to such considerations, while for me form is the primary consideration in a work of art. Again, I always find myself irresistibly drawn to contrapuntal writing, whereas Delius is the most homophonic of composers—the fugue in the *Mass of Life* is unique in his work, and a dismal failure at that. For me, melody is the most important element in the musical synthesis; for Delius it was harmony. But there is one striking and curious affinity between us, namely, a common predilection for similar melodic formulas—curious, because this element, so far as I am concerned, derives unmistakably from Hebridean folk-song, which I came to know before I ever heard a note of Delius, and which Delius never knew at all. There is, for example, a melodic progression in the *finale* of his music to *Hassan* which is almost note for note identical with one of the themes in my *Deirdre*, yet there can be no question of direct influence one way or the other, since my melody existed on paper long before Delius wrote his incidental music to Flecker's play, and he did not see my opera until after he had completed his score.

I can only ascribe this coincidence—and there are others like it—to a common experience: that which is known to mystics as "the state of illumination", a kind of ecstatic revelation which may only last for a split second of time, but which he who has known it spends the rest of his life trying to recapture. It is not necessarily an attribute of great art. Some of the greatest have never experienced it, while many lesser talents have, and some with no talent at all; but those who have experienced it can always recognize the presence of the peculiar quality which appertains to it. The music of Delius is an example, and I was immediately aware of it in the first work of his I heard, in spite of an imperfect performance. I knew, too, the exact moment at which that experience must have occurred in Delius's life, and when I asked him if it were so and if I were right, he was surprised and admitted that I was. The occasion was one summer night, when he was sitting out on the verandah of his house in his orange grove in Florida, and the sound came to him from the near distance of the voices of the negroes in the plantation, singing in chorus. It is the rapture of this moment that Delius is perpetually seeking to communicate in all his most characteristic work.

Nothing Delius ever wrote is a flawless masterpiece. He lives, and will continue to live, by virtue of exquisite passages of almost unendurable sweetness and poignancy, in which he succeeds in recapturing that moment of ecstasy experienced in his youth. Those to whom such moments have never occurred will probably find nothing in Delius. Those to whom they have, will forgive him much for his manifold imperfections, of which no one is more acutely conscious than I, in spite of his intimate, personal appeal to me.

It must have been the recognition of this deep fundamental understanding between us that impelled his wife, Jelka, after his death, to approach me with a view to inducing me to write the "official biography" of the master: a suggestion to which I reluctantly acquiesced out of a sense of duty (for I did not at all relish the task), but only on condition that I should be allowed an absolutely free hand to write as I thought and felt, without concealment of any facts or adverse critical judgments. I insisted on an absolute *carte blanche*, in fact, to which she gave her consent. Nothing came of the project, however, as the result of a letter which I received from her, dated 14th December, 1934.

Grez-sur-Loing.

My Dear Gray,

Yesterday I had a letter from Beecham. He proposes to write the biography himself; in fact he says that most of it is already written in a number of essays on the Delius works, and he wants to do the remaining portions with the aid of a young writer under his leadership. This rôle you could, of course, never accept, and needs a willing collaborator under Beecham's orders. You will, I hope, understand that I cannot do otherwise than accept Beecham's proposal.

I never expected this, as he has already such multiple activities, but of course he holds all the threads of the Delius in his hands and it is natural for him to wish to be associated with him also in a literary way.

Yours ever affectionately,
Jelka Delius.

My projected biography was, in consequence, never written; on the other hand, neither has that of Sir Thomas Beecham yet appeared, nor does it seem likely ever to appear. This is a pity, because no one, obviously, was better qualified than he for the task. After him, since Philip Heseltine was dead, there was no one better qualified than I. But, as I have said, I had no positive urge to undertake the work: it would certainly have interfered seriously with other and, to me, more important projects which I had on hand, and which I would have had to lay aside. The fact remains that it was a book which should have been written, and now probably never will be—the biography of a mysterious, enigmatic personality from the hand of one who knew him intimately, and the critical study of the work of one of the most singular figures in the history of music, written by one who knew it equally well.

Sir Thomas has, apparently, seen fit to decide otherwise. Much relevant and essential material for such a book remains in his hands; but he neither writes it nor, seemingly, is willing to allow anyone else to write it. While I am on the subject, it might be appropriate to mention here the only occasion on which I have had personal contact with the gentleman in question. Although one of the last conductors in this country to become aware of the superlative genius of Sibelius, he nevertheless made up for this lapse by giving a festival devoted to the work of the Finnish master, in 1938, in connexion with which he asked me to undertake the task of providing programme notes for the entire series of concerts—a request to which I naturally acceded in view of my deep attachment to the art and person of the composer. The advance arrangements for the festival, unfortunately for all concerned, coincided with the Munich crisis, as a result of which it seemed for a time as if the whole project would have to be abandoned, or at least postponed indefinitely. Only with the lifting of the menacing shadow of war was it possible to start work; and the short space of time at my disposal for writing the script and seeing it through the press, combined with the formidable dislocation of all normal activities during and after the crisis, combined to make the ensuing weeks something of a nightmare, to say the least.

However, all went well at the last moment, and even more than well. After the festival had run its triumphant course, Sir

Thomas asked me what emoluments I considered suitable in return for my services; to which I replied that I asked for no payment—that it had been a pleasure and a privilege to have been able to contribute, in however small a way, to the success of his admirable venture. He replied by enquiring tenderly as to my favourite brands of cognac and cigars; to which I answered that I was content to leave the choice, in complete confidence, to his impeccable taste and unerring judgment in such matters. . . . .

It only remains to be added in this connexion that, by a curious coincidence Sir Thomas Beecham became the tenant of a furnished flat belonging to my mother at Abbey Lodge, Regent's Park, in the sitting-room of which there hung, over the mantelpiece, a gigantic oil-painting, executed by a now defunct president of the Royal Scottish Academy, depicting my brother and myself at the ages of seven and five respectively. Sir Thomas, I have been told, on reliable authority, used sometimes to sit and contemplate this admittedly deplorable work of art, murmuring as he did so: "Bubbles, Bubbles!" evidently under the mistaken impression that the seraphic-looking little boy in the picture who so closely resembled the advertisement for Pear's Soap, painted by Millais, was a portrait of me. Actually, it was my brother. I was the other figure in the composition—the complete antithesis of "Bubbles"—a glum, brooding, disconsolate little object, wondering what he was there for, hating every moment of the long hours of sittings, and showing it only too clearly in his expression.

Jelka Delius died shortly after writing me the letter quoted above, worn out by the strain and stress of the many years of utter devotion which she had dedicated to the art in which she believed so completely—for I am more than inclined to think that it was the art rather than the man that she was in love with. It would have been surprising were it otherwise, for, as I have already indicated, Delius was a singularly unlovable man, and life with him must have been a purgatory at the best of times, until it became a hell at the worst.

I doubt, in fact, whether there was ever any real, deep, human relationship between these two strange people. Jelka herself was an artist *manquée*, a painter of appalling pictures in which the predominating colour key was a sickly pink, and which hung in scores on the walls of the house at Grez, contributing in no small degree to its depressing atmosphere. She had entirely given up her own art on uniting her life with that of Delius, and sought to realize herself through him and his art—chiefly his art, in which she felt herself fulfilled. He, on his side, received in return the care and attention which he needed in order to achieve his work.

I am confirmed in the belief that such was the basis of their relationship by the fact that he was always insisting that there could be no other possible form of marriage for an artist. The speech recorded by Mr. Eric Fenby (*op. cit.*) was one which he had already made to Philip Heseltine and to me, and no doubt to many others. Its burden was indeed an obsession with him. I quote from Mr. Fenby's version:—

> "No artist should ever marry . . . Amuse yourself with as many women as you like, but for the sake of your art never marry one. It's fatal. And if you ever do have to marry, marry a girl who is more in love with your art than with you."

I think Jelka would have subscribed to that dictum and supported it with a statement of her own complementary belief, namely, that a woman should not marry a man for love of him, but for the work of which he was potentially capable, or for children. They despised love, in fact; and I even sometimes think that Jelka hated Delius the man as much as she worshipped the artist. She had every reason. His selfishness and callousness towards her, in spite of his complete and utter dependence on her for everything, was sometimes horrifying to witness. Yet I only once remember her uttering a single word of complaint, reproach, or resentment against his behaviour during these last terrible years when, in reply to some particularly unkind and unjust remark on his part she said sadly, with beautiful dignity: "I sometimes wonder, Fred, whether you ever realize how unkind you are to me, and how deeply you wound me. If you did, I cannot believe you could do it." But it had no more effect on him than on a stone. He merely rolled his head slowly from side to side, with a sardonic sneer on his tightly pursed lips. Whatever his sufferings—and no doubt they were great—I felt at the time, and still feel, that no human being has the right to inflict such unmerited torment on another one, so utterly devoted as she was. With all my admiration for his art I find it difficult to forgive Delius for such inhumanity. And when one tries to reconcile this trait with the gentleness and tenderness of his best music, one has to confess oneself baffled. Never has there been a stranger or more violent dichotomy.

At the same time, it must always be borne in mind that in herself ultimately she was nothing, possessing only, in superlative degree, the great feminine capacity of self-sacrifice and dedication to an ideal embodied in one person; and that through him she achieved a fulfilment which she would otherwise never have known. She suffered greatly, but with an ecstatic pain, like that of the early Christian martyrs—no woman who has ever lived has had such a highly developed capacity for self-immolation as Jelka Delius—and it may well be that in the balance, when all things are weighed, she accomplished her destiny. She believed implicitly that Delius was the greatest composer of all time, and if she had doubted it for a single moment she could never have endured what she did. Ironically enough, it was the fact that she understood so little of music that enabled her to cherish this fond delusion. In the end she reaped the reward of her long martyrdom and devotion. She lived to experience the triumphant apotheosis of the art of Delius in the great festival devoted to his work which was given by Sir Thomas Beecham in 1929; and she was fortunate in not living long enough to witness the inevitable automatic reaction against it, or to suffer even for a moment the slightest doubt in the reality of her faith and vision. For that reason she may surely be accounted to have had a happy life, and even to have achieved the summit of earthly bliss; but what she had to endure in order to achieve this ultimate felicity seemed, to the eyes of the objective beholder, and even to that of the subjective sympathizer and admirer of the art of Delius, as I then was, and with qualifications still am, wholly incommensurate with the reward. But of that no one can judge save the person concerned.

So far as his views on the married state in connexion with artists is concerned, I must admit that I believe him to be right. In other words, there may be many happy exceptions, but as a rule marriage is fatal to artists unless they have already achieved material success or have independent means. I have seen too many promising artists wrecked on the shoals of matrimony to be able to doubt it.

I have already said that Frederick Delius, considered simply as a human being, was one of the strangest and most inexplicable who has ever lived; and that as an artist also he was singular, unique, unclassifiable. Not the least strange thing about his art is the flagrant contradiction that exists between his early and mature work. With all its beauty there is in the latter an unmistakably morbid quality—and I use the adjective both in its original Latin signification of "diseased" and in its Italian derivative meaning of "over-softness"—which stands in striking contrast to the more virile, energetic, exuberant quality of the former, as exemplified particularly in the Piano Concerto, *Paris*, and other works of the same period. But the contrast is not merely one of thought and feeling, but also of technical mastery. The early works referred to are in many ways much more accomplished than the later ones; so much so, in fact, that the orchestral virtuosity of *Paris* and the pianistic brilliance of the Concerto have, to many admirers, only appeared explicable as the outcome of a collaboration on the part of some hitherto unidentified partner or "ghost".

The suggested explanation is plausible, but I think unsound. Apart from the fact that there is not a shred of material evidence in support of it, I am convinced that the clue to the problem is to be found in the affliction from which Delius suffered, the cause of his blindness, paralysis, and death, and to which it is now possible to refer without giving offence to any living person—namely, syphilis. It is to this source that I attribute the lack of formal balance and critical sense, the technical instability and cloying chromaticism, the pheno- menal egocentricity amounting almost to *folie de grandeur* which characterize his later years. It is significant in this connexion to note that his friend, Paul Gauguin, the painter, whose art is so closely akin, in both qualities and defects, to his own, also suffered from the same malady. Note, moreover, the same striking contrast between the early, virile work of Gauguin in his Breton period and the nostalgic, opulent art of his latter years in the South Seas. The equation is precisely the same in both cases, and I cannot believe that it is a mere coincidence.

I conclude these recollections and observations concerning Delius with an extract from a letter which he wrote me con- cerning my *Survey of Contemporary Music;* not so much on account of its initial testimonial, which was no doubt prompted to a great extent, if not entirely, by the glowing eulogy of his own work which is contained in my book, as because it sums up in a few words his whole simple æsthetic creed.

MY DEAR GRAY,

Many thanks for your book, which you so kindly sent me. I have just finished it and have read it with the keenest interest. I am full of admiration for the sincerity, the breadth and fearlessness of your outlook. As a survey of contemporary music it stands alone. I will not mention your style and erudition, which are of course amazing.

In my opinion there is no music without emotion; it is the first and last essential of beautiful music and intellectuality must only play a secondary rôle. Hence all these researches of quarter tones and atonality will and can lead nowhere. Ugly sounds are not music, nor have they anything to do with music. I have not heard *Pierrot Lunaire* but what I have heard of Schönberg was either weak Brahms or weak Wagner, or very academically constructed ugly sounds. A monstrous orchestra does not make the *Gurrelieder* either strong or original. Musical theorists have as yet never been able to write beautiful music—whether they are called Busoni or Schönberg. The real musical genius writes for no other purpose but to express his own soul, and in so doing finds life's greatest satisfaction and joy.

Despite the naivety of expression, I do not think that Delius was fundamentally wrong in his definition of music. Where he was utterly and preposterously wrong was in denying validity to any and every other kind of emotion than his own. To be unable to find anything in Schönberg or Busoni but perverse intellectualism is wildly absurd. The violent, Strindbergian emotionalism of Schönberg is the first and most important thing about him; the deep feeling of Busoni, though much more subtle and complex, is no less real and fundamental . . .

I first came to know Ferruccio Busoni, in 1922, through Bernard van Dieren, who had for many years been his closest and most intimate friend; in witness whereof it is only necessary to point to the essay on Busoni which is to be found in van Dieren's book entitled *Down among the Dead Men*— probably the finest study of a man and musician that has ever been written.

On looking through my papers for the purposes of this book I came across a fragment of a diary which I kept in a desultory fashion during these years, which gives my first impression of Busoni, and my reactions to his powerful personality. In transcribing these notes, however, I would like to make it clear that my present opinion of him as a creative artist is immeasurably higher than that recorded below. I did not at the time know his best works, and the greatest of all, *Doktor Faust*, was unfinished. But I allow the impression to stand because, in essentials, I do not think I was far wrong in my estimate.

5/11/22

In the course of the week I met Busoni with Epstein and van Dieren, and heard him play to-day at the Wigmore Hall.

His personality is most impressive—a marvellous face; great strength, and yet almost feminine in the delicacy and sensitiveness of the features—very mobile and expressive. His manner, like van Dieren's, is slightly irritating in its formality, stiff politeness and ceremoniousness; a curious contrast to the easy and nonchalant demeanour of Epstein. It would indeed be difficult to find two men more completely contrasted in most essential respects, but one thing they certainly possess in common—a highly developed persecution-mania. For Busoni, as for Epstein, everyone is a potential enemy; even one's ostensible friends must be carefully watched, and never trusted further than one can see them—and not even that far.

Epstein said, after the concert, in his usual direct and abrupt man-ner: "What struck me most, Busoni, when I heard you play for the first time, was the way in which you looked at the audience—with such hatred and contempt"—and Busoni positively beamed with pleasure.

This *méfiance* is all very well, very imposing, very impressive, especially if one is an exceptional being, like Busoni. In our various ways we all have to wear some armour of disdain and contempt, for the sake of sheer self-preservation, even if it should occasionally have the effect of alienating sympathy, and even of sometimes converting a potential friend, or ally, into an actual enemy. Nevertheless, it is a sign of littleness to allow one's personal feelings to disturb or distort what is, after all, done *ad majorem Dei gloriam*. And in Busoni's playing we too often become conscious of this attitude of hostility and resentment directed against the audience, of which he is, after all, the servant. He does not have to play to admiring and enthusiastic audiences if he does not wish to; he could live a quiet retired existence in a country cottage and devote himself to creative work if he really wanted to. But no; he must have it both ways. I have heard Busoni play abominably (not to-day—he was beyond all praise in everything he did) quite deliberately, as if to say "Here you are, you swine; this is good enough for you, who do not know the difference between good and bad."

Which is only too palpably true; the audience applauds equally enthusiastically whether he plays well or badly—and he is incapable of playing badly unless he intends to do so, out of sheer perversity. And on such occasions I say to him, or rather to myself, "Does it never occur to you, *illustrissimo Signore*, that amongst this admittedly absurd collection of people that constitute a musical audience there are a few who are capable of appreciating the best, and who come to hear you because they recognize that you can give it? And then you come on to the platform, scowl ferociously at us who have sometimes paid more than we can afford in order to hear you, put your foot down on the loud pedal, and present a travesty of some work or other for which you have suddenly conceived a dislike."

We are not all swine, before whom you so contemptuously throw your pearls with such a lordly air, as of a pre-Revolution *grand seigneur.* The real nobleman does not have to assert his superiority so blatantly—he makes it felt unobtrusively. *Noblesse oblige*, in fact, and one would have thought that you were too great to indulge in this *parvenu, nouveau riche* gesture of nobility. That you are a great man we know, and are only too ready and willing loudly to proclaim it; but do you have to rub it in quite so hard, to display it quite so violently and insistently? There is something wrong there . . .

Busoni has all the appearance and all the appurtenances of greatness, but there is just something lacking—and I am thinking now more particularly of the composer. He has the grand manner, abundance of ideas, immense technical mastery—every separate element that goes to make a superlative artist, except the unifying synthetic principle, that indefinable but always recognizable something without which all is but sounding brass and a tinkling cymbal— the æsthetic equivalent of what *caritas* is to the Christian faith. Or is it simply faith itself that he lacks? I do not know, but what I do know is that Busoni is just not quite a great composer—and I think that he knows it too, or at least suspects it; and there are all the elements of tragedy in this situation. He is as proud as Lucifer, and at heart as sad.

As a pianist, on the other hand, when he is not being deliberately perverse, he is unique and unapproachable. There is no one to-day who can touch him, and probably there never has been anyone to equal him save Liszt. The degree of his insight into the work at hand is truly astonishing. He completely identifies himself with it, when he wishes to do so. Every note he invests with a peculiar significance which, one sometimes feels, was not consciously present in the composer's mind, and is certainly not apparent in the printed notes, but which one is sure he would have unhesitatingly endorsed if he had heard the performance. Busoni, in fact, on occasion seems to achieve an enhancement of the composer's vision, and adds to it something of his own without distorting it in any way. This is the summit of interpretative genius.

What constitutes the essential difference between a great executant like Busoni, and a great creative artist? For it is evident that the man who possesses such insight into and absolute comprehension of a Bach or Beethoven must in sense be their equal. It seems to be an insoluble problem. But in his own creative work there is always something lacking, which I can only define as ecstasy, which can take many forms. But in one form or another it is the very stuff of poesy and of all art whatsoever. No great art is possible without it; and Busoni's music, with all its admirable qualities, just lacks that indefinable sense of "lift". All his vast, ambitious and elaborate constructions never quite leave the ground, never take the air as, in their very different ways, those of Bartók or Delius do, in a single bar, with effortless mastery.

His aim, his target, is the highest conceivable, but he just fails to hit it. And the very swine before whom he casts his pearls in such lordly and contemptuous fashion are aware of it in their own fashion. Swine are not always fools; on the contrary they are very cunning and have a keen nose for truffles, and a sense for the presence of a great man even when—or chiefly when—their recognition takes the form of a squeal of rage and an impulse to trample him to death. But they do not pay this oblique compliment to Busoni. They admire him as a pianist and ignore him as a composer—and I am not sure that they are wrong.

This, as I have said, was only the first impression made upon me as a young man by the powerful impact of the personality and the art of Ferruccio Busoni; and the essence of that impression was subsequently reprinted in the essay devoted to him in *A Survey of Contemporary Music*. But, as I have said, it is only fair to add that in later years I came to know better, and to entertain a deep respect and admiration for much of his work; especially the great Piano Concerto which sums up his early period, and *Doktor Faust*, which sums up the period of his maturity. Respect and admiration, yes, but love and affection never, and consequently my early impression may be allowed to stand without modification except in details and in degree.

I am inclined to think that the explanation of the basically unsatisfactory nature of Busoni's achievement as a composer is to be found largely in the incomplete reconciliation between two conflicting principles. In the language of Hegel you find in him the two first terms of a proposition, the thesis and the antithesis, but he never arrived at the third term, the synthesis. His father was Italian, his mother German, and the two similarly contrasted elements in his work never became fused into a unified personality. This duality, moreover, was further intensified by a conflict between his love and worship of tradition on the one hand, and his interest in modernistic experimentation on the other. Here, again, were two antithetic terms which never achieved a synthesis in the form of a unified style. The fact remains that Busoni was potentially one of the greatest composers of his age, unquestionably its greatest interpretative artist, and certainly one of its most remarkable personalities; and it will always be to me a great and memorable privilege to have known him and to have heard him play.

Chapter Ten

I T IS in the nature and function of a leading theme to recur, and if it is not mere vain repetition or recapitulation, but serves to lead to fresh aspects of the material, its recurrence is not only justifiable but necessary to the form of a book such as this, which might otherwise easily become desultory and diffuse.

It will have been recognized by now that the main problem of my life, and therefore the leading theme of this book, consists in the duality of nature which leads me alternately to seek its expression in musical sounds and in words—an Hegelian thesis and antithesis which finds its resolution in the synthesis of opera, or music drama, where the two elements are harmoniously combined. But since opera is of all art-forms the least indigenous and the least encouraged in England, it is only natural that there should be a certain element of frustration in my career—if you can call it a career!

Apart from that there is also the duality of creator and critic within the same field of activity; in connexion with which my good friend, Norman Peterkin, of the Oxford University Press, who has acted as a highly efficient midwife to several of my publications, once observed to me despondently: "It's no use, Gray: you have to make up your mind to be one thing or the other. You can't be both a composer and a critic—it simply can't be done." Useless to protest that Wagner, Berlioz, Schumann, Liszt, Debussy, to mention only a few, have successfully combined both functions! Useless to point out, as I have already said, that many painters have also been writers and critics of more than distinction! The fact remains that in this country at least, one is not permitted to combine the practice of the arts of music and literature, or the functions of creator and critic in music.

One of the consequences of having thus been made to feel myself an intruder in both fields, of music and of literature, inhabiting two worlds yet belonging to neither—incurring also the hostility of composers by frequently criticizing them adversely (or by omitting to mention them at all, which is worse) and that of critics by creative pretensions and a perhaps rather tactless habit of suggesting that no one is capable of judging the products of an art which he himself is unable to practise to some effect—as a result of all this I naturally found myself attracted, in social and intellectual relationships, to congenial company in which none of these problems and disabilities applied; namely, that of painters and sculptors. With them I was never made to feel myself as an intruder or an outsider—a writer masquerading as a musician, or a musician with literary pretensions—but was simply accepted as a foreigner in a strange country, and as such, treated with courtesy, kindliness, and good-fellowship. As a young man, in fact, I tended rather to avoid the company of musicians and writers, apart, of course, from a few isolated personal friends. My chief contacts were rather with artists.

First and foremost in this connexion, during the years of which I am now writing (roughly 1917–22) was the sculptor, Jacob Epstein, whom I have already mentioned in the foregoing chapter, in relation to Busoni; and earlier, with reference to my first meeting with Bernard van Dieren which was effected through Epstein's introduction, for which I can never be sufficiently grateful to him.

In the fragment of an old diary transcribed above I wrote, somewhat sardonically, perhaps, about a tendency to persecution mania which he shared with Busoni, and which constituted a bond of understanding and mutual appreciation between them. The observation was, I think, perfectly just, subject to the important qualification that Epstein has had every reason to suffer from it: that it would be very surprising and even unnatural if he did not. I cannot conceive of a better basis for persecution mania than the fact of having been persecuted, and I question whether any great artist of our time or of any time has been so consistently maligned and vilified as Jacob Epstein. The fact that he has fought back vigorously and given in return as much as he has received does not affect the truth of the statement that, from the time of the Oscar Wilde monument in Père Lachaise and the Strand statues, he has been the object of an unremitting hostility on the part of the general public, malevolently fomented by the popular Press. What is worse, he has had also to contend with the equally strong opposition of his professional rivals—natural and understandable, no doubt, but none the less discreditable—and with the more insidious but even more powerful and malevolent hostility of the high pontiffs of the art world: the Roger Frys and Clive Bells and the whole united pullulating cohort of the willowy æsthetes. Epstein, in short, has been confronted throughout his life with a formidable antagonism which he has had to fight on several fronts simultaneously; an unholy alliance between cretins and *intelligentsia*, between the man in the street and the Bloomsbury chorus of male sopranos and lady tenors, between the mandarin ducks of the Royal Academy and the guttersnipes of Fleet Street—to say nothing of the organized opposition of the Church, from Roman Catholics to Plymouth Brethren—and he has beaten them all (worn them down, it might perhaps be more accurate to say) singly, and in combination, by the sheer force of his genius and personality.

The tripartite friendship which existed in these days of which I write between Epstein, van Dieren and myself was a close one, and symbolically embodied in a portrait bust of van Dieren made by Epstein in 1916, which I bought and still possess (one of my most treasured possessions); in the statue of Christ, for which van Dieren was the model until his enforced departure for Holland, when I took his place for the hands, feet and neck, which still remained to be executed (I shall never forget the occasion when Epstein, quite abruptly, and for no explained reason, asked me to show him my feet, and I sheepishly removed my socks and shoes, and he looked at them closely and said: "They will do"); and finally a bust of myself, which Epstein made in 1918—I remember sitting for it at the time of the Armistice. It is not one of his best works and, in any case, is too heroic in conception for the features which it purported to represent and reproduce. (I am no hero.) But to this day I remember only too distinctly the agonies I endured in maintaining, for the Christ statue, for hours on end, the rigid position of the hands which are, in both senses of the word, the *crucial* element in the composition. (I have been a martyr.)

In sitting for the bust, an equally painful ordeal, I was more than compensated for the boredom involved by the interest derived from watching the technical processes of a great master of his craft at work. And when at long last, after some twenty sittings, at the end of which the composition seemed to be achieved and accomplished, I supposed that my pains were at an end, but received instead the discouraging, laconic statement that he was only beginning. . . . [1]

In 1920 or 1921 (I forget which) I accompanied Epstein, at his urgent request, to Italy, with the intention of finding in Carrara, or the vicinity, a studio near the marble quarries from which he could obtain the various shapes and varieties of the material he required for the execution of the works which he had in mind.

The expedition was unfortunately in vain. All the available studios in the district were occupied by monumental masons and other purely commercial sculptors. There were no vacancies to be found and we had, perforce, to return discomfited, but not without spending many pleasant days in the

---

[1] This reminds one of the similar experience of Paul Guillaume, the art-dealer and biographer of Cezanne, who, after sitting for his portrait to the master for an even greater number of sessions, *comme une pomme*, was told by him that he was not dissatisfied with the shirt-front.

course of our quest in that lovely part of Italy, which I had not previously known, on the Gulf of Genoa, between Spezia and Livorne. Especially do I cherish memories of Massa and Serravezza, from whence Michael Angelo quarried the marble which he preferred to the whiter variety of Carrara, and where I saw one of the loveliest women I have ever seen in my life—with a head and features as clearcut and noble in line as on a Greek medallion. There was also a more than memorable occasion when we were staying at a hotel in Livorno and in accordance with the regulations then in force, visitors had to sign the register with, in addition to their names and nationality, also their profession or calling. I naturally entered myself in the book as *musicista* (which in the Italian language signifies a composer, as distinct from *musicante*, who is an executant merely: and from *musico*, a term which derisively combines the two meanings of "musician" and "eunuch"—a not unknown combination but not always appropriate). When the time came for us to leave for the station in order to take train for Florence and we were paying the bill at the desk, there came from an adjacent room the sound of a piano, on which was being played the E Major prelude from the first book of the "Forty-Eight" of Bach, which had always seemed to me to be like a Bellini aria that moves too fast; but on this occasion it was played, as I had always felt it should be, as if it were an operatic *cantilena* from the pen of the Sicilian master himself. I listened, entranced, opened the door of the room from which the sounds emanated, looked in, and saw there seated at the piano a very lovely girl, aged about seventeen, who was obviously performing for the benefit of the young foreign *musicista*.

Pedantically speaking, the land of the Sirens is the southernmost tip of Italy, with Capri its core; but for me the whole Italian peninsula is Siren-land, and in no place nor in any time have I heard more distinctly or alluringly the accents of the "Song the Syrens sang" of which Sir Thomas Browne writes, than that day in Livorno. If I had been alone I would certainly have missed that train. But Ulysses, in the highly inappropriate incarnation of Epstein, was stern and adamantine. "Come along, Gray, or we'll miss the train!" I weakly (or strongly?) acquiesced, and we departed.

I remember, years afterwards, recalling the occasion to Epstein, and he said that of course I should have stayed behind, and left him to continue his journey alone. If he had said so at the time I would undoubtedly have done so, and the whole course of my life might have been changed. But I do know that if I had been alone I would certainly have missed that train—more accurately, I would not even have tried to catch it, and I would have been caught, in the toils of the sirens.

Was the outcome for better or for worse? I cannot say, but I can say that if I had not taken that train I should in all probability be still in Livorno to-day, happy and contented, no doubt, sitting around in the sunshine with a buxom, comely matron and a dozen (at least) squalling brats, instead of trying, no doubt unsuccessfully, to compose and write in our gloomy Nordic land.

The whole issue was once more reopened last year (1946), when I went to Capri, the heart of Siren-land, in order to meet again there Norman Douglas, the living embodiment of all that the pagan way of life represents. And once again the old enchantment, the pull at my heart-strings of the song of the sirens, made itself felt as strongly as on that far-off day in Livorno when the lovely girl transplanted the soul of Bellini into the body of Bach, which is the symbol of anything I have achieved. All the music I have ever written, or at any rate all that is best of it, is the outcome of that *momento del verdad* of which I have already written, and which links up with the sonnet of Gérard de Nerval, and before that with the Chopin Nocturne in early childhood. They all form part of one and the same emotional experiences, constituting the second theme of the symphony, diaphony, or cacophony, as you will, of my life, and consequently of this book.

I sometimes wonder what happened to her. She is most

likely a grandmother by now and has entirely forgotten the existence of the young foreign *musicista* around whom she sought to throw her coils, and so very nearly succeeded, and would have succeeded had it not been for Epstein.

Other memorable and pleasant days spent in his company were in Paris, in Montparnasse, which still existed then as a centre of art and culture, though already visibly wilting in its death-throes. There is no place in the world to-day more dead than that old Montparnasse, which I am glad to have known, even in its decline—the magical days and nights spent in talk and drink and love. *Tempi passati*, and *où sont les neiges d'antan*—only *clichés* are appropriate to such recollections . . .

On one occasion Epstein took me to visit the legendary and fabulous Brancusi in his studio—that saint of art, apostle of pure form, and gentle fanatic of the Platonic idea in the mind of God, for whom sculpture had come to mean complete abstraction from everything human or earthly, the quest of the absolute. At the time of our visit Brancusi was engaged in putting the finishing touches to one of his enormous marble spheroids—like dinosaur's eggs—on which he had been working uninterruptedly for many months, entirely oblivious of the outside world. It is an index to Epstein's all-embracing catholic sympathies that, although in recent years his own development has increasingly led him away from the realm of abstraction to which he was once attracted, he has never ceased to venerate the very different art of which Brancusi is the chief exponent.

Other memorable experiences for which I am grateful to Epstein have been many exceedingly profitable hours spent in his company in the National Gallery and the British Museum; especially in the Egyptian rooms and the ethnographical collection, where I learnt from him to appreciate for the first time the rare and admirable qualities of the art of primitive and exotic races, and particularly of African wood-carvings, of which he himself possesses one of the finest private collections in the world.

At approximately the same time, *i.e.*, around 1916 or 1917, I also became acquainted with Augustus John, with whom I established an equally close friendship. That this was possible was due primarily to the fact that I was a completely obscure and unimportant young man, who, moreover, was neither painter nor sculptor, nor even art-critic, and was consequently immune from the suspicion of having any kind of axe to grind: had it been otherwise I should almost inevitably have been involved in violent hostilities, and forced to take sides in the party politics which were then raging so furiously in the world of art, with Epstein and John as the respective protagonists or adversaries. Actually I am sure that neither of the principals in this absurd state of warfare was in any way responsible for it, and that they were both unwillingly forced into antagonism by the malevolent activity of over-zealous partisans and mis-chief-makers, of whom the ringleader and prime mover was an egregious idiot named Horace Cole, who achieved a certain notoriety as a professional practical joker by hoaxing the Admiralty into receiving him with official honours disguised as the Sultan of Zanzibar, and digging up Piccadilly at midnight by pretending to be a navvy, and sundry other childish tricks of the kind. I readily concede to him a certain wild vein of fantasy in such exploits which entitle him to be regarded as a forerunner of the Marx Brothers, but his activities in the world of Art were an unmitigated nuisance. For some reason or other —more likely for no reason at all—Horace Cole entertained sentiments of the most violent animosity towards Epstein, and lost no opportunity of carrying them into effective execution.

This in itself would have been of no importance but for the fact that Augustus John tolerated him and encouraged him in his buffoonery in the same way that a monarch would grant indulgence to a Court jester. There was nothing more in it than that, but this amused tolerance was naturally construed and twisted into a tacit condonation of Cole's violently anti-Epsteinian attitude, which was unfortunate.

I think myself that Horace Cole was a lunatic, but of the

border-line variety that never gets certified. He was a rich man, and whenever he overstepped the bounds of tolerable behaviour, which was often, his well-filled purse enabled him to escape the consequences which would otherwise have been visited upon him. His envenomed hostility towards Epstein, however, and the lengths to which he would go to gratify it, were beyond a practical joke, and definitely pathological. I have before me, as I write, a letter from Epstein, undated, but which must have been written in 1917. In it he thanks me for an invitation I had made to him to come and stay with me at my house in Cornwall, which he had to decline on account of the fact that he had been called up into the army as the result of an agitation engineered in the Press by Horace Cole, who had even gone so far as to make direct personal approaches to the military representatives of the tribunal before which Epstein's plea for exemption was submitted.

I have not the slightest doubt concerning the substantial, and even integral, accuracy of the letter, for I had a short time before acquired the strongest possible first-hand evidence of the inveterate malignity of Horace Cole towards Epstein, and even to anyone remotely associated with him. On one occasion when I was sitting quietly in the Café Royal, having a drink with some friends, Horace Cole sat down at our table, uninvited and more than unwelcome, and then proceeded to pour forth a tirade of the wildest abuse directed against Epstein and myself, with the most outrageous implications. To such a public affront there are only two possible replies: legal proceedings or physical violence, both of which are highly repugnant to me. As it happened, on this occasion the former alternative did not even present itself: the white light I have already described in other connexions descended like an incandescent veil before my eyes, and I completely lost self-control and normal consciousness. . . .

Horace Cole was a very powerfully built man, with great muscular strength—an asset on which he confidently relied for the immunity which generally attended him in his public displays of offensiveness, but in spite of his greatly superior physical equipment I succeeded—thanks to the white light—in giving a very creditable account of myself before we were finally separated by the professional "chucker-out", who was in these days an indispensable feature of the establishment, and forcibly ejected. I was grateful for this intervention, since if the struggle had gone on long enough his superior physique would undoubtedly have prevailed, in spite of the white light. As it was, I was highly gratified to note, while passing him in King's Road, Chelsea, the next day, that he had become the unwilling possessor of a couple of lovely black eyes, out of which he could not even see me. Shortly afterwards, in order to have his revenge, he stormed the premises in which I was then living, with the assistance of a couple of thugs whom he had suborned, but again got the worst of it; after which he ceased entirely to molest me.

Well, Horace Cole is dead now and we are told that *De mortuis nil nisi bonum.* But since the law of libel effectively prevents us also from uttering unpalatable truths concerning the living, it would seem that the only people one is allowed to criticize adversely are the unborn. I cannot accept such a ruling. I always have said, and always shall say, what I think of the dead without any sentimental gloss, and of the living as much as I can without incurring litigation, which I abhor as much as, if not more than, physical violence. Not for me, if I can possibly avoid it, the martyrdom of appearance in the courts of law—the little I have had to do with them has been more than enough to last me for the rest of my life. So far as the dead are concerned, I am always willing to allow liberal overweight to redeeming features, and to discount the adverse balance, and I should be glad to do so in the case of Horace Cole if it were humanly possible; but, frankly, in retrospect, I cannot find anything to be said in his favour (apart, as I have said, for a certain vein of freakish fantasy in his Marxian practical jokes), a verdict I could hardly wish to pass on any other human being I have ever known.

At any rate, it was this ridiculous and odious mountebank who, more than anyone else, was responsible for the embittered atmosphere which prevailed in the world of art in these days, dividing it into two hostile camps between which I was fortunately able to move freely, like a benevolent neutral in war-time provided with a *laissez-passer* by both contending factions.

While my contacts with Jacob Epstein were chiefly on the æsthetic plane, those with Augustus John were predominantly social, and took place largely in establishments which catered for the thirst that afflicts most good artists, but chiefly in the Restaurant de la Tour Eiffel in Percy Street, off Tottenham Court Road, presided over by Rudolf Stulik, a Viennese *restaurateur* of the old school, and one of the most picturesque figures of an epoch as dead and gone as he is. Alas, poor Stulik! "—a fellow of infinite jest, of most excellent fancy . . . where be your gibes now? your gambols? your songs? your flashes of merriment, that were wont to set the table on a roar?"

The Eiffel Tower was a unique institution; indeed, there was probably no other such place in the world. At one end of the social scale it catered for the most exclusive segment of the aristocracy, even embracing Royalty, sometimes *palam populo* on the ground floor, sometimes *clam*, and most ablatively, in discreet private apartments upstairs; while at the other end, Stulik would befriend penniless artists—feed, clothe, shelter, and succour them without asking a penny in return. In actual fact, such as these were often his best customers, for with a few unworthy exceptions they never forgot his kindness and generosity when success and prosperity came their way, as it frequently did. They returned, paid their debts, and in the end, no doubt, spent in return more than they had ever owed. His worst customers were the richest, the most highly placed in Society, who would incur huge bills, sign them with a lordly gesture, and never meet them, or would give cheques in payment which were promptly dishonoured by the bank. Rudolf

once, in his cups, as he invariably was by a certain advanced
hour of the night, showed me in his office a wad of cheques of
about the bulk of a volume of the telephone directory, many
of them signed by some of the most illustrious and respected
names in *Debrett's* and *Who's Who*, all endorsed with the
ominous letters "R.D.", amounting to well over a thousand
pounds.

But so long as things went well, which they did for a long
time, Rudolf did not greatly care. He regarded bad debts with
philosophic detachment, as part of the *métier*, and recouped
himself for his losses at the expense of his few honest customers,
who formed a slender intermediate layer of financial support
between the impecunious artists and the defaulting aristocracy,
by charging outrageous prices for everything he provided. One
tolerated this, and meekly paid, whenever one was able to afford
to go there because, after all, the place had a character of its
own, the creation of its genial proprietor; and also because,
as it can now be safely revealed, seeing that Rudolf is long dead
and beyond the reach of so-called justice, he blandly ignored
the licensing laws of the country and permitted those clients
for whom he had a personal regard to stay so long as they liked,
into the small, and even the large, hours of the morning—a
privilege of which I frequently availed myself to the utmost
limit of my capacity in more senses than one, and even
beyond it.

Many, indeed, were the joyous evenings one spent in the old
Eiffel Tower, in the best company not merely of London but
of the world; since foreign artists and other personalities of
distinction in various walks of life would automatically gravi-
tate there in the immediately post-War (No. 1) years, when
austerity and its concomitant satellites were almost as much in
evidence as to-day after World War No. 2.

I always occupied a particularly warm spot in Rudolf's heart
because, by a pure accident, I happened to be the first customer
to enter his restaurant after his release from the internment
camp in which he had languished during several war years—

for, as I have said, he was an Austrian, and therefore technically an "enemy subject". He never forgot this coincidence and went out of his way to pay me special consideration on account of it; a particular instance of which occurred one evening, when I was dining alone in modest fashion at a large table, while a party consisting of five or six boisterous and wealthy would-be patrons entered and rudely demanded accommodation. Apart from the table at which I was seated the only other one available was a small one for two persons; and I naturally suggested to Rudolf that I should transfer myself there and thus make room for the newcomers. In spite of my acute embarrassment, and the ill-concealed resentment of the party concerned, Rudolf firmly refused to allow it. "Mr. Gray," he said in his inimitable Viennese accent which I shall not attempt to reproduce, "you are not only my customer, but my guest; not only my guest, but my friend! You will please to stay where you are; you will not move—I do not allow you to move! They can go somewhere else! I do not want them here! Mr. GRAY, I AM A VIENNESE! !"

It is true that at the time the incident occurred he could well afford to do as he liked. His little restaurant was enjoying a fashionable vogue, but the frequent repetition of such quixotic gestures must to some extent have been responsible for the subsequent decline in his fortunes and eventual eclipse. In the days of his adversity the quality of both the food and the wine deteriorated lamentably—only the preposterous charges remained at their high level—but one was only too willing to pay them, when one could afford to, in memory of former days and in homage to his superb panache, à la mode de Cyrano de Bergerac.

After the restaurant was closed at legal hours to the normal clientele and only the select few remained behind, one of us would suggest, diffidently and with the utmost tact and circumspection, that he might rest from his culinary labours, sit down at table with us, and partake of a glass of wine; to which he would always haughtily reply: "I *never* drink with my

customers" (pause) "but to-night I shall make an exception."
This solemn ritual, which was invariable, was set to music in
an admirable piece of recitative with piano accompaniment,
composed by Eugène Goossens, who was at that time one of
the regular *habitués* of the establishment, which reminds me
that among the many nuptial feasts celebrated there was that
of his gifted and adorable sister, Sidonie Goossens, the finest
harpist of our time, on the occasion of her betrothal to Hyam
Greenbaum, potentially one of our greatest conductors, who
died tragically before his gifts achieved recognition. Among
many other such festive occasions were the wedding ceremon-
ials of Constant Lambert, Thomas Earp (concerning both of
whom more anon) and the present writer—his first matri-
monial venture. . . .

The central figure of the convivial company which habitually
congregated there in order to enjoy good food, wine, and conversation was, of course, Augustus John, for whom a table was
kept in perpetual reservation in the same far corner, every
night, even when he did not arrive to occupy it. Woe to the
innocent, uninstructed newcomer who, perceiving this empty
table in an otherwise congested restaurant, would make his
way to it and seat himself there!

It was chiefly at the Eiffel Tower that I came to know
Augustus John intimately, and many were the gay evenings
that one spent there in his jovial company and in that of the
many brilliant men and lovely women who clustered around
him like moths around a candle—an object of illumination,
incidentally, which one used to burn not only at both ends, but
simultaneously in the middle as well, in these late nights and
early mornings. But how good they were so long as they
lasted, which was quite a long time!

The old Eiffel Tower of blessed memory has gone, like so
much else, and is now a dreary Greek restaurant. The other
old haunt of my youth, the Café Royal, still exists in name, but
in nothing else except that one can still, by chance, meet an
occasional civilized human being there, chiefly in the back bar.

Later, when I became more actively involved in the musical world, my habitual resort was Pagani's, in Great Portland Street, a stone's throw from the Queen's Hall. That has gone, too, destroyed by incendiary bombs during the last war. In Paris, my beloved Foyot vanished shortly before the war, and by a curious chance I dined there on the night before it closed down for ever. When I visited Paris last, in 1946, I made my way to Montparnasse, hoping to find some old familiar anchorage: they were all gone—the Petit Trianon closed, Lavenue disappeared; but what was worse, the places which still existed under the same names which I had known, were mere shells and ghosts of their former selves. Death is better than survival as a Zombie. Paris to-day is for me a city of Zombies, of beings who appear to be alive but are not. The old life, vitality and gaiety—they have all gone. "All have gone for ever."

To revert to the subject of restaurants, I have known most of the finest in Europe. Leaving out those of Paris, which everyone knows, even people who have no appreciation or understanding of food or wine, simply because they are automatically taken to them in the normal course of events: and passing over with a bare, but highly appreciative mention such celebrated resorts as the Chapon Fin at Bordeaux and the equally famous restaurant at Aix-les-Bains of which I have forgotten the name—to say nothing (although one ought to say a lot) of the Luna and Fenice at Venice, I do not hesitate to say that the noblest establishment I have ever known which caters for this particular aspect of human desire was the restaurant of Otto Schwarz in Riga—a relic and remnant of old Tzarist Russia, left intact by a sheer miracle throughout the bloody civil wars, with the alternating triumphs of White and Red, and enjoying a brief surcease or respite, an Indian summer, in the short-lived republic of Latvia, before its final submersion by the Tartar hordes. Of all restaurants I have ever known that of Otto Schwarz was the unexcellable, the *nonpareil*.

Having said all this, I hasten to assure the reader that I only mention such resorts in order to show that I am highly appreciative of the best that life has to offer, in the way of both food and wine, because that is part of the psychology which, after all, is the chief subject of the book; with the important qualification, which is equally characteristic, that I am perfectly content with a chunk of bread and a piece of cheese.

At the same time, I deliberately refrain from attempting any description of the Lucullan joys I have experienced in the course of my life. There is no form of reading more dreary and boring than that which consists in the recording of the dishes and their excellence enjoyed by the writer—and that applies to wine as well and to other human pleasures, as I shall shortly proceed to demonstrate. Such experiences, delectable though they are, cannot be made the material of a work of art, save in the hands of one or two supreme and unique masters. The whole of the human alimentary canal, in fact, from top to bottom, is closed to æsthetic traffic except for two great literary artists—Petronius at one end and Rabelais at the other. No other writers have been able to make great literature out of either aspect of the subject (except, perhaps, for one or two passages descriptive of gastronomical delights and excesses to be found in the pages of Gogol's *Dead Souls*). I hasten to add that I have no wish to discourage the production of informative works devoted to the topics in question—on the contrary, such treatises are of crucial value and importance, and contribute greatly to the amenities of life. I am here only concerned to submit that they cannot aspire to the condition of literature.

The same observations and strictures apply to an equally important and significant aspect of life—the act of love. If there is a more tiresome category of would-be literature than the gastronomic or excretory, it is assuredly the pornographic. I have read, eagerly and assiduously, most of the products of the human pen which can be said to belong to this category, but I have been bitterly disappointed, and have never yet found one which was not supremely boring, except for the memoirs of Casanova; but one reads him rather for the story of his escape from prison in Venice, his relations with Voltaire, Rousseau, Catherine and Frederick the respectively Great, and others, than for his interminable, monotonous amours, each one of which resembles its predecessor and successor. The *Monsieur Nicolas* of Restif de la Bretonne has engaging passages, but one tires of the book long before one comes to the end; and as for the Marquis de Sade, one is tired of him at the very beginning, because in the first pages he has already exhausted the entire limited gamut of sexual experience and perversity —it is one long, continuous *fortissimo*, like the music of Tchaikovsky, but without his *diminuendi*. And again, as with Casanova, the Divine Marquis only becomes interesting when he discusses politics or philosophy, on which topics he displays an original and interesting mind.

It was Arnold Bennett, I think, who said somewhere that the greater part of life, and the most important aspects of it, simply cannot be written about at all, and I fear he was right. My original purpose and ambition in essaying this book was, in fact, nothing less than an attempt to disprove this dictum, to achieve the first autobiography that had ever been written which told the whole truth about the writer and everybody with whom he had come into contact, without concealment. At the same time I clearly realized from the outset that such a project could not possibly attain publication during the lifetime of either the author or any of the persons mentioned in the book; but I was quite cheerfully prepared to accept that condition. It was not until after I had started that I realized the impossibility of accomplishing the project, even if one possessed the combined pens of Petronius, Rabelais, Swift, Saint Augustine, Jean-Jacques Rousseau and a few others— on the level of a work of art, that is. An engrossing pathological document is no doubt possible, but I was not, and am not, interested in producing that.

I was reluctantly forced to the conclusion, in fact, that in the seemingly easy but essentially difficult art of autobiography, selection and elimination are even more important than in any other form. I find myself thinking particularly at the moment of *My Life and Loves* by Frank Harris, a writer not entirely devoid of talent, though grossly over-estimated in his day. There is nothing to be said for the book; it is not merely vulgar but, what is much worse, supremely boring and badly written—pornography at its dullest. The sad truth of the matter is, that in order to write tolerably well about one-self and one's relationships to others, one is compelled to confine oneself to the barest superficies of life: the psychological equivalent of the ninth part of the iceberg which protrudes above the surface of the waves. Then, after thinking of Frank Harris and his squalid confessions, I contemplate the opposite extreme, as exemplified in *A House in Bryanston Square*, by Lord Algernon Cecil, written in a style so exquisite that, compared to it, Walter Pater is mere Billingsgate; and in which the central figure is so ethereal and disembodied that her feet never touch the earth—she does not come to life at all.

Between these two extremes, of putting too much in and leaving too much out, both of which result in artistic failures, there is the third method in autobiographical writing which achieves artistic success at the expense of truth, involving distortion and misrepresentation of facts, which is the method of Strindberg. No such women could possibly exist outside the latter's fevered imagination, although, God knows, I have had to cope with some passably Strindbergian females in my day.

The fact remains that to write a full and accurate account of one's own life and intimate relations with others, and at the same time achieve a work of art, is impossible, I now believe. No one has ever come nearer to that inaccessible ideal than Salvador Dali in his *Secret Life*, and for that *tour de force*, if for nothing else, I reverently salute him. He has denuded himself and exhibited himself more completely and shamelessly to the public gaze than any other writer who has ever lived; and yet, even so, how incomplete is his revelation! What a great deal he leaves out! How reticent is his account of his relations with

Gala, for example! Even Henry Miller is positively coy in dealing with certain aspects of life.

What even Salvador Dali and Henry Miller cannot achieve I do not propose to attempt, and it will have been noticed that while I do not seek to conceal, but have rather tended to emphasize, the important rôle that relations with women have played in my life, I have confined such recollections to those which were never consummated and never even came within measurable distance of fruition. These alone lend themselves to artistic treatment; the important and crucial experiences I have not attempted, and shall not attempt, to treat. Discreet hints and subtle suggestions must suffice. Such deep personal issues cannot, so far as I at least am concerned, be made the substance of good writing; mere pathological exhibitionism as such does not interest me, nor, I am sure, would it interest the reader. I have no ambition to be a second Frank Harris, a second Salvador Dali, or a second Henry Miller. On the other hand, the etiolated idealism of the opposite extreme, as exemplified in *A House in Bryanston Square*, repels me equally, and I have too much self-respect to indulge in the distortions of truth and actuality which, in the hands of Rousseau or Strindberg, achieve æsthetic validity.

These observations are by no means as wild a divagation as might at first sight be supposed. However far I may seem to stray from my tonic key and progress through remote modulations, I always have firmly at the back of my mind the moment of my return to it, which I now proceed to execute.

One of the many agreeable aspects of my friendship with Augustus John consisted in the Petronian parties which he used to give in his studio in Mallord Street, Chelsea, and many were the occasions on which I was privileged to be present. It so happened, one day, when on the point of completing the full score of my first opera, *Deirdre*, after months of hard work during which I went nowhere, saw nobody, and lived like a hermit in a cell, I received an invitation to attend one of these delectable functions. I hesitated, but, as always, succumbed to temptation and accepted; with the result that once more I encountered Fate in siren form, not on this occasion that of the Mediterranean of *Pausilippe et la mer d'Italie*, but of the siren of the North, Queen Thamar. But whereas Epstein rescued me, quite inadvertently, no doubt, from the toils and wiles of the siren of the South, Augustus John signally failed to save me from those of her Nordic sister. I fell, and the whole course of my life was changed. Before embarking on this new movement of my symphonic development, however, which demands a new chapter, I revert momentarily to the point from which I departed in the present one; but in doing so I hope I have made it clear that few people are in a better position than I to answer that "puzzling question" raised by Sir Thomas Browne in his *Hydrotaphia: Urne-Burial* as to "What Song the *Syrens* sang", which he admits is "not beyond conjecture'. It is certainly not beyond conjecture, for I have heard it many times; and whether the sirens belong to the South or North, East or West, whatever language they speak, the sounds they utter are recognizably the same, and the only way to avoid hearing them is to go through life with one's ears plugged with wax—which is not my way. I have accurately transcribed their song in the episode of the encounter between Saint Anthony and the Queen of Sheba. These are the authentic notes they sing, as I happen to know, and no one better. Since I am speaking of the Queen of Sheba, the arch-sovereign of the realm of sirens, who has haunted my imagination ever since I can remember, this is the appropriate place in which to refer to an experience which I once had in connexion with her. Being once in hot pursuit of one of her many transitory embodiments, or incarnations, I had occasion to visit a certain hostelry, famous for the number of crowned heads it has sheltered, in order to establish contact with the lady in question, who, I had been informed—wrongly as it happened—was dining there that evening. I entered the restaurant and went from table to table earnestly scrutinizing the features of every woman present, and seeking in vain the object of my desires, until the manager came forward and asked me, with no doubt pardonable asperity, if I were looking for any particular person. Whereupon I replied: "Yes, I am searching for the Queen of Sheba;" to which he responded stiffly: "I regret to say, sir, that Her Majesty is not at present in residence . . ."

Apart from the unforgettable Mallord Street festivities I retain a particularly lively recollection of a Christmas celebration which took place at John's country residence at Alderney, near Poole, in Dorset, in the early 'twenties. It was the occasion of one long, enchanting Kermesse, of the Flemish school, the pleasures of which were due not only to the more than lavish hospitality of my host, but also in large measure to the gracious presence and personality of my hostess, the presiding genius of the household—Dorelia.

Of Dorelia John I would find it difficult to write in measured terms; but since I do not even propose to make the attempt, the issue does not arise. It is impossible to write of such a peerless woman except in superlatives, which I shall now proceed to employ. From the first moment I saw her—apart, of course, from the innumerable representations of her lovely person which are among the finest examples of the master's art, I conceived for her a deep romantic attachment, entirely devoid of any trace of gross, or even normal male desires; an experience I had never known before, and never have since. I never before even conceived the possibility of entertaining for a beautiful woman an absolutely pure and platonic devotion. Platonic is, perhaps, the wrong word: the quality of emotion involved was perhaps more akin to that of the Middle Ages than to that of pagan antiquity, to that of the mediaeval troubadours who were able to combine a capacity for ideal, romantic adoration for one inaccessible woman, with a very normal behaviour towards all other women, to say the least.

At any rate, my attachment to Dorelia (or Dodo, as she was familiarly called, and with justice, seeing that such heroic women as she are as utterly extinct in the modern world as that species of bird) was one of humble worship and adoration of a very beautiful woman, who was at the same time extremely intelligent and, what is perhaps even rarer than either, a rich, harmonious, exquisitely poised personality. If she ever reads these lines she will perhaps be surprised to learn of the ardent idealized homage she inspired in the breast of the preposterous young romantic I was in these days—and, thank God! still am, in spite of a certain inevitable middle-aged dilapidation.

When I think of the wives of the great artists I have known, I am never sure whether the latter are to be congratulated on account of their good fortune, or praised for their fine choice and judgment. Alternatively, did the women choose them and ruthlessly impose themselves? As I say, I do not know; the fact remains, whatever the answer, that of all men I have ever known I have never known any so supremely blessed in this important conjunction as the greatest—Bernard van Dieren, Ferruccio Busoni, Frederick Delius, Jean Sibelius, Augustus John and Jacob Epstein. I used to believe, with Ernest Renan, that *la femme est la consolation des pauvres*, but it would seem that he was wrong and I with him. The truth is, I suppose, that one cannot generalize on such issues, for one can certainly think of examples of great men who have been supremely unfortunate in this respect. I can only say that in my personal observation it has been otherwise—the greatest have had the best, the most favoured have had the consolation prize as well as the supreme one.

The further issue arises, however, and is not so easily set aside, namely: to what extent do, or did, the artists mentioned owe their achievement to their partners? I am not, I hasten to assert, suggesting for a moment that women are the "inspiration" of great art—that is mere romantic trash and twaddle. No artist of any significance has ever created anything of value out of his sexual attachment to a woman which he would not have done quite as well without her. But it happens to be true, nevertheless, that no artist can do his work and wrestle with the business of life at the same time. They are both whole-time occupations, and no one person can cope with both. Many a potentially great artist, I know, has been irretrievably sunk for lack of this material practical background, and I can certainly think of at least one in the above-mentioned list of the felicitous who would never have achieved what he did had it not been for his wife—Frederick Delius, than whom no man more utterly incompetent in the business of life, or incapable of looking after himself in any way at all, has ever lived.

By a strange coincidence it happens that on the very day on which I am writing these lines (5th March, 1947) I have read with something of a shock a brief statement in a newspaper to the effect that Jacob Epstein's wife, Peggy, has suddenly died. No man can ever have had a more loyal and devoted life-partner. I can well believe that towards enemies, real or imaginary, she could behave ruthlessly, but I can only speak of people as I find them, and over a period of thirty years I can honestly say that I never had from her anything but kindness and courtesy.

To some extent, I admit, she had a soft spot in her heart for me, on account of her deeply ingrained sense of racial loyalty, which she managed somehow to reconcile with her inter-national Communistic leanings. She was a Red of the Reds, but she was also a Scot among Scots, carved like a monumental statue, as if by the master's hand, out of Aberdeen granite. Whenever I met Peggy Epstein I always felt very acutely that man is the weaker vessel—as indeed he is, and no one could make the proposition so devastatingly clear as she. But so far as she was concerned, I could do as I liked: I could do no wrong in her eyes, however badly I might, in fact, behave, because of my one saving grace, my one redeeming feature—I was a fellow-Scot and therefore immune from the censure which would otherwise, and no doubt rightly, have attended me.

On the occasion of the above-mentioned Christmas festivities at Alderney, the John family was represented in strength, but such is its magnitude that one never meets them all together. If one did, the effect would no doubt be overwhelming; but I have known them all separately, at one time or another, and in varying combinations and circumstances: Caspar, with a more than distinguished career in the R.A.F.; Henry, a would-be Jesuit father, who disappeared suddenly in mysterious and tragic circumstances and was never seen again; David, who began life as a would-be architect and eventually became an orchestral oboist; Robin, an expert in foreign languages, who has hardly ever been known to speak a word in any of them, his capacity for silence being equal to that of the giraffe, which has never been known to utter a sound; Romilly, a would-be poet, who seems to preserve an equally giraffe-like, Trappist silence of the pen; Edwin, a would-be boxer, who has since, I understand, reverted to ancestral type and become a painter; and last, but not least, two charming and delectable daughters, Poppet and Vivian, who between them stole my heart away; but they never knew anything about it—they were much too young at the time.

Gifted and charming though they all are (or were) in their various ways, one always felt that, with the exception of Caspar and the girls, they were all rather borne down and oppressed by the weight of their father's dynamic personality and formidable renown. To have an illustrious parent is by no means an advantage, except possibly in material circumstances; psychologically, it must be a tremendous handicap to be always thought of, and always to think of oneself, as the son of someone instead of as one's own individual self; and when to that is added a personality as strong as that of Augustus John, the resultant accumulation of adverse influences must have been overwhelming in its oppressive force. If it had been my fate to have been the son of a great man, I think I should have changed my name by deed poll and taken refuge in a foreign country: only in so doing could one have achieved a personality of one's own. (Think of poor Siegfried Wagner . . . what a fate!) Daughters, on the other hand, can acquire prestige, glamour and enhancement of their personalities through such circumstances.

One particular incident stands out in my recollections of this Christmas celebration of a quarter of a century ago. Augustus and I, after an unusually quiet day, repaired at dusk to the local public house, in his car. After we had duly refreshed ourselves—but not unduly—we left the establishment and took our seats in the car, he of course, being at the wheel. We started off, but after a few convulsive grunts and snorts the engine stopped dead. The self-starter refused to function, so Augustus got out in order to wind up the crank in front of the engine, which he accordingly did, having forgotten that he had left the clutch in gear. Since the car was standing on a slight downward incline, the result was that as soon as the engine started the car started, too. Augustus, not quite realizing what was happening, nor understanding why the machine should suddenly start into motion, tried to check its course by pushing against it, but it gradually gathered momentum and he disappeared under the wheels, leaving me to cope with the situation.

It was a pitch-dark night; I was completely unacquainted with the mechanism of the machine, and in the process of frantically pushing and pulling every lever I could lay my hands and feet on, I only succeeded in braking and accelerating simultaneously. With a roaring, strangled yell like that of a wounded elephant, the car continued to gather impetus, until fortunately a substantial brick wall put a welcome end to further progress; whereupon, to my inexpressible relief, Augustus crawled out from underneath the car with no more serious injuries than a few bruises, and asked in a pained and plaintive voice why I had done it—evidently under the impression that a sudden maniacal whim had impelled me to take his place in the driver's seat and attempt to run him down.

He might easily have been killed, for it was a very low-built *chassis*, but Augustus has always lived a charmed life where cars are concerned, and his driving has always been wildly unorthodox in my experience. He has told me subsequently that in this respect—if in no other—he is a reformed character; but I am not sure if he is the best judge of this, and should require corroborative evidence before I again entrust my valuable life to his hands on the wheel, for this experience was not unique. I remember only too well another and later occasion when we went together on a tour of South Wales. When asked afterwards by a friend how we had got on, Augustus replied with a sardonic smile that I had started out on our journey in a mood of suicidal depression, but that he had effectively cured me of it, and by the time we had returned I was only too glad to be alive. It is perfectly true—I was. No one is more ready and eager than I to enter on a discussion of the relative merits of Paolo Uccello and Piero della Francesca, but not when taking a sharp corner on two wheels at forty miles an hour in the gathering dusk, without any lights, on the wrong side of the road, with a precipice on one side and a cliff on the other, to say nothing of defective brakes and an unreliable steering-gear.

I recommend anyone suffering from suicidal depression or a distaste for life to induce my illustrious friend to take him for a spin in the country and I guarantee that when he returns— if he ever does return, which is problematical—it will be as a yea-saying Nietzschean lover of life; and the same applies to my equally old and dear friend Jack Moeran the composer whose driving has a similarly Nietzschean life-desiring effect on the passenger. I am further reminded in this connexion of Norman Douglas who told me once that when as a young man in Paris he found himself afflicted by suicidal depression he would visit the Morgue, which in these days was open to public visitations, and would thereafter return homewards cheerfully reconciled to the prospect of continued existence.

Other guests besides myself at the memorable Christmas party to which I have alluded above, apart from the family, were Sophie Fedorovitch, who has since achieved fame as the creator of many admirable stage settings for the Sadler's Wells

Ballet Company; Trelawney Dayrell Reed, who looks (or looked in these days) like an El Greco saint, though behaving very differently, and has distinguished himself chiefly by his erudite history of the game of "shove-ha'penny" and by the notoriety he acquired in pre-War days by attempting to shoot down an aeroplane which flew so low as to disturb his tranquillity; and Francis Macnamara, one of the most remarkable and lovable persons I have ever known, and probably the most fantastic, which is saying a great deal.

At the time I met him first he was engaged on the production of a quarterly publication called *The Wessex Review*, to which he was practically the sole contributor under fantastic anagrammatical pseudonyms such as "African Maskerman" and "Marianna Camscarf", in the concoction of which he must have spent as much time as in the writing of the essays to which these signatures were attached. The primary object of his activities, so far as one could discover, was a Chestertonian kind of decentralization and regionalism with, as its ultimate object, the establishment (by force of arms if necessary, though he was by nature genial and pacific) of an independent kingdom of Wessex, which was to be administered in accordance with a theory of monetary values and an economic system which he had evolved. He expounded his theories at great length and with great eloquence, to all and sundry, in speech and in writing, but even expert professional economists, whom he impressed by his patent sincerity and erudition, had to confess themselves unable to understand what he was talking about.

The same thing happened in connexion with a book on Dante to which he had devoted a vast amount of time and labour. On completion it was duly submitted for publication to the Oxford University Press, and passed through the hands of the greatest Dante scholars of the age, all of whom, I understand, were greatly impressed but utterly mystified.

Francis Macnamara, indeed, lived in a world of his own creation as all great men do, but unlike others he was unable to communicate his vision or to make himself understood to anyone but himself. The personal world he inhabited was by no means anarchical or illogical; on the contrary, it was subject to very strict laws and discipline, but it bore no relation to anything else in human experience. Everyone who came into contact with him had reverently to admit his incontestable sincerity and his complete grasp of the subject of his discourse; but all alike had to confess to a complete inability to follow his mental processes. He was the absolute embodiment of the celebrated phrase of Rabelais'—*Chimaera bombinans in vacuo.*

The reason for his choice of Wessex for the centre of his wild activities and as the destined cradle of his system of thought, is to be found in a theory which he developed at length in an essay, in accordance with which civilization progresses in a definite direction westwards, at a definite speed. Having ascertained that in the period 2000–1000 B.C. the centre of civilization was in Memphis, in the preceding millennium in Babylon, and in the succeeding millennium in Greece and then in Rome, he claimed to have discovered that these places lay as nearly as makes no difference in one straight line, and were separated from each other by more or less equal distances; while the time taken for the spirit of civilization to pass from one point to another was regular and unvariable. By means of exhaustive calculations he was thereby able to deduce the conclusion that the line of civilization was due to pass in the year 1923 through a village in Dorsetshire in which he was living—or else he went there because he knew that it would pass through there at that time.

As might be imagined, Francis was addicted to the Hegelian trinity of thesis, antithesis, and synthesis, which he attempted to carry into execution in every aspect of life. For example, if he would embark on a drinking bout, which he did fairly regularly, he would intersperse his alcoholic potations at regular intervals with copious draughts of strong black coffee—a process which he used to call "balancing Christ with Mohammed". As I have always intensely disliked the latter, and in any case am indifferent to coffee, I never followed him in this strange exercise, and indeed on more than one occasion strongly remonstrated with him for practising it, regarding it as an heretical interpretation of the Hegelian doctrine leading inevitably to the negation and cancelling out of the thesis and antithesis, rather than to the desired synthesis.

For a long time we used to meet with almost ritualistic regularity at that impressive establishment in High Holborn, near the corner of Chancery Lane, which is the headquarters of the illustrious house of Henekey, like a Gothic cathedral, with its dim religious light and vast columns of gigantic vats towering up to the ceiling, with little alcoves lining each side like confessionals, in which, attended by a waiter whom Francis averred to be the reincarnation of Niccolo Machiavelli (and certainly his physical resemblance to the Florentine Secretary was more than striking) we would dispose of innumerable goblets of superb Amontillado, which wine Francis devoutly believed to be the original Tar-Water of Bishop Berkeley, for whom we both entertained an equally deep veneration, and would hold endless discourse upon the nature of the universe— a topic on which both of us were eminent authorities.

In later years I entirely lost touch and sight of this lovably preposterous person, to my infinite regret. In accordance with his belief in the regular, steady march of the spirit of civilization in a westerly direction, he calculated that it would traverse Ireland, and from there take its final departure for the New World. So to Ireland he went, and waving a hand in reverent salutation to the irrevocable passing of European culture, bidding the Life-Force a fond farewell from our shores, he died. I sometimes like to think that his ghost, as in the film of René Clair, has gone west, in the company of the spirit of civilization; but I am more inclined to believe that he would have preferred to stay behind, like the true Quixotic, Rabelaisian, Chestertonian European he was, and go down with the sinking ship—for sinking it undoubtedly is.

It only remains to be added, in connexion with Francis

Macnamara, that he was the godfather of my daughter Pauline, whom he held tenderly in his arms at the baptismal font of the church under the water tower at Notting Hill Gate, where G. K. Chesterton was also baptized (and which is the scene of the greatest battle fought in the famous war between the armies of Notting Hill and Kensington); and that his actual flesh-and-blood daughter is the wife of Dylan Thomas, probably the most gifted poet of our time in this country, who also enjoys the somewhat dubious and equivocal distinction of being the only person with whom I have ever danced. This strange and momentous occurrence took place in the Gargoyle Club, in Soho. Later on in the same evening, in some obscure night-club, we compared notes on the state of our respective livers and, as each stoutly maintained that his was in the worse condition, we then and there, in a spirit of bravado, exchanged them. Since then I have felt very much better and he, I gather, decidedly worse. So I would appear to have had the best of the bargain up to the time of writing. There is probably not much to choose between them; we are both Caucasian Prometheans to whom the eagle comes regularly for his mid-day meal.

My respect for the poetry of my unique Terpsichorean partner is great; my understanding of it frequently defective. In fact, I do not always know what he is talking about, and I am not sure that he always does himself—and I do not mean this in any derogatory sense. I believe that, to a great extent, his poetry is a form of automatic writing, as probably the best poetry is. But of his technical ability there can surely be no question, and there is nothing automatic about that.

One day, in the back bar of the Café Royal, when we were exchanging drinks, and, with great tact and circumspection, the latest bulletins from the battlefields of our respective livers, Dylan said abruptly: "There are only two good poets in this country to-day," to which I naturally replied, "Who is the other, Dylan?" His answer was: "Roy Campbell, of course!"— an answer which gave me great joy, because this had always been my firm conviction, quite apart from the fact that the poet in question is one of my oldest and best friends. (It might be truer to say that he is my friend because I admire his work so much.) And if all else fails, and my music is unplayed, my books unpublished or forgotten, I know I shall attain to a tiny modicum of vicarious immortality through association with this admirable poet, who has enshrined my name in his verses, coupled with the name of the great painter who was our common friend.

> "Far from the stuffy haunts of the genteel
> Let the gay Muse prepare the epic meal,
> And set me down with John or Cecil Gray,
> So swift to wing the moonlight hours away,
> While to our jests the rafters rock and roar
> And chairs and tables canter on the floor
> To swagger in the great Valhallan halls
> Till care, a wreck, beneath the table falls!"
>   (*The Georgiad: a satirical fantasy in verse.* 1931.)

It will be gathered from this quotation that our relationship was not maintained on an exclusively intellectual level. We both were (and still are) particularly addicted to Chianti—a finely matured Aldobrandini was our preference—of which we would consume innumerable *fiaschi* on the frequent occasions of our meeting, which invariably took place at a little Italian restaurant of the name of Poggioli, in Charlotte Street, off Tottenham Court Road, which has vanished in the course of the years, giving place to an establishment quite other, like all the pleasure resorts of my youth.

I particularly remember one occasion when Roy and I, together with a few other friends, after having liberally partaken of the admirable Aldobrandini, repaired to his flat near by, where we decided to play a football match. (Curious, incidentally, are the effects that our major poets have upon me: I dance with one and play football with the other—two things I never do under normal circumstances.) My recollection of the event being slightly hazy, not entirely owing to the distance of time which separates me from it—about twenty years or more—I recently asked Roy for the benefit of his recollections, to which he replied as follows:—

MY DEAR CECIL,

. . . That football night with Popovitch, Brookes, and General Booth's grandson, we had two callers. One was Mr. Eames, the caretaker of the block, who came to protest at the din; and the other was a short little man in private's uniform who I thought was trying to gate-crash on the party. When I was at hospital in Mombasa I was reading a book of Lawrence's (T. E.) letters and saw the photos of him, and to my horror they seemed to ring a bell and I was reminded of this fellow I saw down the stairs that night. He was my benefactor and got my first book published, when I knew nothing about him. I am sometimes haunted and conscience-stricken . . . Do you remember breaking the bed to make the fire?

Yes, I remember it vaguely, but I do distinctly remember the quiet, unobtrusive little man in uniform, and when I met T. E. Lawrence some time later at one of Augustus John's parties in Mallord Street, I also had the uneasy feeling of having met him before somewhere, but how or when I could not tell. I also have certain qualms of conscience regarding the incident, for in reading *The Letters of T. E. Lawrence* I came by chance across a letter of his to Jonathan Cape, the publisher, warmly praising my book on "Peter Warlock". I only hope he did not recognize me as being one of the disturbers of his night's repose —it must have been about three in the morning. . .

In the writing of this book I have been struck, with increasing frequency, by the number of coincidences that have occurred in the process; how, when I was thinking or writing of such and such a person, I would receive a letter from him or her, or encounter them in the street, after a lapse of perhaps twenty years or more, or read of their death. So it happened, as I have said, in the tragic instance of Peggy Epstein, as narrated above. On such occasions I experience a curious, eerie sensation of my dead past coming to life again, like a corpse which gradually becomes warm and begins to palpitate; I remember things and people that I thought I had entirely forgotten, and so it was with the odd trio mentioned in the letter of Roy Campbell.

The grandson of General Booth—of the Salvation Army—

takes me back to the days of my early youth and my brief sojourn at Edinburgh University, where he was a fellow-student. We found ourselves sitting side by side at a dreary lecture which was being delivered by Professor Charles Saroléa, on the *Chanson de Roland*, and discovered in each other the only two reasonably civilized and cultured persons present. We met, quite accidentally again, in London, some ten years later, and renewed our friendship. He has led a strange life, beginning with an atmosphere of religious fanaticism in his youth, and then becoming involved in the worlds of music, literature and art, successively but without success, from a worldly point of view. It is again many years since I saw him, but I have heard that he is now on the stage.

Ivan Brookes, when I knew him, was a painter, and I remember a picture of his representing a couple of uncommonly handsome fish, reposing on a plate, which hung on the walls of the Eiffel Tower restaurant. I lost sight of him also, but have learnt indirectly that he has since taken to religion, and after a short spell in the Anglican halfway house, has become a devout Roman Catholic—the precisely opposite course of development to that of his friend Booth, who started in a religious career and ended up as an artist. I knew them both in their transition periods, when they were chiefly interested in enjoying life, as I was.

The third member of this odd trio of Musketeers, to which I was the d'Artagnan, was Sava Popovitch, a Serbian painter, who believed amongst other things that he had discovered the secret alchemical formula for the production of great works of art, given which, he maintained, any reasonably intelligent person could produce a masterpiece. The secret resided in the mathematical progression of the Golden Measure or Proportion which goes back to Pythagoras, and the application of which, Popovitch maintained, could be recognizably demonstrated to be the guiding principle in all superlative works of art, from the earliest times up to the present day. It also followed, naturally, that any picture which did not embody the formula could not possibly be a good picture, whatever seemingly attractive qualities it might otherwise possess. Roger Fry, I have been told, was at one time considerably impressed by the Popovitch theory and sought to put it into practice; but, so far as I am aware, neither of them succeeded in producing the masterpiece so passionately sought—*La Recherche de l'Absolu.* Masterpieces are not so easily—or, paradoxically, are more easily—accomplished.

In the course of his quest of the absolute, however, he became involved in several equivocal activities, as all alchemists and would-be magicians invariably and inevitably do. I remember very distinctly one occasion when, on meeting him in the Fitzroy Tavern in Charlotte Street, which was then one of my favourite ports of call, he seemed to be unnaturally and unreasonably opulent. I jestingly commented on the unusual phenomenon and hinted darkly that he was probably in the pay of the Russian Secret Service. He looked at me with horror and apprehension, and I realized at once that what I had meant as a joke was the actual truth. Naturally I said nothing about it to anyone, but I was not surprised when, a short time later he was accused of espionage. I forget the details of the subsequent proceedings, but I remember the substance, which amounted, briefly, to the fact that he had accepted a certain sum of money from Moscow in return for which he was to furnish the designs of the latest British tanks. He did precisely nothing about it except to send to an agent in Berlin a few blue-prints of obsolete models which he had copied from perfectly accessible sources; the moral of which would seem to be that, as I have always suspected, the Secret Service activities of every nation are wildly inept and unproductive of any important result.

The fact remains that Popovitch was thenceforth under a dark cloud, and eventually returned to his native country, where he was at the time of the German invasion. He characteristically went out of his way to insult a German officer in public and was summarily shot on the spot.

A few days ago, on the 7th March, 1947, to be precise, I was standing in the back bar of the Café Royal partaking of a final drink before closing time, as is my wont. The fuel crisis was at its peak, and the sole illumination was that provided by two or three guttering candles placed in saucers on the bar, as if on an altar, shedding a dim religious light by which the barmen —Jimmy, whose clerical features suggest that he has missed his vocation and should have been a priest, and Johnny, who resembles an acolyte—discharged their duties, in the white robes of their august calling. I stood there, meditatively sipping my drink, and trying to recall and reconstruct my memories of these far-off days and of these three odd figures in particular, when there entered a person entirely unknown to me, for the purpose of a quick final. In the course of a conversation, which naturally revolved round the dismal *dégringolade* of the times in which we lived, the stranger gave utterance to a piece of pseudo-Gibbonian prose which runs as follows:—

> "Such was the degeneration of the age, that even the Queen of Sheba herself preferred the titillations of the chief of the eunuchs, to the ponderous buttocks of the Roman pro-consul."

It is surely more than a coincidence, and even decidedly uncanny, that this complete stranger should recite this piece of ribald nonsense at that particular moment, seeing that a setting of these very words by me, in four-part harmony, was the theme-song, and often battle-cry, of those three boon-companions and myself a quarter of a century ago. After which formidably Proustian (but I hope not so boring) parenthesis I return to my point of departure—Roy Campbell.

Whatever the facts may be concerning the football match in Roy Campbell's flat, one fact should be established, namely, that the first person to discern the merits of Roy Campbell's poetry was not Colonel Lawrence, but Philip Heseltine ("Peter Warlock"), who published several of his poems in *The Sackbut*. When we add to this the further fact that Roy Campbell's most intimate friend during his scholastic sojourn at Oxford was a young musician named William Walton, one cannot fail to be struck by what must be more than a coincidence. Indeed, Roy Campbell is of all modern poets, and probably of all poets who have written in English, the most musical, not even excepting Swinburne or Tennyson; and, as with both these forerunners, his verse is literally unsettable to music, because it is already so full of music that it repels any further addition. No composer has yet succeeded in setting Tennyson or Swinburne satisfactorily to music, and I doubt whether anyone has ever even attempted to set Roy Campbell. No one would be so foolish as to attempt it, for it simply could not be done. He himself is comparatively indifferent to and uninterested in music, but so far from this being in contradiction to the musical nature of his art, it is rather confirmatory; for if he had been gifted with musical capacities he would have been a composer and not a poet. He uses words as composers do notes; his treatment of the language is orchestral. That is why his greatest admirers are to be found among musicians, as I have frequently noticed. They regard him as one of themselves: they are *plus Royalistes que le Roy*, in fact.

As evidence of the attachment and understanding which subsisted between Roy Campbell and the first person to recognize his talent, I append the following poem, which is to be found in the volume entilted *Mithraic Emblems* (1936):—

Dedication of a Tree
To "Peter Warlock"
This laurel-tree to Heseltine I vow
With one cicada silvering its shade—
Who lived, like him, a golden gasconade,
And will die whole when winter burns the bough:
Who in one hour, resounding, clear, and strong,
A century of ant-hood far out-glows,
And burns more sunlight in a single song
Than they can store against the winter snows.

This lovely little elegy, written in memory of a dead friend, who was mine as well, leads me back to its subject, and to the book which we wrote in collaboration during the years of which

I have been speaking: a study of the life and work of *Carlo Gesualdo, Prince of Venosa, Musician and Murderer*. He dealt with the music of this singular personality, I with the biography, which entailed a vast amount of research.

The story of how this undertaking was conceived and carried out is in itself of great interest as an example of the functioning of what may seem to be coincidence, but is in reality preordained, in some mysterious fashion, I am convinced.

Philip came across the first clue, in connexion with a quotation from a madrigal of Gesualdo, which is to be found in Dr. Burney's *History of Music*, which the author described as "exceedingly shocking and disgusting to the ear", but which seemed to us to be not only astonishing in its harmonic daring for the time in which it was written, but also of intrinsic expressive beauty; and we thereupon resolved to find out more concerning this singular composer.

Shortly after this resolution I happened to be reading a volume of short stories by Anatole France, entitled *Le Puits de Sainte Claire*, one of which deals with *L'Histoire de Donna Maria d'Avalos*, who was murdered by her husband, a Prince of Venosa—another member of what must have been a remarkable family, I thought. I next came across a reference, also seemingly by chance, to a Prince of Venosa in the unlikely context of the German romantic writer, E. T. A. Hoffmann, in his *Serapionsbrüder*:—

> "*O ruft euch doch nur jenen Venusinischen Prinzen ins Gedächtniss, dessen Campanella erwähnt! Der gute Furst könnte nicht anders zu Stuhle gehn als wenn er vorher von einem dazu ausdrücklich besoldeten Mann erklecklich abgeprügelt worden!*"

Stranger and stranger, I thought—what a family! On checking up on Hoffmann's reference to the Neapolitan philosopher Campanella, in the Reading Room of the British Museum, I found in his *Medicinalium juxta propria* (*Libri tertii, cap. III, art. XII, Monstrosa cura*) the following passage:—

> "*Princeps Venusiae musica clarissimns nostro tempore cacare non poterat nisi verberatus a servo ad id adscito.*"

This discovery was electrifying—the composer of this extraordinary music was obviously identical with the Hoffmann-Campanella gentleman who was unable to go to stool without being soundly beaten. But more was to follow. When browsing through the entrancing pages of Brantôme (*Vies des Dames Galantes—Discours premier, sur les dames qui font l'amour et leurs cocus*) I came once more across the story of one Maria d'Avalos, married to a Prince of Venosa, who murdered her on account of her infidelity. Was it possible that he also was identical with the bizarre figure I had already discovered? To cut a long story short, he was. Dr. Burney's Prince of Venosa, who wrote music like late Wagner or Delius at the end of the 16th century, the Prince of Venosa who murdered his unfaithful wife under more than usually revolting circumstances, and the Prince of Venosa whose constipation could only be removed by means of flagellation—they were all one and the same person. Philip and I realized that we were on the trail of one of the most fantastic figures of his age, or of any age, and certainly quite the most fantastic in the entire history of music, besides being completely unknown, unmentioned even in Grove's *Dictionary of Music and Musicians* and the *Oxford History of Music* (grave derelictions which have been rectified since the publication of our monograph in 1926).

Philip, being an expert on old music, undertook the task of following up the track from that angle, while I, with my knowledge of Italian language, history and literature, pursued our prey from the biographical side, in which task I received valuable assistance from Norman Douglas, and also Sacheverell Sitwell, who made the suggestion that I should get into touch with Salvatore di Giacomo, whom he knew to be an authority on the period and locality with which I was concerned.

I duly did so, and was deeply touched by the enthusiasm and practical assistance which the venerable scholar gave to our project, without which, indeed, it might never have been realized, or would at least have been much more imperfect and incomplete than it was. The trouble he took on my behalf was boundless and inestimable. He had documents copied for me from the archives of the city of Naples, he chartered a photographer to make a hazardous journey by mule with his apparatus to the remote and inaccessible village of Gesualdo in order to take photographs of the castle and the convent there; in addition to which he surreptitiously abstracted from a library in Naples, of which he was the custodian, the only available extant copy of a rare publication called *Memorie Gesualdine*, which he sent me—all this with no other guarantee than my word that I would return the book and pay the expenses involved in the other operations.

Generous and trusting gestures such as these would go a long way to restore one's sadly shattered faith in human nature, were it not for the fact that they would not be possible to-day: faith in mutual personal integrity is a thing of the past, to which Salvatore di Giacomo belonged. He had no personal motive in all he did for me, nothing but a disinterested love of music, literature and history; and I deeply regret that he did not live long enough to enable me to meet him in the flesh and thank him in person. Our book, however, was dedicated to him. It was the least we could do; but unfortunately, also the most, for he stubbornly refused to consider any question of remuneration for all the trouble he had taken on our behalf, beyond the payment of the mere bare expenses incurred. (The book is now out of print and completely unobtainable, but my biographical section has recently been reprinted in a volume of collected essays.)[1]

This is not the end of my intimate relations with Carlo Gesualdo, Prince of Venosa, Musician and Murderer, and the beautiful Maria d'Avalos. A short time ago I was approached by my distinguished and talented friend, William Walton, with a view to the provision for him of an operatic libretto. After considering an endless variety of possible subjects, it occurred to us that there were the makings of a great opera in the story of Carlo Gesualdo and Maria d'Avalos. As a matter of fact,

[1] *Contingencies and Other Essays*. Oxford University Press. 1947.

I had on several occasions toyed with the idea of writing such a libretto for my own purposes, but had always laid it aside again out of a feeling that I was not able to do complete justice to it: that it required qualities which I did not by nature possess. But it seemed to me ideally suited to William Walton, and I accordingly set to work and produced a libretto. Unfortunately it still remains unset. Whether the composer felt that it was a failure or merely unsuited to him, or alternatively that he did not feel equal to the task, I do not know—a bit of each, perhaps. I still think often of attempting to set it to music myself and probably in the end I shall do so, if Walton does not; and he does not seem likely to do so at present, if at all. My difficulty consists in the fact, already mentioned, that I did not feel that the subject was entirely suited to me; and this aspect of it became intensified as I wrote the libretto, which was intended, not for myself but for the very different Walton, affording opportunities for musical developments of which he is supremely capable, but I, up to the time of writing, do not feel myself to be.

I end this chapter with a *coda*—how difficult it is to rid oneself of the musical habits of a lifetime!—by referring to my old friend, Matthew Smith, the painter, who in an odd thematic way knits together the many diverse strands involved in it. Like me, he has always been a close friend of both Augustus John and Jacob Epstein; unlike me (who, as I have said, was a mere negligible foreigner in the world of the visual arts) by virtue of an artistic stature equal to theirs. He was also the intimate friend of Bernard van Dieren and, strangely, of Frederick Delius as well, whose near neighbour he was when, for many years, he lived in Grez-sur-Loing. In addition, he was kind enough to act as witness and signatory to my third and last marriage; so it will be seen that he is closely interwoven into the texture of my life, although we actually meet very seldom. But when we do, he seems to provide a kind of thematic link connecting all the various aspects and phases and movements of the symphony which is my life. Finally, he provides an instructive illustration of the strange duality of man and artist with which we have been concerned so often in the course of the foregoing pages. In his work he is violent, fierce, relentless; in his life he is the mildest, gentlest, kindliest mortal I have ever known—like Bartók in this—and the complete antithesis to Delius.

Chapter Eleven

IN THE last chapter I signalled the momentous change which took place in the course of my life, as the result of a chance encounter at a party of Augustus John's in Chelsea. The period of youth, irresponsibility, and wild-oat sowing was at an end. My modest financial resources, while more than adequate to a gay bachelor life, were unequal to the strain of marriage and parenthood, and I consequently was compelled to seek some means of making money to supplement them. Robin Legge and Herbert Hughes, who were in charge of the musically critical department of the *Daily Telegraph*, were kind enough to put work in my way, and for some years after marriage my chief energies were given to that most detestable, pernicious, contemptible, and parasitic of all human activities —attendance at concerts for the purpose of writing notices about them. Before embarking on it, however, I was able to bring to completion a project which I had long held in mind, and to which I have already obliquely referred, namely, the writing of *The History of Music*.[1]

I had started work on the project as early as 1916, but it was not until I was approached by Mr. C. K. (*Basic English*) Ogden, with a contract in his hand, for such a book, to form part of a series of volumes he was engaged in editing, entitled *The History of Civilization*, that I concentrated exclusively upon its completion and execution. This involved several years during which I literally lived in the Reading Room of the British Museum, from opening to closing time, and retired to

[1] *The History of Civilization.* Edited by C. K. Ogden, M.A. Kegan Paul, Trench, Trubner and Co., Ltd. 1928.

rest no further away than to Bury Street, on the opposite side
of the road from the Museum, where I had rooms in a house
which has since disappeared as a result of having received a
direct hit from a bomb in the recent hostilities. For months
on end, indeed, my orbit frequently did not extend beyond the
hundred yards that comprised the British Museum, the
"Plough Tavern", and my rooms in Bury Street for work,
recreation and sleep respectively.

Such was my life in these years, between 1924 and 1927,
roughly; and a very happy time it was in many ways. There is
something peculiarly congenial to my temperament in the life
of a secluded scholar or historian. It appeals strongly to the
mediaeval monk who, unbeknown to my friends, male and
female, boon companions or bed-partners, constitutes such an
important part of me. There is, indeed, in the scholastic life,
when pursued ardently and to the exclusion of all else, an
intense form of intoxication which is almost physical. Frequently, on emerging from the British Museum at closing
time, in the gathering dusk, after a whole day spent in concentrated labour, to the sound of the screeching and screaming of
the innumerable flocks of birds which have made their abode
in the upper niches and cornices of that noble edifice wherein
I have spent so many hours, days, weeks, months and years of
my life, I would reel like a drunken man, in a kind of ecstasy
born of excessive indulgence in the heady torrents which pour
from the fountains of beauty and knowledge—more intoxicating, and more insidious in their intoxication, than any wine or
spirits distilled by man—and I should know, having freely and
frequently partaken of all varieties of inebriation.

The historian and research worker constitute a very positive
side to my personality, in fact. It is perhaps not going too far
to say that I was an historian before I was anything else—in
witness whereof I need only refer to the portentous series of
historical treatises I wrote around the age of sixteen or so.

During that period practically my sole excursions outside
the magic circle I have delimited were to Westminster

Cathedral, whither at one period I would repair daily in order
to attend Mass and study the ritual music of the Roman
Catholic Church, so little known even to otherwise erudite
musicians, scholars, and critics. The musical director at that
time was Father Long, the successor to that very great
musician, Sir Richard Terry. If lacking the supreme genius of
his predecessor, he nevertheless endeavoured to carry on the
tradition established by the latter, and freely allowed and even
encouraged me to make scores from the parts of old masses and
motets completely unknown, for the purpose of performance—
and some very strange works we unearthed and had performed,
to the mystification and, no doubt, acute discomfort of normal,
unmusical participants in the divine rite.

After Mass was over, which was, most conveniently, about
opening time, I would adjourn with members of the choir to a
neighbouring public-house where, to the accompaniment of
innumerable pints of bitter, we would discuss the finer points
of the work that had just been performed, and its relation to
and difference from the music of other members of the school to
which it belonged. In this way I came to be more intimately
acquainted with such music than most historians who have
written on the subject without ever having heard a note of it;
and not without pride I record the fact that when the book
was eventually published, Sir Richard Terry wrote a review
of it in which he said that:—

"although Mr. Gray disclaims any qualifications as a period-specialist
I can only say that I have not seen the case for plain-song and poly-
phony (my own special period) more clearly and illuminatingly
presented."

It is also of interest to note that when I met him shortly
after for the first time, the course of conversation clearly
indicated that he took it for granted that I was a member of
the Roman Catholic Church. He was surprised and slightly
disconcerted to discover that I was not. "I would not have
thought it possible," he said, "for anyone who was not a
practising member of our community—and not merely a

convert, but one born and bred within the fold—to understand the music and the rite of the Mass, and the intrinsic nature of Gregorian chant, in the way that you do."

I am not altogether surprised now that he should have assumed me to be a Roman Catholic, for on re-reading the book I am struck by the very orthodox Catholic view-point expressed throughout: a result, unquestionably, of daily attendance at Mass, for purely musical purposes to begin with, but ending up with a definite psychological pull towards the Faith which had given birth to that music, which is only natural. Indeed, it would be surprising were it otherwise, considering the powerful attraction exercised by the Church of Rome on very much stronger minds than mine even without the close, diurnal contact which I maintained with the ritual over such long periods of time.

Looking back, in fact, on these days I realize now, which I did not then, that I was standing on the threshold of the Church, on the verge of conversion but never quite taking the decisive, final step. Nor do I think I ever shall now, although my instinctive sympathies with the Roman Catholic Church remain intact and very strong indeed. It is the only form of organized religion that I could ever possibly embrace, but even so I would rather have none. I have always preferred the exteriors of churches to their interiors, and the objective study of religion from outside rather than direct participation inside. In this connexion, incidentally, I have noticed that those who are inside want to get out, while those outside want to get in—a perpetual two-way traffic stream of apostates and converts. Which of the two is at present the larger? It would be interesting to know. There are no reliable statistics. About equal, I should say; but if the balance inclines in one direction more than the other, I am disposed to think that at the present moment it is slightly in favour of the Roman Church, for the first time since the Counter-Reformation. On the other hand, the churches of the *via media* are fast melting away. In religion, as in politics, the choice is between extremes, and the fundamental issue is the same in both. Protestantism and Liberalism are both irrevocably dead—Roman Catholic or atheist, Conservative or Communist are the only alternatives if you wish to take sides one way or the other. For myself, as already sufficiently indicated, the alternative does not present itself; I am essentially a spectator, a non-participant. I can no more subscribe wholeheartedly to any political doctrine than to any religious creed.

The History of Music conformed with my normal *tempo* of laborious gestation and rapid parturition—about twenty years of the former and one of the latter. Nevertheless, the confinement, though comparatively brief in point of time, was not an easy one. I took more trouble and pains in the writing of that book than I have ever taken before or since with anything I have ever done; a Flaubertian diligence of never less than eight hours a day without intermission, an effort which exhausted me for some time to come. Indeed, it was not solely financial pressure which impelled me to devote myself for the next few years to the comparatively light and lucrative occupation of journalism, but also the imperative need for relaxation after a period of intense strain; I could not have undertaken any major task for some time afterwards even if I had wished to do so.

I have already said that *The History of Music* was part of a preconceived trilogy, dealing with the music of past, present and future, of which the first (*A Survey of Contemporary Music*)[1] had already been published and the third, called *Predicaments*[2] was destined to appear some years later. I have always been as much a traveller in time as in space, in fact, and have lived as much in the past and future as in the present— rather more so perhaps, both in my work and in my personal life; tending to look back and ahead more than to enjoy the fleeting moment.

I believe, myself, implicitly in the conception of time as

[1] Oxford University Press, 1924.
[2] Oxford University Press, 1936.

constituting a fourth dimension, and in the possibility of travelling as freely in time as in space, like the protagonist in that early romance of H. G. Wells, called *The Time Machine;* for I have done so myself, and not merely in my books but also in life through the agency of that strange substance known as *cannabis indica*, Indian hemp, or hashish, with which I experimented on a few occasions when I was a young man; the most remarkable property of which is perhaps its power to destroy the time sense and to enable one to pass through what seems to be a thousand years in a split second, or to move freely through past, present and future.   It is a profound metaphysical experience, in fact, proving the truth, to him who partakes of the substance, of Spinoza's dictum to the effect that "the present consists of a section of the past which is remembered and a portion of the future which is anticipated".   Equally phenomenal, too, is the power of auto-suggestion it confers upon one, in virtue of which he can experience with realistic intensity any fantasy that he cares to indulge in.

On one occasion when I had been experimenting in this direction I had been reading beforehand a short story by Théophile Gautier called *Le Club des Hashischins*, in which he describes how, under the influence of the drug, he had the illusion of seeing the hands of the clock on his mantelpiece travelling backwards.   I willed myself to undergo the same experience and it duly occurred.   I watched the hands of my clock slow down, stop, then begin to move backwards, first slowly, then with gradually increasing and finally vertiginous momentum until they revolved with the rapidity of the propeller of an aeroplane.   I felt myself becoming younger, as the timescape flashed past me in reverse, like a palindrome; I caught distorted, evanescent glimpses, transitory visions of my past life.   I was in Italy, then in Cornwall, Birmingham, Bad Nauheim, back at school, first in England, then in Scotland; I looked down at myself and saw that I was a small boy in kilts. The *tempo* rapidly increased, and I suddenly realized with a panic of horror that I was nearing the portals of life and was about to cross the threshold into the limbo of non-existence from which I had emerged. With what seemed to be a tremendous effort of will I managed, in the nick of time, to reverse the process. The hands of the clock, at which I had been fixedly staring, slowed down in their backward course, stopped, and then resumed their normal movement. I sighed with a relief which, however, was short-lived, for the same fiendish *crescendo* which had taken place in reverse now occurred in forward motion; I re-lived my life again from the beginning, flashed past the present, and felt myself rapidly growing old, decrepit, until I found myself at the point of death. In an agony of fear I succeeded once more in reversing the process and willed myself back to the point from which I had started the so-called present; and, coming to rest there, I observed that the hands of the clock were in precisely the same position as that in which they were before I had started on my wild career through time. The whole fantastic experience of my journey back to the womb then forward to the tomb, then back to the point from which I had set out, had been instantaneous. I had, in fact, experienced a simultaneous vision of the whole of my life spread out before me as in a picture, but with one important difference, which is fraught with metaphysical and psychological significance—the flash-back through the past presented recognizable, identifiable features, but the flash-forward was completely meaningless and unintelligible.

In other words, the actuality of the conterminous extension of existence, past, present and future, can only be clearly apprehended in retrospect; the apprehension of the future remains unintelligible until it becomes part of the past. This only became clear to me when, many years later, I came across the celebrated prophetic writings of Nostradamus. No one who has read them with an objective and unprejudiced mind can possibly fail to recognize the fact that he clearly prophesied events which were destined to occur centuries after his death, but only seen as in a glass darkly; for example, the flight of Louis XVI to Varennes and his arrest there through the agency of a chandler with the highly improbable name of Sauce—it was all clearly foretold by Nostradamus and can be found in the editions of his prophecies published in his lifetime or only shortly after his death, so that there is no possible loophole for the rationalists in any attempt to explain away, as forgery, a coincidence of which the mathematical odds against its occurrence would require the use of figures more astronomical than those involved in the measurement of the distance between this planet and Betelgeuse, calculated in inches.

The fact remains that to his contemporaries, and no doubt equally to himself, the prediction was completely meaningless and unintelligible. Nostradamus unquestionably practised a form of automatic writing, which more than probably, to my mind, was the outcome of the state of trance induced by the use of *cannabis indica*. He wrote down as well as he could the dark and incoherent visions which he experienced when under the influence of the drug, but they remained meaningless until interpreted in retrospect, until they had become the historical past.

The future then, it would seem, can be foretold, but not apprehended. The facts can be established, but not the co-ordination and interpretation which alone make the facts significant. If you travel backwards through the time-landscape you can recognize it; if you travel forwards you cannot. The discrepancy is no doubt due to the element of free-will which subsists in some mysterious and inexplicable fashion at the heart of pre-destination; with which solemn thought let us again set the hands of the clock backwards, without the aid of the mysterious oriental herb this time, and stop at the point at which I left off in the preceding chapter: with marriage and the adoption of the career of a music critic.

With regard to the first aspect of the situation I propose to say nothing, in accordance with the observations made earlier in these pages concerning the virtual impossibility of writing well about such intimate personal relationships, beyond saying that I am not by nature a family man in any of its aspects, as husband, father, or son, or brother, although I have tried very hard. It has been as Dr. Johnson has it in another connexion: "Sir, it is like a dog walking on its hind legs. It is not well done, but you are surprised to find it being done at all." The strain and effort have always been wildly incommensurate with the modest results attained. No, family life is decidedly not my *forte*, but the greater part of my life has been spent in trying conscientiously to cope with its demands, always fighting a losing battle, a rearguard action, and in the particular case in question very much a retreat from Moscow.

As for Fleet Street, I am afraid that I am no more suited to it than to domesticity, and again the dictum of Dr. Johnson is highly appropriate. In the first place, my whole temperament and mentality are incompatible with those which make the successful journalist. My mind, as I have already had occasion to observe more than once, works slowly and deliberately, over a long period of time, and is averse to improvization; the journalist must think quickly and rely on improvization at the very last moment possible. All good journalism, I know, for I have been acquainted with many of the genial tribe which produces it, is written with one eye on the clock and the other on the door through which the messenger-boy is due to emerge in order to seize your copy, page by page, as you write it. No good journalist ever thinks about his job until the very last moment: he knows from experience—and it is a very important psychological fact—that only when he is literally "up against the clock" can he produce good journalism. It is only under this extreme pressure that he can function: sheer urgency and absolute necessity alone can cause his pen to flow in the requisite manner. If he is given time to think and re-write, he may produce an essay which may or may not be good literature, but it will assuredly not be good journalism. He must also be able to write in such a way that if his copy is too long for the amount of space available, it can be drastically cut without making nonsense.

It will be understood, then, that I never became a good

journalist. I was absolutely reliable and conscientious, and never once failed to produce my copy in time, but I always went through agonies in the process; and my style of writing was such, by nature, with one sentence leading inevitably and logically to the next, that it was impossible to cut without disastrous consequences.

How I used to envy my professional colleagues who, after a concert or opera would pause, exchange greetings, chat nonchalantly and then stroll off in leisurely fashion to write their various contributions; while I with anguish and trepidation in my heart, would start thinking about what I was going to write even before the performance, continue worrying about it during its course; and then, no sooner was it over than I would rush off frantically and agonize over my notice, rewriting it several times until I was reasonably satisfied with it, only in order to see it torn to shreds and reduced to utter nonsense by the Procrustean sub-editors in accordance with the ruthless dictates of space! I could not blame them for this; I recognized the difficulties under which they nightly laboured in order to reduce a mass of material to the trim columns we read every morning. The fault, I realized, was chiefly mine, but that did not make it any better, but rather worse.

The climax of the horror came when I was sent to "cover" the festival of The International Society for Contemporary Music at Oxford on behalf of *The Daily Telegraph*, for which I was chiefly writing then; and to telephone my lengthy contributions, replete with Polish, Hungarian, Czecho-Slovakian and other outlandish names, which I had laboriously to spell out, to the office in London. Since I detest the telephone in any case and never employ it if I can possibly avoid doing so, I went through the torments of the damned. One particular disability associated with my use of this instrument consists in the fact that if I have to spell out a name like Szymanovsky, which I frequently had to do, by means of the orthodox technique of "A for Apple", etc., I had to search desperately for the appropriate formula for each letter and could only think of obscene words; which, since the recipient in London was invariably of the female gender, I could not employ.

Still, I managed to acquit myself honourably. Later, I combined the post of a junior contributor to the above-mentioned journal with the senior post of London critic to *The Manchester Guardian;* writing snippets concerning events of chiefly minor importance for the former, and long notices about major events for the latter.

Between these two incompatible forms of journalism, for neither of which was I by nature suited, I led a miserable existence for some years, which was only mitigated by occasional vacational visits to the Continent. Apart from some of the work I did for *The Manchester Guardian* and contributions to *The Nation and Athenaeum*, to which I was also the music critic for some years, I consider these years to have been almost totally wasted, apart from one fortunate circumstance which was, to a great extent, the outcome of my journalistic activities. In 1929 it had been arranged to spend Christmas with Sergei Mamontov in Tallinn (or Reval) in Estonia, where he was director of the opera. Since Sibelius, for whose work I had for so long entertained so great an admiration, lived only twenty or so miles away on the other side of the Gulf of Finland, I conceived the plan of visiting him at the same time. I therefore suggested to my chief on the music staff of *The Daily Telegraph*, Herbert Hughes, that I should travel to Finland on behalf of the paper and interview the composer, writing other articles at the same time on musical conditions in the Baltic countries. He readily fell in with the suggestion, which was also accepted by the Editor, and in consequence I was able to travel to Finland and establish personal contact and cordial relations with the master, which, in addition, were to stand me in good stead when, a year or two later, I undertook the commission offered me by the Oxford University Press to write a book[1] about him.

It was with considerable trepidation, none the less, that I

[1]*Sibelius.* (Oxford University Press. 1934.)

crossed over from Tallinn to Helsinki, on the last day of the year (1929). I was ostensibly approaching Sibelius in the capacity of a professional journalist, in order to obtain from him an interview for my paper; and I had already been warned that of all the species into which *homo sapiens* is divided, that of *homo diurnalis* was to Sibelius the most repugnant.

Our first meeting had a very sticky start. His English not being good, and my Finnish and Swedish non-existent, we floundered about in a curious macaronic language compounded of French and German. After a few minutes of polite, but very strained, conversation in this idiom, I must have made some observation which pleased him, for he suddenly exclaimed in wonderment: "But, Mr. Gray, you are not a journalist—you are a musician! Why did you not say so at the start?" He became a different man, jumped up, shook hands with me warmly, produced a bottle of whisky from the cupboard, and from that moment onwards all went well. When we parted it was arranged that I should lunch with him the next day at the hotel where he always stayed on his visits to the Finnish capital. (Normally he lives in the country, some twenty miles away, at Järvenpää, where he leads a life of complete solitude and seclusion, in striking contrast to his visits to Helsinki.)

The occasion will always be one of the memorable and agreeable experiences of my life. Not only did he prove to be the perfect host in all that pertains to the table, but the intellectual feast he spreads before his guests is even more magnificent, if that were possible. Most musicians are apt to have one-track minds. However interesting their conversation may be in speaking of their art, and more particularly in speaking of themselves and of their own achievements, they are, as a rule, singularly uninteresting and unilluminating on other topics.

Sibelius exhibits precisely the opposite tendency—of himself and his work he speaks diffidently and unwillingly. One quickly realizes that he prefers to discuss any and every other subject on earth, and does—literature, philosophy, psychology, painting, politics, science. The time passed as if by enchantment. Suddenly, on looking around the restaurant, I noticed that we were the only people present and, glancing at my watch, discovered that it was about six o'clock. Murmuring a few words of apology for having outstayed my welcome, I made as if to depart; but my host appeared mildly surprised at the suggestion and prevailed upon me to stay for dinner, which we duly consumed at the same table. We did not separate until seven o'clock in the morning.

This was my first, but by no means my last, experience of such prolonged sessions, which, I subsequently learnt, were a normal feature of Finnish social life and a particularly favourite predilection of Sibelius, in connexion with which many entertaining stories are told. I cannot resist the temptation of telling one of them here.

On a similar occasion to that which I have described above, the conductor Kajanus, one of Sibelius's most intimate friends, sought to excuse himself and take his departure, as he was due to conduct a concert at Petrograd next day. The others present protested that the occasion was not one to be sacrificed to such sordid material considerations, and pressed Kajanus to telephone through to Petrograd and cancel the engagement. Seeming to comply with the suggestion, Kajanus left the table, but went to the station, took train to Petrograd, conducted the concert, and returned to Helsinki, where, on re-entering the restaurant, he found the company still seated at the same table, engaged in the same animated discussion. On seeing him, Sibelius mildly expostulated with him, saying: "That was surely a very long telephone call of yours, Kajanus!"

To give any adequate idea of all the wisdom and wit—enigmatic, gnomic, aphoristic, paradoxical—which flows from Sibelius on such occasions as from a perennial fountain, would be impossible. But there is one particular conversation I had with him which I remember very vividly and distinctly, and which I select from among many such recollections on account of its peculiar relevance to recent circumstances.

It was, of course, during the inter-war period and, like many of my compatriots—and I still think not entirely without justification—I was indulging in bitter criticism of the trend of British foreign policy. "You must allow me to disagree with you, my friend," said Sibelius quietly, lighting another cigar (incidentally, if anyone alive is more addicted to cigars than Mr. Churchill it is Sibelius, with whom he shares other tastes in common). "I have frequently noticed that your fellow-countrymen are given to violent abuse of your foreign policy on the grounds of its blundering folly and ineptitude. It seems to be one of your national sports. But, believe me, we on the Continent do not share your views. If we sometimes criticize your foreign policy it is on quite different grounds: because it is so subtle, so astute, so far-sighted, so Machia-vellian. Reflect for a moment. If it were truly as you say, how do you account for the fact that in your long history you always win your wars, and that you always triumphantly emerge from every crisis? Luck? No—not every time: it is not possible! Listen. I am being very serious. To-day the world is passing through what is perhaps the most critical phase in all human history. It may be difficult for you in your island to realize to what an extent the peoples of the world-look to England. If England fails, all is lost; England is the lynch-pin of civilization. And England will not fail—of that I am convinced. When the crisis comes, as come it will, England will find herself again, and will save the world for civilization as she has done before."

So much for the man and the shrewd, far-sighted student of history and human nature. As for the composer, I have already written so much about him elsewhere that any further con-sideration of his music here would be redundant. There is, however, one point of interest which may profitably be con-sidered—the element of mystery in his development. Up to his sixtieth year he continued to pour out a profusion of works of every kind—he was one of the most prolific of composers. In 1925 he capped his immense output with what are perhaps his two greatest works: the symphonic poem, *Tapiola* and the

Seventh Symphony. Since then he has written, or perhaps more accurately published, nothing. Now, in his eighty-second year he has, for more than twenty years, remained silent. What is the explanation?

The facts, so far as I know them, are as follows.

An Eighth Symphony exists, or did exist, I have been assured by a pupil and friend of the master, Bengt de Törne. Arrangements were made for the performance, orchestral parts were prepared; but at the last minute, Sibelius withdrew the work and locked it away in his desk. Such is the story, or legend—for with Sibelius it is difficult to separate fact from legend. He is one of these rare figures around whom myths and legends begin to collect even during their lifetimes. There is no surer earnest of enduring fame.

As to the reasons for this self-imposed Trappist silence I can only conjecture that, rightly or wrongly, Sibelius had come to the conclusion that he had said all he had to say, and that any further utterance would be superfluous repetition of what he had already said. If this interpretation is correct, it only enhances his greatness. One cannot think of any other figure of his outstanding eminence who has thus voluntarily abdicated, at the height of his powers, except Rossini.

Finnish hospitality, as already indicated, is, or was in these days, a formidable proposition, especially at the time—New Year—when I first visited the country. Lunches imperceptibly merged into dinners, and dinners into lunches; and as it remained dark until eleven in the morning and became dark again by about two-thirty in the afternoon, I completely lost all sense of time, not knowing whether it was a.m. or p.m. or what day of the week it happened to be. As often as not, I would be up all night and in bed all day without knowing which was which, and it really did not matter, since they were virtually indistinguishable. After what must have been about ten days of this hectic, phantasmal existence it was with a certain sense of relief that I succeeded in extricating myself from it and recuperating from the effects of Finnish hospitality in the comparatively sane and normal land of Sweden, in Stockholm, whence I returned home *via* Copenhagen and Hamburg.

When I re-visited Finland some two years later, with the commission for the book, in order to obtain biographical material and to study the unpublished and otherwise inaccessible works of the master, I travelled by sea, from Hull to Helsinki. It was an appalling voyage, with a fierce gale blowing all the way. The ship arrived some twenty hours late, but Sibelius was waiting for me on the quay-side. "You must be very tired after your terrible journey," he said; "we shall have a quiet evening and meet again for lunch to-morrow, after you have had a rest." Alas, for good resolutions! It was again seven o'clock in the morning before we separated, and so it went on as on the former occasion, except that, as it was only autumn, it was possible to distinguish day from night. What I should like to know is this: do (or did) the Finns live like this all the time, or only when offering hospitality to foreign guests? Whichever the answer, they are a race of supermen, and the fact that Sibelius has attained to the age of eighty and more without showing any ill effects, is a living proof of it. But even so, when or how do they ever get any work done? That is the mystery to me.

On my return to England I straightway embarked upon the writing of my book on Sibelius—a task which was interrupted in mid-course by the tragic death, at his own hand, of my very dear friend, Philip Heseltine. The shock to me was a terrible one, all the more so because up till that time (1930) I had been singularly immune from the ravages of death. No one before to whom I was deeply attached had died, only acquaintances and unloved relations—not even in the 1914–18 War. Up till the age of thirty-five, in fact, Death had left me absolutely untouched, *virgo intacta;* since when he has never left me alone, and nearly all my old friends have fallen like the leaves of Vallombrosa, leaving me clinging to a branch, a lonely, sere and yellow leaf, sad and desolate.

For many years after the tragic event Philip Heseltine haunted not only my waking, but my sleeping thoughts: sometimes for nights on end I would dream of him, to such an extent at one period that I was afraid to go to bed, and would often wake up in my arm-chair in the early hours of the morning. Even after I had sought to exorcise his sad ghost by writing a memoir of him, he still continued to return to haunt me in my dreams; and there is an element of wry and macabre comedy in the fact that on such occasions my chief emotion was one of acute embarrassment at having written a memoir of him—for in these dreams I always remembered having done so—while all the time he was walking around and talking as if he were still alive. I would wake up feeling a perfect fool on such occasions, so vivid was the sense of his continued existence.

Many years have now passed since he thus haunted me in sleep, and his unquiet ghost, I feel sure, is now at rest; but he still haunts my waking thoughts as much as ever, and not mine alone. The most extraordinary thing, indeed, about that extraordinary man is the tenacity of his survival in the minds and memories of those who knew him. Even to-day, more than fifteen years since his death, whenever two or three of them are gathered together, the conversation will imperceptibly but infallibly turn upon him. In the memory of his friends he is as alive now as he ever was when he trod the earth, and so he will continue to be until the last of us are dead.

Perhaps even more remarkable is the tenacity of his hold on the memory of his enemies: they seem just as unable to forget him as his friends. A good example of this involuntary kind of tribute is to be found, as I have already had occasion to observe, in the pages of Sir Osbert Sitwell's autobiography (Vol. II, *The Scarlet Tree*). After dismissing his songs as "Wardour Street" and saying that "his knowledge in other directions in which he was said to be learned was often nugatory", Sir Osbert goes on to say:—

"I remember, in Venice, his telling me how painting did not interest him, but only mosaics; it then transpired that he had just come from

Sicily, but was unaware of the presence in that island of the great mosaic churches of Monreale, Cefalu and the Capella (*sic*) Palatina."

Well, some of Peter Warlock's songs may deserve the epithet of "Wardour Street", just as some of Sir Osbert's writing may reasonably incur the reproach of being an effete survival of the 'nineties. Secondly, I do not know of any direction in which his erudition was held to be considerable by himself or anyone else, apart from music, except Elizabethan literature, and in that field it was by no means "nugatory". Finally, if Philip really said that he was not interested in painting he can only have been trying to pull the elegant Sitwellian leg, in which he seems to have been successful. For the rest, he was never in Sicily in his life. It is true that in 1921, returning from North Africa to Naples on his way to Venice and Budapest, his ship touched at Palermo, or Catania, or Messina, but he did not land save for five minutes in order to enquire about some missing luggage; there was no time for anything else, so he could not possibly have had the chance to become acquainted with any of the mosaics so superciliously mentioned by Sir Osbert. The evidence for the above statements comes from an irrefutable source, namely, that of Philip's travelling companion, Mr. Gerald Cooper. And if it is necessary to talk of Wardour Street, what about "it then transpired" as being Fleet Street at its worst? As for the Capella Palatina, *capella* is the Italian for a she-goat, which I cannot think was meant to be a recondite jest on the part of Sir Osbert. I assume that he intended to refer to the Cappella Palatina—Wardour Street Italian, in fact, though actually they have better Italian in Wardour Street.

It is unfortunate that a writer of talent, whom I sincerely admire, as I think I have shown in an earlier chapter, should condescend to fire off such a malicious squib at a man of equal if not greater talent, who has been dead now for nearly twenty years. The misfortune, however, is chiefly that of the author, because no one who reads this book will be able entirely to believe anything that Sir Osbert says in future; which, of course, I hasten to say, would be entirely unjust. But people who launch boomerangs should not be surprised when they return to their point of departure—which they invariably and inevitably do.

In this connexion I am reminded of the various autobiographical writings of Mr. Clifford Bax. In his admirable volume, entitled *Inland Far*, there is a portrait of an unsuccessful painter called Murray Paterson, which I immediately recognized as being a portrait of my old friend, Eric Robertson, to whom I have referred on pp. 99 *et seq*. But there were certain details in the portrait which mystified me, and I asked Clifford Bax if he had any evidence or corroboration for them. He quite candidly admitted that he had made them up: that his conception of the art of autobiography involved the heightening and improvement on reality. In other words, for him the writing of one's memoirs is a kind of intermediate *terrain* situated between truth and fiction: a category corresponding in its way to the kind of fiction which is really disguised autobiography—in fact, there is little difference between them.

This seems to me to be perfectly legitimate, so long as the method and approach are clearly indicated to the reader, as in the case of Proust, who, we know, is all the time writing his life thinly disguised as fiction, and no doubt taking considerable liberty with facts. All I want to make clear is that it is not my method or my ideal in the present book. I tell the truth and narrate the facts as I know them to the best of my ability. If there are any errors of fact contained in these pages they are due to defective memory or faulty judgment, but not to deliberate intent.

Speaking of Clifford Bax, it is surely a remarkable coincidence that he should be my next-door neighbour in Albany, while his brother, Sir Arnold, is my near neighbour in Sussex. But since these relationships belong to recent years and I have set the term of this book at the momentous year of 1939—apart from occasional brief time-excursions over the frontier—I do not propose to discant upon them here and now: some other time, perhaps. . . .

The dramatic circumstances in which my career in Fleet Street came to a sudden end, after several years of hard labour, were as follows.

On one of my few free nights I had arranged to dine with friends at the *Escargot Bienvenu* in Greek Street, which since the eclipse of the "Eiffel Tower" had become my favourite restaurant and was also presided over, and still is, by an equally genial host—Alexandre Gaudin, a *restaurateur* of the same noble order as my old friend, Rudolk Stulik. I was looking forward to the occasion, like a schoolboy to the holidays, but just as I was about to leave the house the telephone-bell rang, and on answering it I was told that a colleague had suddenly become indisposed and would be unable to fulfil his engagement for that night, and would I kindly take over in his place. It was one of those questions which, according to Latin grammar, would have been of the *nonne* category, expecting the answer "Yes". I had always wondered, as a schoolboy, what happened if you asked a *nonne* question and received a *num* reply, and now I learnt. It happened that I had just been reading that immortal, though little known, masterpiece of story-telling by Herman Melville, called *Bartleby*, in which the chief character of that name, a hard-working clerk in a solicitor's office, after a long term of faithful service, on being called upon to perform one of his customary routine tasks, replied quietly, gently, but firmly to his astounded employer: "I would prefer not to," and made a dignified exit.

In reply to this peremptory request, then, or rather command, I heard myself, to my own astonishment, repeat quietly, gently, but firmly, the words of Bartleby: "I would prefer not to." There ensued a moment of blank, incredulous silence, followed by a gasp of amazement. "But surely, Mr. Gray, you do not mean to say that you do not *want* to?" I merely repeated, quietly, gently, but firmly: "I would *prefer* not to," and replaced the receiver. A few minutes later the telephone call was repeated, with an added accent of menace, but my reply remained the same: "I would prefer not to."

It was as if a great burden had been lifted from my shoulders. I once more breathed freely; I felt a free man again whatever the consequences might be. I decided that, while I was at it, I might as well make a clean sweep of my decks, and sat down to write a letter to *The Manchester Guardian*, resigning my post on that paper also. The fact is that, for some time past I had come increasingly to loggerheads with my opposite number in Manchester, Neville Cardus; it had become as impossible for us to work together as for two *prime donne*. There was not room for both of us on the same paper, and after the tragic death of Edward Scott (the son and successor of the great C. P. Scott) in a boating accident, who had very gallantly supported me on more than one occasion, I decided that it was better to abdicate gracefully, of my own free will. My energies could be more profitably devoted to other purposes than to a petty rivalry with an unworthy antagonist in a field in which I was not really interested.

So ended my career in Fleet Street. I have since, in times of financial stress, made several half-hearted attempts to get back there, but my proffered services have always been politely declined. I have since heard—I do not know with what truth—that there is in Fleet Street a kind of unofficial *dossier*, or black book, in which are recorded the names of renegades and individualists, excommunicant and untouchable. If such a compilation exists, I do not doubt that my name is in it. But such moments of financial stringency apart, I have never regretted the decision made for me by the Bartleby of Herman Melville. Such is the power of great art. The life of a music critic is soul-destroying. The art critic, the literary critic, the dramatic critic, are all perpetually engaged in the consideration of new work, good or bad; but nine-tenths of the music critic's life is spent in listening to everlasting repetitions of a bare handful of threadbare masterpieces, with the inevitable result that he is not in a fit state to judge the remaining tenth. That is why all music critics (with the solitary exception of Ralph Hill) look like Zombies.

I can understand only too well that poignant story of the first violinist in a French orchestra which was playing under a great conductor. In the course of the first rehearsal the latter noticed on the face of the leader an expression of deep distress which on occasion seemed to be the outcome of physical pain. The conductor stopped the rehearsal and solicitously inquired whether the player was ill. No, he was perfectly well. Was it possible that he (the conductor) had offended him in some way, in which case he offered all due apologies? No, it was not that. Perhaps, then it was his personality that was not sympathetic? On the contrary, his personality was more than congenial. "Is it, then, my interpretation of the work with which you disagree?" "By no means; I think it is faultless." "Then tell me," cried the conductor, in utter despair, "what is the matter with you? The look of suffering on your face makes it impossible for me to go on—it upsets me too much!" To which the player replied sadly: "*Ce n'est rien de personnel, monsieur; c'est tout simplement que je déteste la musique.*"

The real motive behind my voluntary renunciation of a fairly lucrative career was the plain and simple truth that I was beginning to detest music. "Even the Queen of Sheba herself," if one had to sleep with her at least twice a day for years on end would become infinitely nauseating, and that is what happened to me. It took me some considerable time to recover and re-discover my soul, which had become sadly damaged in the process.

The more specific sources of my misery in these years during which I must surely have made penance for all sins formerly committed, and also anticipatorily for any I might subsequently commit, consisted in a curious fatality by which I was almost invariably deputed to attend any concert at which that admirable artist, Myra Hess, was playing the Schumann Piano Concerto, as a result of which, even to this day, I cannot again listen to the work, although I used to be very fond of it;

and secondly, an even very much drearier fatality which led
me through an infinite number of remote suburbs in order to
endure amateur performances of *Merrie England*—I must have
undergone at least twenty such excruciating ordeals. The worst
of them all, however, which still shakes me in retrospect, was
a concert performance of Gounod's *Faust*, with the principals
in fancy costume and the chorus and orchestra in evening dress.
Have I suffered?—a *nonne* question to which, I am confident,
there is no possibility of a *num* reply.

No, decidedly, journalism is not, never has been, or will be,
my vocation. At the same time, I confess to what I hope will
be regarded as pardonable pride in the fact that I served on
The Manchester Guardian, the greatest newspaper in the
world, and gave satisfaction to the extent that I was earnestly
entreated to reconsider my decision and withdraw my resignation. But my soul was sick, and my mind made up.

While we are on the subject of journalism, let us travel back a
few years again on our time-machine. In the early 'twenties
Orage, the editor and creator of *The New Age*, resigned, and
the paper fell into the hands of a collection of cranks devoted
to the furtherance of the seemingly now defunct financial
system called Social Credit, associated with the name of one
Colonel Douglas. The great reputation that the journal had
once enjoyed—and justly—dwindled gradually towards nothing, and the circulation correspondingly. I was then a regular
contributor as music critic, and my mercurial Serbian friend,
Sava Popovitch, under the pseudonymic pen-name of R. A.
Stephens, was the art critic. One A. E. Randall was not only
the dramatic critic, but also provided most of the other con-
tents of the paper. Together we decided on a *coup d'état*, a
palace revolution, in order to save the paper and restore it to
its former eminence. We believed, and not without justification, that if all the leading contributors, which we were,
effected a lightning strike, the editor would not be able to
carry on and would be glad to hand the paper over to us for a
reasonable sum, which I was prepared to find. But the plot

failed. At the last moment, by some desperate expedient, the editor was able to find sufficient collaborators to tide him over the crucial period.

In retrospect I am wholeheartedly grateful for the failure. To have been committed to the production of a weekly journal would have been a whole-time task, allowing for no creative activity whatsoever, as I subsequently learnt from Clifford Sharp, the erstwhile editor of *The New Statesman*, who told me that he had never been able to take a holiday from the moment that he had accepted the post—no sooner was one number produced than he had at once to start work on the next, and so on for year after year.

Another journalistic venture with which I was closely associated in these days—the 'twenties—was *The Calendar*, a monthly publication of which the editor was Edgell Rickword, a poet of great distinction and the biographer of Rimbaud, who has since deserted the Muse in favour of Left-wing political activities: a sad renegation and a great loss to poetry. Among other contributors and associates were Bertram Higgins, who similarly renounced poetry for propagandist activities of a Right-wing tendency; and Douglas Garman, another poet, who also abandoned art for politics, and is the brother of Mary Campbell, the wife of Roy Campbell, the poet, and of Kathleen Garman, who has served as a model to Epstein in many of his works. How oddly things, and people, link up, making a pattern! Finally, there was Wyndham Lewis. . . .

When I was living in Hillsleigh Road, Notting Hill Gate "under the great grey water tower that strikes the stars on Campden Hill", as G. K. Chesterton has it, I used to repair, every Saturday morning, to my bank in Queen's Road, Bayswater, in order to cash a weekly cheque before closing time at noon. Invariably when bound upon this errand, at about eleven-thirty, I would pass a very remarkable figure of a man. Whatever the season of the year, whatever the prevailing climatic conditions, he would invariably be enveloped in a large dark overcoat, with the collar turned up, a large black sombrero with the brim turned down, and gloves; so that practically all one saw of his person was a pair of eyes which peered out, with a basilisk glint, through formidable horn-rimmed spectacles, upon a hostile world through which he passed as one engaged on a secret mission—as, no doubt, he often was.

One day it happened that, on returning from my bank, I paid a visit *en route* to a public-house facing Kensington Gardens, between Queen's Road and Notting Hill Gate, at the corner of Ossington Street, named "The Champion"; and on entering found there, to my surprise, Roy Campbell engaged in earnest talk and drink with the mysterious stranger who had become something of a *Doppelgänger* to me, and was introduced to him—Wyndham Lewis.

To be frank, I had long suspected, without being absolutely certain, that the portentous, menacing, sombre, disquieting apparition which I was wont to encounter in my weekly visitations was none other than the painter and author of that name whose work, of course, I knew well. From the days of *Blast*, just before World War No. 1, I had followed his activities with increasing interest and respect; and from his novel *Tarr* onwards, which after several re-readings I still consider a masterpiece, up to the unfolding of the long series of impressive volumes on which he was then engaged, beginning with *The Art of Being Ruled* and *Time and Western Man*.

It is psychologically interesting, by the way, that I should have instinctively divined his identity solely from a knowledge of his work: for at the time when I frequented art circles he had become a complete recluse, and I had never knowingly set eyes upon him before the days of which I am now writing. Only Wyndham Lewis could look like that, I felt, and I was right.

At the same time I was not particularly anxious to make his personal acquaintance, having heard so much, apocryphal as well as real, no doubt, concerning his aggressiveness and cantankerousness, and the *mille e tre* feuds for which he had become legendary. Had he not, indeed, deliberately adopted the signature of "The Enemy" in his multifarious activities? Anyway, his formidable reputation as a master in the gentle Whistlerian art of making enemies was such that I was content to enjoy his intellectual coruscations without making any attempt at personal contact. Besides, with many of his ideas, however greatly I admired the brilliance and cogency of their presentation, I was deeply at variance. In particular, his *parti pris* for the arts of space, and his prejudice against the arts of time, and music especially, was hardly of a nature to endear him to me. In fact, despite my objective admiration for his intellectual gifts, I felt more hostile than sympathetic, from what I knew of him from second-hand.

After this first-hand personal encounter I was surprised to find that in personal relationships, so far as I, at least, was concerned, this violent polemist, the enemy and hostile critic of all and sundry, including even those who had formerly been his best friends, was the most genial, affable, kindly and courteous of men. It is true that, as I have already had occasion to observe in another context, our spheres of action were so widely separated that no kind of professional rivalry, no clash of personal interests, could intervene to disturb our friendly relations. He could not possibly suspect me of any hostile intent, and could therefore divest himself in my company of the weighty and cumbrous defensive armour which he otherwise habitually wore.

Many were the occasions on which we used to come together, sometimes in the local public-house, more often in his rooms in Ossington Street in the evening—Mr. Lewis's ten-o'clocks, but unlike those of Whistler, *p.m.* not *a.m.*, and lasting into the early and even late hours of the morning; during which the oracle, like the Bailiff in his *Childermass*, would hold forth without intermission on any and every subject under the sun, moon and stars, to an entranced and highly select audience which, in addition to myself, generally included Constant

Lambert, Thomas Earp, William Gaunt, and R. H. Wilenski, with an occasional odd intruder in addition.

I have known many admirable talkers in my time, but I can say without hesitation that Wyndham Lewis was the most brilliant, witty and profound of them all. The only serious rival to him that I can think of was Bernard van Dieren; but it must be admitted that on occasion the latter was apt to become oppressively long-winded and to over-elaborate his thesis in the manner of Coleridge, to say nothing of a similar tendency to divagate and modulate from one theme to another until he ended up in an entirely different thought-world from that in which he started. This Wyndham Lewis seldom did: his power of developing a line of thought and returning to it logically, however far afield he might seem to have strayed, was truly impressive, and the object of my constant admiration and astonishment. Whatever else Lewis may be, he is the unsurpassable *improvvisatore* of the spoken word.

It is true that when I look back on these magnificent coruscations I can for the most part only recall their brilliance, the dazzling pyrotechnic display of squibs, rockets, and Catherine-wheels which he set off in such bewildering profusion hour after hour, without stopping for a moment. I have often subsequently, however, recognized in print various themes and turns of phrase which I had first heard orally in these Ossington Street Nights; but I would not know whether such were the spontaneous outcome of the moment, which he afterwards recorded, or whether he was reciting to his audience the result of the preceding day's work.

Whichever the explanation, there was always a complete identity between Lewis the talker and Lewis the writer. In both he was essentially the *improvvisatore* with all the virtues and the faults that go with it: the wealth of invention and imagery, coupled with a complete lack of shape or form. This may seem to be a contradiction of what I have said above, namely, that he was supremely able to develop a line of thought and return to it logically, but actually there is no contradiction.

That gift is something entirely different from the constructive sense which perceives the end in the beginning and the beginning in the end, even before the artist starts work. In spite of all his eulogies of classic form, Lewis is, of all writers, the least capable of conceiving a work as a complete and rounded whole.

Look at his books and you will see what I mean. His beginnings are uniformly superb; the preliminary *coup d'archet* is that of the master, and commands instant attention. There is little in modern English literature to equal, and less to excel, the opening pages of *The Childermass* or *The Apes of God*. But each of these remarkable books gradually disintegrates as it progresses, and ends in spouting cascades of rhetoric, foaming torrents of words. They do not end, even: they merely stop. It is significant to observe, in this connexion, that *The Childermass*, undoubtedly Lewis's most ambitious and important conception, bears on the fly-leaf the announcement that the second and third parts of the work would appear in the course of the autumn of 1928. That is a long time ago—twenty years, and they have not yet appeared; nor does it seem likely now that they ever will, unless Lewis is a Goethe and his "Childermass" a Faust. But I doubt it.

This is symbolical of Wyndham Lewis in every respect: the magnificent initial gesture; and the subsequent decline and ultimate *dégringolade;* for just as this sequence is to be discerned in each of his works, regarded separately, so it is to be found in the pattern of his career viewed as a whole. He deliberately set himself out to be a leader in the worlds of both artistic creation and political action, and his incontestable gifts entitled him to be so regarded and accepted during the uneasy chaotic years of the inter-war period, at the turn of the 'twenties and thirties, when everyone, feeling the impending approach of disaster, turned desperately from one side to another in search of the man who could lead them out of the *impasse;* and for a time it seemed possible that Wyndham Lewis could fill that rôle. His masterly and devastating critical analyses of art, politics, sociology and philosophy, which he poured out in one volume after another in rapid succession, diagnosing with unerring instinct the causes of the present discontents and the shortcomings of all alternative proposed solutions, all went to suggest that he might be the guide for whom the world was waiting, to whom all were looking.

Now, I am far from being one of those who take the line of saying that it is easy enough to criticize and destroy, but difficult to achieve anything positive and constructive. The critic has a perfect right to point out what is wrong in a work of art or state of society without being called upon to provide something better, just as one is justified in saying that a dish is badly cooked in a restaurant without being under the obligation to take the place of the *chef* and teach him how to cook well—that is not one's business. But Wyndham Lewis, whether intentionally or not, always led his readers to expect that once he had completed the necessary preliminary work of demolition and destruction, he would proceed to the formulation of a positive, constructive, creative philosophy. He attacked, formidably and convincingly, every institution in every sphere of human activity, and after having levelled it all to the ground and pulled everything to pieces, he bowed politely, coughed apologetically, and took his departure—not only metaphorically but literally, when the final crash came in 1939.

I firmly believe, and shall always maintain, that Wyndham Lewis has one of the finest minds of his generation, and that he was potentially a great leader, but when it came to the final issue he invariably evaded it. For some years before the war I had come to the reluctant conviction that his inability, or refusal, to commit himself to any clear-cut attitude towards anything, apart from a purely destructive one, had become permanent.

Wyndham Lewis is like a deep-sea fish: depending for his existence on a formidable adverse pressure, a superincumbent mass of hostile resistance. Place him in a position of power and responsibility, bring him to the surface, in fact, and he becomes ineffectual and blows up. *Nolo episcopari* is his secret motto, in the ultimate resort; but at the same time he desires power. All his life he has been fighting to achieve it in one way or another, always building up movements, schools, groups, with a mole-like pertinacity and a Machiavellian diplomatic subtlety, only to destroy them, one after another, by his own hand. He does not wish to stand alone, but he cannot brook rivals. Always he has systematically turned upon and rent his closest associates and most devoted disciples, in the revolutionary style intiated by Robespierre and carried on by Stalin. He has relentlessly exercised this political technique in the field of art and philosophy. All his friends and collaborators have, sooner or later, come under the lash of his pen, and have been led in a tumbril to the guillotine in his books, one after another: James Joyce, Ezra Pound, T. S. Eliot, the Sitwells, Edgell Rickword—it is unnecessary to continue the list, for it contains the names of all who have associated with him at one time or another.

He is even prepared to round upon himself, deny himself, contradict himself, to veto his own veto, in fact, rather than find himself in agreement with anyone about anything. For example, after having valiantly and effectively assailed romanticism in all its forms and in every sphere of activity, in a long series of volumes—in his view, indeed, one gathered that romanticism was the hydra-headed monster which it was his sacred mission to destroy—he allowed himself to be so irritated by T. S. Eliot's assumption of the banner of classicism that he executed a complete *volte-face* and contradicted everything he had ever written on the subject by saying, in his *Men Without Art*, that "it would be mere effrontery, or buffoonery, in an artist of any power amongst us to say that 'as an artist I am a classicist'. With all of us—and to this there is no exception—there are merely degrees of the opposite tendency, at present labelled romantic."

To agree with Lewis in anything was, in these days, automatically to incur his opposition, in fact; and during the period when I knew him best and met him most, my friends and his former friends, would express surprise at our intimacy, shaking their heads, to the refrain of "You wait, you will see. No one can remain on friendly terms with Lewis for long. Sooner or later he will attack you suddenly, without warning, for no reason whatever, as he has always attacked everyone who has ever been on friendly terms with him. Above all, be careful never to do him a good turn—that is the one thing which, above all, he will never forgive you for."

Well, perhaps I never did him a good turn, but we always remained the best of friends, to the bewilderment of all who knew us both; for it would be difficult to find two persons more fundamentally opposed to each other in all essentials. But it was this very antagonism, temperamental and intellectual, I am inclined to think, which formed the basis of our friendly relations—the attraction of opposites to which I have already referred on several occasions in these pages.

Apart from that, however, with all his phenomenal versatility, Wyndham Lewis had one formidable blind spot—a complete inability to understand or appreciate the art of music; and since the art of music was his Enemy No. 1, this shortcoming must have caused him considerable inconvenience, and I sometimes think that I may have been of some use to him in piloting him through these dangerous, unfamiliar seas. To change the simile, in the same way that a blind man needs a helping hand or a dog to guide him, so the tone-deaf Lewis needed the assistance of friendly ears in his excursions into the hostile territory of music. The extent to which he needed it is shown by the fact that he seriously regarded George Antheil as an important contemporary composer, on the testimony of Ezra Pound, whom Lewis, erroneously, I need hardly say, believed to be an authority on music.

Why anyone ever took poor Ezra seriously on any subject whatsoever I am unable to discover. When I came across his early volumes of poetry, *Canzones* and *Ripostes*, while an undergraduate at Edinburgh University, I was impressed and excited, and I still think there was something there. But when I met him a few years later in London, I was sadly disillusioned. His genuine youthful sensibility had given place to a bombastic, arrogant, perverse charlatanism which steadily gathered momentum, until it culminated in the crisis which brought him to the mental home in which he is now confined—a grim example of what is liable to happen to one who disregards the dictates of his inner nature and strives to create a fictitious personality. The real Ezra Pound was a wistful minor lyricist who dwelt in mediaeval Provence; the self of his dreams and ambitions was a daring modernist and leader of contemporary movements; and the outcome of this violent dichotomy is not altogether surprising: was, perhaps, inevitable. It will have been noticed, I think, that I am interested—possibly to an excessively morbid degree—in madness, since I fear it more than death. When once discussing the subject not long ago with my friend, Peter de Polnay, in his stately manorial establishment at Boulge Hall, in Suffolk, the ancestral domain of Edward Fitzgerald of Omar Khayyam fame, I was reassured when my genial host observed in his characteristic drawl: "My dear Cecil, neither you nor I will ever go mad. We are too humble. It is only the arrogant who become mad." And there is great truth in that. It was poor Ezra's inveterate arrogance that led to his overthrow.

This perpetually recurring subject of the dichotomy which seems to exist in every creative artist, whether manifested in a simple conflict between the man and his work, or in the more complex variety which can be traced equally in both, leads us back to Wyndham Lewis, in whom this duality is developed to an exceptional degree. I am more than inclined to suspect that the explanation of his hesitancy and inability to commit himself to any definite and positive line of thought or action, apart from the purely destructive, is to be found in a deep, uneasy sense of self-doubt, and even humility, to which his violent pugnacity serves as a carapace. The more I got to know Lewis the more I came to realize that behind the aggressive exterior which he chose to present to the world there lay concealed an infinite variety of complexities and subtleties and contradictions.

Ultimately, I think, he is an embodiment of the *Geist wer stets verneint*, in spite of the fact that in every picture or drawing he has made, in every line he has written, in everything he does, one can immediately detect the presence of an exceptional mind and a supremely gifted and original personality. Yet it all seems just to lack that undefinable quality which many infinitely lesser figures possess, but which is unmistakable and cannot be counterfeited, the only thing that really matters—the creative fire. In this respect he greatly resembles Busoni.

I have already mentioned the name of Thomas Earp as being that of one of the chosen few who regularly frequented the Lewisian symposium, but I had known him for a long time before. Indeed, he is the oldest of my extant friends, for I first met him, in 1916, through the agency of Philip Heseltine, with whom I was at the time sharing a studio in Battersea; they had been at Oxford together. Since then we have maintained contact at irregular and sometimes lengthy intervals.

Of all people I have ever known, Thomas Earp best exemplifies and embodies the characteristics which I so greatly admire in Chinese philosophy, especially of the Taoist school, and of Lao Tzu in particular. Actually, he is much more consistent than the Master himself. I have already quoted in another connexion the poem of Po Chü-i[1], in which the latter takes the philosopher to task for saying that those who speak know nothing, while those who know remain silent, and then writing lengthy works. Thomas Earp does not lay himself open to this reproach. It is true that he has published a few slender volumes, and that he writes art criticism for a daily newspaper, but these activities are only pursued for the most regrettable and necessary of reasons—in order to make a living. He would infinitely prefer to remain silent, and the work which he pro-

[1]See page 162.

duces for its own sake, or in order to please himself alone, he puts away in a drawer and forgets, with true Taoist indifference.

Another Chinese trait which he shares with me resides in his unrepentant, unashamed delight in the joys of the bottle, and many have been the occasions in London and Paris on which we have gratified it together. I particularly remember one of them when he, Augustus John and I were sitting together in the "Eiffel Tower" restaurant discussing a bottle of Rudolf Stulik's best, and in answer to my own question: "Why does one drink?" I replied: "In order to escape from myself, I suppose." To which Augustus demurred, saying: "On the contrary, I drink in order to become more myself;" to which Thomas responded, quietly and gently: "I drink because I like it," which seems a very much better reason than either of the former alternatives, and probably very much nearer the truth in all three cases.

Another link that we possess between us consists in the formidable slowness and extreme exiguity of our output. I have spoken of my elephantine parturitions, but his are mammoth-like. Ever since I have known him he has been busily engaged on a life of Stendhal; but it has not yet seen the light. He is a poet of high accomplishment, but apart from early work none of it has appeared. In this connexion an additional bond between us is our common admiration for Gérard de Nerval, of whose six sonnets, *Les Chimères*, he has made a translation which is one of the finest examples of that difficult art in modern times, but they remain unpublished.

I share this fastidious distaste for publicity and everything concerned with it, though I am far from being such a consistent exponent of it as Thomas Earp. It is unfortunately true that *il faut vivre* in spite of Talleyrand's acid retort: "*Je ne vois pas la necessité,*" and it is also essential that a composer should hear his work at least once in order to make sure that his tonal values and sense of balance are correct—a problem which does not arise in the practice of any other form of art, not even drama, which similarly requires interpreters in order to come fully to life, but can nevertheless achieve a simulacrum of reality by means of the printed page, whereas music cannot. But apart from the regrettable necessity of making money on the one hand and testing one's technical capacity on the other, I neither see, nor have I experienced, the necessity, or even cherished the desire, of achieving publication or performance of anything.

I find it difficult to induce even my best friends to believe that I am genuinely indifferent in such matters. I would have thought it readily understandable that by the time an artist had finished with a work that he had carried about with him for more years than he cared to remember, the last thing on earth he would want would be to have anything more to do with it, except for one, or both, of the good reasons above mentioned. So it has been with me, at any rate; and so it is with Thomas Earp, and this perhaps is our greatest bond in common; our activities, for what they are worth, are devoted wholly and absolutely *ad majorem Dei gloriam*. Others may be actuated by exhibitionistic cravings, but not we, who are both of us failures in terms of worldly values and wish to remain so, for the best of all possible reasons, namely, that success and fame, under modern conditions of vulgar publicity, stinks—no sane man who has seen so much of it at close contact as I have could possibly desire it for himself.

This is no mere sour grapes on my part. Whenever I have been the recipient of any compliment on anything I have ever done, deserved or undeserved, I have never experienced any other emotion than that of acute embarrassment and almost physical discomfort. As for fame, I can think of no more unhappy and tragic figure than T. E. Lawrence, who so acutely desired it and, at the same time, despised it, and himself for wanting it: who, in the unkind but devastatingly true words of Philip Guedalla, "was always backing into the limelight".

Apart from anything else, who in his senses would choose to be in the position of the Priest of Nemi, who slew his predecessor and was doomed to a similar fate at the hands of his

successor—which is the destiny of the fashionably successful
artist in present times? His reign is short and uneasy. I have
never known a famous man of my acquaintance to be really
happy. Unless he has the fortune to die young, he will almost
inevitably live to endure the misfortune of seeing himself
eclipsed, forgotten, or vilified. An even greater misfortune is,
of course, to outlive this inevitable reaction and become a
Grand Old Man, a stuffed owl like Thomas Hardy.

It is interesting to note, incidentally, in this connexion, how
few composers, compared to other artists, ever live long enough
to achieve this dubious distinction, and how few of the greatest
ever even achieve the normal or natural span of life. Verdi is
practically the only Grand Old Man that music has to show;
nearly all other great composers have died early in life or in
middle age. Music, in fact, would seem to be one of the most
dangerous of human occupations or professions, together with
that of publican: the expectation of life is probably shorter
than in any other. I think it likely that there may be a good
scientific explanation of the phenomenon, namely, that the
emission of beautiful sound-waves causes vibrations as harmful
to the operator as those which emanate in the world of light-
waves from X-rays . . .

A very different figure from that of Thomas Earp whom I
encountered at the same time and place, through the same
agency, and in the same circumstances, was Robert Nichols; he
also had been at Oxford with Philip Heseltine, and he contributed a short study to the book which I subsequently wrote
about Philip, dealing with the early days when they were
undergraduates together.

I thought it an excellent piece of work, a sensitively realized
impression which was also finely written. I remember saying
so once to Gerald Cooper, who had also known Philip well, and
was surprised and somewhat disconcerted when he disagreed
with me and said that it was only too obvious that Robert
Nichols, while ostensibly writing about Philip, was only using
him as an excuse for writing about himself; and on re-reading

his contribution to my book in that light I was reluctantly compelled to admit that there was considerable justification for the criticism, and that Nichols had, in a subtle fashion, contrived to present himself as being the central figure in the picture.

I do not suppose it was deliberately and intentionally done, the plain fact of the matter being that he was congenitally incapable of writing, talking, or thinking about anyone or anything in the world except himself. He was the most completely egocentric personality I have ever encountered in my life. If he were to write a description of the solar system, he would contrive to place himself at the centre of it.

His graphomania was a part of, and on the same gigantic scale, as his egomania; and he continually plagued his acquaintances with interminable letters written in such an abominable script that it was impossible to decipher them. This illegibility was, of course, merely a symptom of his egocentricity. He took it for granted that his greatness was so incontestable that the enraptured recipients would be prepared to devote days, if necessary, to the deciphering of his missives. I was only one of the many who were thus afflicted, and have still to this day a number of letters from him which I have never had the ability to decipher, or the energy and patience to attempt it.

Great though his craving was for fame and success in the immediate present, it was as nothing compared with that which he entertained for future immortality. Never did any man live, not even Goethe, who had his eye more consistently cocked on posterity. You always felt in his presence, in everything he said or did, that he was addressing his potential biographer, his Boswell, standing at his elbow, carefully noting down everything, or registering it all in his memory in order to write it down subsequently. In consequence, he never in my experience behaved naturally; he always seemed to be acting a part, which however exciting to him, was supremely boring to all his friends. I was not, by any means, the only person who winced and fled on seeing Bob Nichols bearing down upon

him with a purposeful glint in his eye and an impending
unspoken monologue upon his lips, of which the sole topic was
himself, his genius, his love affairs, and so on, interminably.

The basis of his emotional and intellectual life was genuine,
but he intensified and magnified it until it became a lie. No
single human being could possibly have supported such a
gamut of emotions, combining the introspective self-pity of
Chateaubriand and Lamartine, the histrionic attudinizings of
Byron, and the demoniacal frenzy of the early Berlioz, as he
did, day after day, for twenty years to my personal knowledge
and experience.

That he felt intensely I do not doubt; but all his emotional
violence was derived from art, not from life; it had no relation
to reality. I remember only too well one occasion on which he
had called on me and poured forth an agonized description of
his tragic fate: of how he was homeless, without a roof over his
head, penniless and starving, not knowing where his next meal
was coming from. I listened sympathetically, but knowing
him as well as I did was not surprised to see him the same
evening at the Café Royal, treating himself more than royally
to an excellent dinner, including a bottle of Burgundy. The
poet knew how best to salve the wounds inflicted on his soul.
At the same time, I do not believe that the whole tale of woe
to which I had been treated was pure invention. He was undergoing some domestic trouble or other, in consequence of which
he was staying with a friend, or at some hotel. I quite believe
his sincerity when he said that he did not know where his next
meal was coming from, but this was simply because he had not
decided whether to go to Oddenino's, the Monico, or the Café
Royal. The reality of his situation had no relation to what he
built up from it. His habit of self-dramatization had become
second nature—he could not help it.

In one important and crucial respect, however, life imitated
art only too successfully. The very first day I met him, in 1916,
he told me that he had only a short time to live—he was
already a compendium of all the poets and musicians who had

died young—and he was continually writing poems in the all-too-familiar Rupert Brooke vein of self-pity—"When I am dead think only this of me", etc. I was suitably moved and impressed; but after the same speech, with variations, had been repeated every time we met over a period of nearly twenty years, I became very tired of it and increasingly sceptical—until he suddenly died, prematurely. It was with something of a shock that I realized that perhaps I had misjudged him all these years, and that he really had all the time been a sick man, and on the verge of death. On the other hand, was it not possible that the part he had played for so long had become a reality? I speak with an uneasy conscience here, for I myself am frequently obsessed with death, and no doubt have frequently bored my friends in the same way that Robert Nichols did. After all, what does it matter? We all begin to die from the moment we are born, and it is far from certain that a long life is preferable to a short one. What is certain is that of all sins self-pity is the most insidious and contemptible, the least sympathetic. I have myself been a great sinner in this respect in my youth, as great as Robert Nichols. If I am to-day, as I hope I am, more or less cured of it, I owe it to his example in front of my eyes: he has helped to save me from my worst self, and for this I am grateful to his memory.

Apart from all that, he was a poet of genuine talent, and some of his work will surely survive. His little-known satire, *Fisbo*, incidentally, reveals a vein of bitter, sardonic wit which one would not have expected from him, and stands in the direct royal line of succession to the satires of Pope, Dryden and Byron. It is in its way, I think, a masterpiece. Finally to his credit, be it said that I never knew him to do an unkind turn to anyone, which is a rare distinction among artists to whom back-stabbing is, as a general rule, not only an agreeable and congenial activity, but also a recognized part of their technical equipment.

Another poet, also recently deceased, with whom I was on friendly terms, was W. J. Turner. I had always entertained a great admiration for his work long before I met him, and I still consider him one of the finest poets of his generation. Apart from that, his play, *The Man Who Ate the Popomack* and his practically unknown slender volume of prose, entitled *The Aesthetes*, seem to me, in their different ways, to be superb achievements. In his capacity as music critic, on the other hand, I was less able to accept him. His appreciation and sensibility were acute, but his complete lack of technical knowledge, to which he frankly confessed, frequently led him into strange aberrations. His ecstatic prostration at the feet of the pianist Artur Schnabel, for example, was always completely unintelligible to me, and he could be incredibly silly on the subject of Bach. No one, on the other hand, had a finer perception of the intrinsic qualities of Mozart, concerning which he wrote more profoundly and wisely than any qualified music critic in this country. But the particular bond between us lay in our common fanatical admiration for the art of Berlioz, which was also the cause of a transitory discord in our personal relations.

On meeting him one day I confided to him my intention of writing a book on Berlioz, adding that if he also had such a project in view I would willingly abdicate in his favour, since there was hardly room for two such books on the same subject in English appearing at the same time. He earnestly assured me that he had no such intention; whereupon I started work. After I had devoted some six months of hard labour to the undertaking, I was disconcerted to see the announcement in the papers to the effect that a Life of Berlioz by W. J. Turner was shortly to be published.

Whether he had already started work on it before I told him of my intention, or whether he then and there decided to forestall me, I do not know; but I rather suspect the latter, for the outcome was a hasty, botched, and careless piece of work. If only he had been honest with me I would not have stood in his way, he would have written a better book, the cause we both had so much at heart would have benefited, and I would not have wasted six months of—to me at least—valuable time and energy. My book on Berlioz is the only important undertaking I have ever begun that I have not brought to a conclusion. But one of my few redeeming features is an inability to keep up a grudge for long, and within a short time we were once more on friendly terms.

The last time I saw him was when I was standing outside a public house called "The George", at the corner of Mortimer Street and Great Portland Street, with Michael Ayrton, and Turner passed us. I thought he looked ill, and two or three days later he was dead. And then I remembered suddenly that the last time I had seen Robert Nichols before his death a couple of years earlier was in precisely the same place—a strange coincidence. And the last time I saw Philip Heseltine before he died was in "The Portland", about twenty yards away. That neighbourhood is, for me, thickly populated with ghosts, to say nothing of the ghosts of Pagani's and of the Queen's Hall round the corner. Leslie Heward and Hyam Greenbaum, the two most gifted conductors of their generation in this country, are two other dead friends whose spirits haunt this ghost-ridden locality. . . .

But let us now return to the land of the living. When I first met William Walton through the agency of Philip Heseltine—it must have been in 1918, the last year of World War No. 1—he was a shy, diffident, awkward, inarticulate, rather devitalized young man, and I frankly admit that I was not greatly impressed either by his personality or by the work of his which I saw. But Philip thought otherwise. "You will see," he said to me one day, "that youth will go a long way;" and he certainly has fulfilled the terms of that remarkably clairvoyant prediction.

What strikes me as chiefly noteworthy in his career, looking back to nearly thirty years ago when I first met him, is the slow, sure, steady way in which he has built himself up into a mature, self-reliant personality out of such comparatively unpromising beginnings, and in his art has acquired a formidable technical capacity which was lacking in his early days, by dint of sheer unremitting hard work. If ever anyone has deserved success it is William Walton; no one has ever worked harder to attain it, and I hope he enjoys it now that he has got it, unlike most of those I have known who have similarly achieved that ambition.

The quality I chiefly admire in William Walton, apart from the dogged tenacity with which he has realized both his latent artistic potentialities and his ardent desire for worldly success, lies in his infinite capacity for accepting criticism, and learning from it—a very rare quality indeed, and one that he possesses to a greater degree than anyone I have ever known.

Every artist naturally wishes his work to be as perfect as he can make it, and consequently in moments of doubt he frequently invites the opinions of fellow-craftsmen or critics for whose opinion and judgment he has respect. But seldom indeed does he take such advice or criticism well when the verdict on his work tends to be adverse. Most artists only invite extraneous opinions in order to be reassured, to have their misgivings allayed, or to elicit approval. Walton, on the contrary, positively invites adverse criticism—that is what he wants. He is not interested in receiving facile compliments, and would not thank you for them if you were to proffer them.

I am thinking particularly of an occasion when he brought to me his symphony, which was in the throes of parturition, in order to play it over to me, stipulating in advance that I would give an absolutely honest opinion without any regard for his personal feelings or *amour propre*.

I consented reluctantly, and was not at all happy about it, because however ruthless and implacable I can be in written criticism of someone with whom I have no personal relations, I am apt to be a coward when it comes to passing adverse judgments orally on friends. On this occasion I am glad to say that I was able to praise the work unreservedly without a guilty conscience, except for one section in the slow movement,

which I condemned equally unreservedly. So far from being
annoyed, the composer was genuinely grateful, and in the
sequel I was glad to see that the offending section was ruthlessly
expunged from the final version. I do not suppose that he
underwent this painful operation solely on my advice; indeed,
I do not doubt that he consulted several other critical practitioners for their opinions before coming to the decision, and
rightly so. But I maintain that such humility and readiness,
even eagerness, in soliciting criticism is a very sure sign of an
artist of great integrity, who puts his work before his own
personal feelings and pride.

It is true, of course, I hasten to add, that one can very often
agree with the substance of an adverse criticism, and yet leave
the work unaltered, either because one cannot improve upon
it or because, with all its defects, it performs a necessary
function with regard to the whole. One's faults are irrevocably
bound up with one's virtues, and the antiseptic of criticism, if
indiscriminately applied, may eliminate the good as well as the
bad, the fertile pollen together with the malignant pests. A
work is not always improved by accepting well-meant and even
well-founded criticisms.

Another equally admirable and equally rare quality consists
in Walton's generosity towards fellow-composers. Indeed,
I know of many cases in which he has gone out of his way—
and often a long way out—in order to render assistance, sometimes financial, sometimes by recommending publication or
performance in influential quarters of works by even formidable
rivals, and in other ways as well. (I know of at least one such
case in which his help was gratefully accepted and repaid with
more than usually shameless ingratitude.) I speak from
personal experience, since it was largely as a result of his
enthusiastic recommendation that my music-drama, *The
Women of Troy*, was accepted for performance by the B.B.C.
a few years ago.

These two outstanding characteristics—the desire for and
the capacity to accept adverse criticism, and generosity to

fellow-artists—point to the central factor in Walton's personality, which consists in an absolute devotion to the cause of art,
or rather of music; for he is not, I should say, greatly interested
in the other arts, except possibly architecture. (Have I not
seen a beautifully constructed model dream-palace made by
his own hands, to be built to his own specifications on the Gulf
of Naples, near Posilipo, his spiritual home, where Gesualdo
also had a palace—*rends moi le Pausilippe et la mer d'Italie*—
which is largely the reason why I wrote my libretto for him?)

Assuredly he is not one of the martyrs or saints or heroes of
art. Apart from his very normal appetite for fame and appreciation, he enjoys the good things of life as much as almost everyone outside monasteries and lunatic asylums; and in order to
obtain and enjoy them, he does not hesitate on occasion to
write music for films or plays which he would not otherwise
have written. Such music he writes with fluency and rapidity,
in striking contrast to the slow, painstaking laboriousness with
which he produces the work to which he attaches importance.
He is indeed, of all artists I have ever known, the most *meticu-
lous* in the original and exact sense of this much abused word,
i.e., he writes with fear in his heart, and with profound humility
and self-distrust. In fact, I do not believe that in essence he
has changed at all from the shy, diffident youth I first knew
about thirty years ago, in spite of and behind the impressive
Façade of fame and success he has since built up. And no one,
in his heart of hearts, has a deeper or more sympathetic
understanding of those who have followed their star, oblivious
of material reward and success—I think that he sometimes even
envies them—and certainly no one is more acutely conscious
of being in the invidious position of the Priest of Nemi . . .

From William Walton to Constant Lambert the transition
is not merely easy, but inevitable; for not only have they always
been close personal friends, but their names have always been
coupled together as being those of the two most gifted English
composers of their generation. At the same time, they are so
strongly contrasted in most essential respects that the Plutarch-

ian method of comparison is, perhaps, the best one to employ in order to bring out the salient characteristics of both.

William Walton, I have said, is a musician first, foremost and all the time; and in so far as he is attracted outside the orbit of music it is in the direction of architecture—indeed, it is the architectonic quality in his work which largely conditions his fine formal sense. Constant Lambert, on the contrary, is by no means a musician "pure and simple". The son of a distinguished painter and the brother of a distinguished sculptor, he frequently suggests and implies in his work the presence of pictorial and graphic elements. I have said of Roy Campbell that if he had not been musically tone-deaf he would inevitably have been a composer; similarly, I suspect that if Lambert had possessed even the most elementary degree of technical accomplishment in the direction of colour or design he would have been a painter rather than a musician. There is something eminently pictorial in his most characteristic works, such as the *Rio Grande*, with its rich, opulent, deciduous colouring; the dark, black, Célinesque quality of the piano sonata, inspired by long, cat-like, nocturnal prowlings through the suburbs of Paris; the *Aubade*, which is a reproduction in sound of a Dutch landscape; the Hogarthian characteristics of so many pages in his *Summer's Last Will and Testament*, to mention only a few examples.

Apart from that he is also a writer of distinction, in witness whereof is his brilliant book, entitled *Music Ho!* and innumerable contributions to periodical publications, to say nothing of his poetic accomplishments in the form of the limerick—his series of fifty devoted to double bishops (bishops with two or more dioceses, like Bath and Wells)[1] being undoubtedly one of the most monumental achievements in this difficult and exacting form.

Again, even within the sphere of music, while Walton con-

[1] A recent incumbent of this exalted position, incidentally, was my former headmaster, who died in the odour of sanctity leaving a mere £215,000 odd—slightly more than St. Francis of Assisi.

centrates exclusively on composition and only occasionally conducts his own work, Lambert divides his energies by devoting a large proportion of his time to conducting—too large a proportion, I think personally, but the fact remains that his conducting is not merely a source of livelihood, but a positive form of self-expression, as much a part of him and as necessary to him as piano playing was to Liszt or Busoni. Composers make, as a rule, bad conductors, and conductors bad composers. Lambert is well-nigh unique to-day in his superlative capacity in both directions. He is not merely one of the most gifted composers of our time, but also one of its finest interpretative artists, capable of entering wholeheartedly into the innermost essence of forms of art diametrically opposed to his own, even positively unsympathetic to him personally, and giving first-rate performances of them.

This duality is as characteristic of his private personality as of his public artistic activities, for he exhibits in himself a disconcerting blend of the most opposite extremes imaginable —a *fin de siècle* Frenchman with morbid *faisandés* tastes, and a bluff and hearty roast-beef-and-Yorkshire Englishman; Baudelaire and Henry Fielding combined, Purcell and Eric Satie, Ronald Firbank and Winston Churchill (to whom he bears an uncanny physical resemblance, to say nothing of the Emperor Nero); these are only a few of the similes which occur to my pen in a vain attempt to present a picture of his capacity for combining characteristics commonly, and reasonably, conceived as opposite and irreconcilable.

This schizophrenic, Manichean, ambivalent dichotomy is attributed by its somewhat (and no wonder!) harassed possessor to the fact that the date of his birth coincides, horoscopically, with the moment of the change from the zodiac sign of Leo to that of Virgo. It must indeed be highly disconcerting to alternate between, and combine in oneself, the characteristics of a British Lion and a French *demi-vierge*, of John Bull and Marianne; but the most surprising feature of the phenomenon resides in the fact that in his work at least, he succeeds in achieving a satisfactory reconciliation between the two disparate elements in his psychology.

In his early years the French element was naturally in the ascendancy as the result of an adolescence passed in the atmosphere of the hectic, feverish, restless 'twenties, with the Russian Ballet of Diaghilev and the French school of composition as the preponderant influence; the English side has steadily grown in strength with the passage of time and is now, I should say, in the ascendant. The balance between the two, however, as I have said, is maintained with surprising success in all that he does. He constitutes a typical exemplification of the Hegelian trinity of two opposing subjects combined into a unity. The English and the French (or Russian) elements unite to form something which is not merely a combination of the two, but something new, and different from both.

Here I conclude my little portrait gallery of memorable people I have known. This book is already too long, and would become interminable if I were to attempt to do more than mention, *en passant*, the names of Boris de Chroustchoff, a descendant of the *boyar* mentioned in the Boris Godounov of Pushkin and Moussorgsky, an eminent bibliophile and the greatest living authority on edible fungi, who hates work even more than Norman Douglas or I, and with whom I once walked from Bayonne to Carcassonne, and got lost in the High Pyrenees *en route;* of Kaikoshru Sorabji, the Parsee composer, whose aversion to fame and publicity are even greater than that of Thomas Earp or me, for he resolutely refuses to allow anyone to perform a note of his music on pain of death, or worse; or Oliver Strachey, the brother of Lytton, whose knowledge of Purcell, Handel and Mozart excels that of any professional musician I have ever known; of Nina Hamnett, who brings with her wherever she goes a nostalgic breath of the old spirit of Montparnasse and Fitzroy Street in the 'twenties; of Alan Rawsthorne, the most gifted composer who has arrived on the scene in England since Walton and Lambert, with whom I share (together with Lambert) a strange attraction to aquariums and their fascinatingly enigmatic inhabitants; of Patrick Hadley, who, apart from his admirable musicianship, enjoys the unusual distinction of being the only person I have ever met who, so far as I can discover, has not an enemy in the world and is equally liked by the most dissimilar and mutually hostile people. I am not sure, myself, whether I should like to be without enemies, like Peter Schlemihl, a man without a shadow; without them one's sword can lose its edge, one's pen its point, one's tongue its barb and sting. They keep one fit; without them one is apt to run to seed—not that I see any signs of that happening to Patrick Hadley, but I know that, personally, I owe almost as much to my enemies as to my friends: without them I should be less than I am. I am grateful to all the friends who have given me so much and to whom I hope I have given something in return; but I thank also my equally numerous enemies, to whom I am sure I have always been able to pay back with compound interest all that I have received from them whenever I have cared to take the trouble, which is seldom.

I could extend the list of my friends indefinitely, and add to it a choice selection of enemies, but it is time to have done, and to revert, in conclusion, to the completion of the portrait with which I started—that of myself. Before doing so it will be necessary to touch for a moment upon a topic hitherto deliberately avoided and postponed, which, as the 'thirties progressed, gradually assumed an ever-increasing importance—namely, politics.

When I was in Italy immediately after World War No. 1, in 1919, I was interested to observe the emergence of a new social or sociological phenomenon in the form of a movement called Fascism, which consisted primarily in a reaction not so much against political Communism as such, which was then in the ascendant in Italy, as against the state of chaos and anarchy which followed in its wake. Fascism, indeed, in its origins, was not a positive, formulated political creed at all—this development came very much later, and only gradually.

It began, and acquired a following, as being essentially a *rappel à l'ordre*, a call for discipline, and as such was exceedingly sympathetic in many of its aspects.

It was very easy for its subsequent legitimate political opponents to jeer at this aspect of the movement and to say that the only thing Fascism achieved was to make the trains run to time for the benefit of wealthy foreign tourists. But apart from the fact that the tourist trade was probably the most important industry in Italy, the extent to which the lives and livelihoods of the native inhabitants were utterly dislocated and disorganized by prevailing conditions could only be appreciated by direct personal experience of them.

I can give a very cogent instance. I had occasion one day to take the train which ran from Syracuse to Messina, in Sicily. I had been warned by the hotel porter that it would be utterly absurd to arrive at the station at the scheduled time of departure—the train was bound to be several hours late: had, in fact, never been anything else for years. But I have a complex about trains, and one of my worst and most continually recurring dreams is concerned with missing them; accordingly I ignored the advice and arrived at the station at the official hour of departure and found the train waiting. On asking diffidently at what time it was likely to start, I was proudly informed that it would leave at the precise hour specified in the official time-table—which it duly did. My mystification was progressively increased as the train slowly rolled up the coast, stopping at each scheduled station and taking on board no passengers: I had it almost entirely to myself. On arriving at my destination, I received the simple explanation, namely, that the train was running precisely twenty-four hours late, and that after waiting for some twelve hours or so, all other intending passengers had given up hope and returned home.

This is a true story and, no doubt, a funny one; but it certainly was not funny to have to live under such conditions, which were always steadily worsening. All normal and natural

activities were coming to a gradual standstill, and it was the
exasperation and resentment caused by this state of affairs that
gave Fascism its popular backing and ultimate power.

In addition to all that, it must be remembered that in the
early 'twenties Communism in politics was closely allied to
extreme Left-wing activities in the field of the arts; and after
the agile adventurings in revolutionary directions which are a
natural and normal concomitant of adolescence, I had come to
entertain a profound distaste for all such tendencies, and to
crave for the return, or rebirth, of an art based upon the
elements of form, balance, proportion, restraint and stability,
as opposed to mere experimenting for its own sake, and the
hysterical destructive subversiveness which in art had come to
be loosely identified with Communism in the political field.

In consequence, it is hardly surprising that I should have
found myself in considerable sympathy with the ostensible
ideals of the new movement, which, I must repeat at the risk
of redundance and over-emphasis, was in its early stages
sociological rather than political, and æsthetic rather than
philosophic. As an artist—or rather a would-be artist—I felt
myself to be a Fascist, and on my return to England I brought
back with me half a dozen black shirts (gondolier shirts, which
I had bought in Venice), and proceeded to flaunt them in the
streets. I was, in fact, beyond any question, England's first
Black Shirt. I regarded myself as the standard-bearer in the
vanguard of the new movement that no one outside Italy had
as yet noticed, which aimed at the restoration to supremacy of
the threatened ideals of Latin Europe—the ideals of faith,
discipline, form, culture, tradition, which were being increasingly menaced by the rising tide of extra-European and non-
Latin values, or rather lack of values, represented by Teutons,
Slavs and Anglo-Saxons; by Germany, Russia, the U.S.A. and
the British Empire.

Alas for youthful idealistic illusions! When I returned to
Italy shortly before the March on Rome and Mussolini's
assumption of power, I was already sadly disenchanted by what

I saw—an army of horrid little thugs swaggering about the streets cocooned in weapons, blackguarding and blackmailing all the decent inhabitants of the country.   But the final disillusionment took place in Venice at this time, when a street battle between Fascists and Communists took place near the railway station, in which the former were victorious. They rounded up their defeated adversaries and marched them back as prisoners to the Piazza San Marco, where both victors and their prisoners joined together in singing lustily the Fascist war-song *Giovinezza*, with the former Communists out-rivalling their conquerors in the enthusiastic vociferousness of their rendering. It reminded me irresistibly of a game I used to play as a child in which, once you were captured by the opposite side, you became one of them, and as zealous, loyal and fanatical in serving your new allegiance and in attempting to catch your former comrades as you had been in the opposite camp.

It is, of course, an endearing trait in the Italian character, and to no one more than me, that a political dispute should resolve itself thus into an harmonious, operatic, Verdian *ensemble*. But a more serious aspect of the phenomenon was revealed to me later, after the accession to power of the *Fascisti*, when, in conversation with a hotel proprietor whom I had previously known in the turbulent days of the Communist ascendancy, I recalled these times, observing that surely now conditions had improved; to which he hesitatingly agreed, with a sigh, saying: "Yes, Signore, it might seem so; but the trouble is that the *Communisti* who made all the trouble in 1919 and 1920 are the *Fascisti* of to-day. The same people are in power: they have changed their coats, but otherwise there is little difference, so far as we are concerned, except that, perhaps they are more efficient in their present rôle. You see that gentleman there," he said, pointing to a peculiarly unpleasant-looking specimen sitting in a corner of the lounge, drinking a *grappa*; "he is now the local party leader, but he was once—and not so long ago—a leading Communist."

As a result of these experiences I returned to England

sadly disillusioned with Fascism and with politics altogether;
I put my black shirts away in a cupboard and never wore one
again. They have in the course of the years all been eaten by
moths. I afterwards came gradually to realize that the
phenomenon I had witnessed was not by any means confined to
Italy, but is of universal application. To change from a
Communist to Fascist, or *vice versa*, is the easiest thing in the
world, like turning your coat. It is still the same coat, although
it may look different—though not actually so very different.
Ultimately there is very little distinction between Communism
and Fascism: they are basically one and the same thing. As I
have said elsewhere, in an essay entitled *Contingencies*;[1]

> "The new order of the immediate future is clearly adumbrated by
> many thinkers, chief among them Nietzsche, Karl Marx and before
> them Hegel, who is the Janus-faced father of both Communism and
> Nazism by way of the Marxian dialectical materialism on the one
> hand and the doctrine of the absolute totalitarian state on the other.
> They are in fact twin births. Their superficial hostility is that of
> brothers, springing from the fact that they understand each other
> only too well, and have so much in common. The greatest hatreds
> and antagonisms are those of affinities, of relations. No wars are more
> bitter than civil wars."

As in music, I might have added, in which real discords only
occur between adjacent semitones, not between widely
separated intervals.

In this connexion I remember very well an occasion shortly
before the last war broke out when I developed this thesis to
some friends in Pagani's, among them Patrick Hadley and Alan
Rawsthorne. The latter vehemently disagreed with me, saying
that there was one major and crucial difference between the
two, namely, that the Soviet *régime* had no imperialistic
ambitions. I shook my head sadly and observed prophetically:
"Wait, my dear Alan, you will see, you will see." (Dr. Hadley,
I hope, will bear witness.)

The day will come, several centuries hence, when historians
of our period will find as much difficulty in understanding the

[1] *Contingencies and other Essays.* Oxford University Press. 1947.

fratricidal political conflict between Communism and Fascist-Nazism as we to-day find in understanding the Catholic-Protestant religious conflict of the 17th century. "What on earth were they fighting about?" we ask ourselves in perplexity. They were only sects of the same religion, with more in common than they had of difference. So to-day in the political world, the two contending forces are only different forms of the same totalitarian ideology, and will in time to come be virtually indistinguishable from each other in the light of the historic eye. "What were they fighting about?" historians will ask themselves, for even at the present moment anyone can see that they have very much more in common than either has with the old 19th-century liberalism which is, if not completely dead, at least unmistakably moribund.

The pact concluded between Russia and Germany in August, 1939, which precipitated the war (a fact now conveniently forgotten) was clear evidence of the truth of this contention. Most people were surprised and stunned by it, but not I, for I had expected it and would have been surprised had it been otherwise. But no one could have been more surprised and intellectually disconcerted than I (except, perhaps, the Russians) when Hitler suddenly executed a complete *volte face*, tore up his Treaty with Russia and invaded her. I was faced with the alternative that either Hitler had gone mad or I had got everything wrong. Being essentially a modest person I diffidently assumed the latter alternative; but subsequent events have conclusively shown that the former explanation was the true one, and that the unedifying spectacle we have been witnessing has been that of two brothers, rival heirs—one of them mad, fighting each other over the dead body of their father for the possession of his estate. One of them would seem to have got the better of the other, but the resultant assets, if they are ever realized, will prove to be very much less than if they had been intelligently shared instead of being made the issue of a sanguinary litigation. The quarrel, quite obviously, was of Hitler's making; Russia was only too willing to come to a peaceful and amicable agreement and share the proceeds equally and fairly. So far as the future is concerned I venture to predict that Russia and Germany will come together once more; that just as in Italy the Communists turned Fascist overnight, so the Nazi elements, which are still the most powerful in Germany, will throw in their lot with the Communists. In a word, they have more in common together than either has with the effete liberal plutocracy of the West as exemplified in America, England, or France; and even in these countries the tide is flowing strongly against the established order. It may turn again—tides always do; but not in the immediate future. At any rate, there is no sign of it at present.

The picture of contemporary politics is best presented in the form of a circle with four equidistant points on its circumference, A, B, C, D, with the point A opposite to D, and B to C. A represents the old 19th-century liberal ideology, which is dead, or dying. To the right of A lies Conservatism, represented by the point B; to the left, Socialism, represented by the point C. When you progress further round the circumference from B and C, becoming respectively more left and more right, you meet at the point D, which represents Fascism, Communism and Nazism, virtually indistinguishable from each other and all at the opposite pole to Liberalism. The ease with which it is possible to pass from one to another is exemplified in the persons of the historical protagonists in the drama—in Mussolini and Stalin, both of whom began as international Communists and ended up as leaders of supernational imperialist States, and in Adolf Hitler, who consciously sought to unite the two trends in one. The whole process and progress, however, was anticipated long ago by Richard Wagner, who began as an extreme Left-wing disciple of the Russian internationalist Bakunin, and ended up as the founder of Nazism by writing *Die Meistersinger von Nürnberg*—Nuremberg, the chosen centre of the Nazi movement.

My own personal position in all this will by now, I hope, be fairly clear: namely, that I am unable to identify myself with any "ism" whatsoever in politics any more than in any other direction; either with Liberalism, Conservatism, Socialism, Communism, Fascism, or Nazism: any more than with Catholicism, Protestantism, Buddhism or Mohammedanism in religion; or Classicism, Romanticism, Realism, Surrealism, or Impressionism, or any other "ism" in art.

For me, every "ism" represents an aspect of truth, but one which is fragmentary and exclusive of all others. Each one is a facet of the whole, or a segment of the circle; but the whole truth is the complete circle in which all conflicting "isms" are harmonized and reconciled; and the finest minds in all categories, of religion, politics, or art are those in whom are combined the greatest number of facets and segments, those who approach nearest to God, Who alone is The Whole. It will have been noticed that none of the biographers or critics of William Shakespeare has been able to tell us whether he was a Catholic or a Protestant, or an atheist: a conservative or a liberal or a revolutionary: a classicist, a romanticist, a realist, or an idealist. He was all and he was none—and the two things are ultimately the same. The symbol which denotes the whole, the complete, the absolute; and the symbol which denotes nothingness and negation, are one and the same—the circle, which is everything, or zero, the serpent with its tail in its mouth—O.

Everything or nothing. *Aut Caesar aut nihil;* this is my motto in all things, and I can no more subscribe to any formulated political creed than to any single religious or philosophic system, or any æsthetic manifesto. Relative truth lies everywhere, and absolute truth nowhere save in the mind of God; and I am too much a student of history to be able to take sides in any political issue with any conviction. It is a quarter of a century and more since I made a fool of myself over *Fascismo;* I learnt my lesson. I hope that some time the day will come, though it will not be in my time, when it will seem as absurd and as wrong to go to war and kill each other in defence of a political "ism" as to-day it seems to be in defence of a religious "ism", or an æsthetic "ism"; though I must admit that I should like to see artists feeling so intensely about their art as to be ready to shed their blood in defence of their convictions.

The only political conviction I have to-day is a very simple one, and I have already quoted it elsewhere in these pages, but it will bear repetition.

"If there is righteousness in the heart there will be beauty in the character. If there is beauty in the character there will be harmony in the home. If there is harmony in the home there will be order in the nation. If there is order in the nation there will be peace in the world." (Chinese philosopher.)

If an able ruler is a good man I do not care what label he wears round his neck—he will be a good ruler. Similarly, I do not believe that an evil man, however able he may be, can possibly be a good ruler, however lofty and elevated his ostensible principles may be.

No political slogan to-day will save the human race. All that is needed is a change in the heart of man, and I see no sign of it. All one can hope for is a miracle. I believe in miracles—sometimes.

At the time when I was taking politics seriously, in the early 'twenties, the general intellectual current in this country was quite otherwise. Largely in consequence of a natural reaction from the conflict of 1914–18, politics were out of favour in the circles of the *intelligentsia*. The prevailing tendency of the age was directed towards the enjoyment of the passing moment and averse to any kind of dogmatic doctrinal discipline. With the advent of the 'thirties, by the time I had satisfactorily solved, for myself at least, all political problems and issues in the fashion outlined above, the *intelligentsia* began to develop an increasingly lively political conscience, which led to what is best described as the Great Schism; as a result of which a tendency manifested itself to split up into two hostile camps. It had at last dawned upon them that the orthodox pre-war liberal democratic order had broken down beyond any hope of restoration. The larger section moved to the Left, but these greater numbers were more than counterbalanced by the individual importance of those who took the opposite course, exemplified in different ways by such otherwise diverse and incompatible figures as Yeats, Eliot, Chesterton, D. H. Lawrence, Wyndham Lewis, Ezra Pound, Roy Campbell. All around I saw my most intimate friends and associates donning some preposterous kind of semi-military fancy-dress uniform, which give them immense pleasure. I was left standing alone, disconsolately, in the middle of the road, like John Ford, "with folded arms and melancholy hat", abused by both sides for my non-committal attitude.

I had been through it all already myself: I knew the answers. I have said before that it is my melancholy destiny to be always a step in advance of my generation, and in nothing is this more perceptible than in politics; and it is one of my major misfortunes to be something of a minor prophet, like Habbakuk (*capable de tout*)—a misfortune, because I am invariably right when I foresee and prophesy woe and desolation, and generally wrong when I take a more relatively cheerful view of things.

Why is it, I used to ask myself, that even the most intelligent, witty and sensitive persons invariably talk the crassest nonsense whenever they open their mouths on the subject of politics? And this applies equally to Left, Right and Centre. Because politics *are* nonsense, always have been nonsense, and always will be nonsense—an occupation for second-rate minds and no more. Compare such deservedly eminent statesmen and politicians as Disraeli or Winston Churchill with Shakespeare or Milton: they are not in the same category.

I once had the interesting experience of being a fellow-traveller on board ship with Lloyd George: it was a Blue Star liner, named the *Avelona Star*, bound for South America at Christmas time in (I think) 1928 (though it might have been 1927). After all I had heard of his magnetic personality and the irresistible charm he radiated, to which even his bitterest opponents succumbed in spite of themselves, I was disappointed, but not really surprised, to discover that all his legendary magnetism amounted to very much less than that of many a second-rate artist you could meet any evening at the Fitzroy Tavern or in a public-house in Chelsea or Bloomsbury; while his intellectual powers and general culture were no more than those of the little Welsh attorney he was. In the technique of administration pure and simple he was notoriously incompetent. Yet it is to men such as he to whom the destinies of the human race are confided. What can you expect?

As the 'thirties gradually rolled on towards the catastrophic climax which I felt to be inescapably imminent, my one preoccupation was the completion of the various artistic projects on which I had been engaged for so long, and little of which existed on paper. One of these was the completion of my trilogy of musical history, past, present and future; the others were the writing of my two music-dramas, *The Temptation of Saint Anthony* and *The Women of Troy*, by which, more than anything else I have done, I hope and expect to be judged.

Chapter Twelve

IT WAS in Cornwall, in 1917, as I have already observed in that context, that I first came across Flaubert's masterpiece, and thereupon straightway resolved to set it to music. In Flaubert and in his Saint Anthony, which is a self-portrait, I saw myself reflected—magnified, no doubt, but not distorted. I have already written much concerning the attraction of affinities and opposites, and Gustave Flaubert, more than any man who has ever lived, is my absolute affinity. If I believed in reincarnation (which I do not) I should certainly believe myself to be the reincarnation of Flaubert; and to anyone who should reproach me with arrogance in making such an assumption, I would only make the humble reply that the doctrine of reincarnation implies as great a possibility of degradation as of amelioration. I only suggest that, whatever the relative proportionate stature, my key and tempo are identical with his: that my virtues and faults, on however much lower a plane than his, are the same. A tiger and a cat belong to the same species, whatever their dimensions; that is all I wish to imply.

More especially in reading his letters I have always had the uncanny sensation of having written them myself, so exactly do my thoughts and emotions harmonize with his; and although I have said above, and repeat again, that I do not believe in reincarnation, I have always carefully refrained from visiting Rouen in case I should be tempted to seek the pavilion in the garden at Croisset where he worked and which, I am told, still survives. I also lived with my mother as he did, with a pavilion at the end of a garden, in which I wrote my *Temptation of Saint Anthony;* and I am quite frankly afraid to go there for

303

fear I might recognize it, or imagine that I did, which would be worse.

The story of the temptation of Saint Anthony is one of these rare subjects, like Faust and Don Juan, which are of universal import, and appeal equally to the imaginations of artists of all categories—writers, painters and musicians—and are realizable in any and every medium; and in the same way that the chance encounter of the young Gustave Flaubert, in Genoa, with one of the many great pictorial masterpieces devoted to the subject, by Peter Breughel, led him to the conception of his *Tentation de Saint Antoine*, which occupied him on and off for the greater part of his life; so it was the reading of his book which, in its turn, like a lightning flash, suddenly revealed to me the idea of my music-drama, which has similarly obsessed me also for the greater part of my creative life.

So far as I am aware, no other composer has ever tried his hand at this subject, which calls out even more insistently for musical treatment than Don Juan, or Faust, which have received so many musical tributes. This neglect is all the more surprising in view of the fact that at the time of its publication in book form Flaubert notes with interest and surprise, in one of his letters, the fact that the work particularly elicited the appreciation and praise of musicians. I can only suppose that an inscrutable Providence reserved it for me; and so far from being arrogant, such a supposition is in reality a sign of humility, since my chances of survival would, no doubt, be small if I had to compete with a Mozart or a Strauss, a Liszt or a Wagner, in dealing with the same subject

Like the book on which it is based, it is in one single scene, observing the Aristotelian unities of time and place, lasting approximately two and a half hours, constituting a unified organism from first note to last, and evolving in its entirety from one thematic germ as the oak tree does from the acorn.

In this respect it is unique in music, so far as I am aware, and this is a mere objective statement of fact which involves no question of æsthetic merit. Bach's *Art of Fugue*, which similarly evolves from a single subject, lasts only about an hour and a half; while Wagner's *Rheingold*, which is approximately the same length as my Anthony, playing without a break, is certainly not a unified organism developing from a single thematic germ. In addition, it is as large in its orchestral and vocal demands as in length and formal dimensions, requiring twelve soloists—three sopranos, two contraltos, two tenors, two baritones, three basses—full chorus and large orchestra. *The Temptation of Saint Anthony*, in fact, is probably the largest organic structure in the history of music; but I hasten to repeat that this is a mere statement of fact, of tape measurement, of statistics, and involves no æsthetic implications. It may be a very bad work, but that would not affect the truth of these purely objective observations, in the same way that it is correct to say that St. Peter's is the largest church in the world without necessarily implying thereby that it is the most beautiful—which of course it is not, by any means.

The Temptation of Saint Anthony is conceived and executed with a view to visual realization, although its performance as a dramatic cantata, like Berlioz's *Damnation de Faust*, is perfectly feasible. The ideal medium for which it was primarily written is a combination of stage and cinema, Saint Anthony himself being personified by a real, living singer and actor, and his visions presented as phantasmagoria, projected upon a backcloth film screen.

The place of action is the desert of the Thebaïd, at the summit of a mountain, on a platform shaped like a half-moon, enclosed by huge rocks. The hermit's cabin stands in the background. Some ten paces away from it there is a cross, and at the other end of the platform an aged and twisted palmtree leans over the abyss, for the sides of the mountain are sheer, and the river Nile seems to form a lake at the foot of the cliff. The sun is sinking. Saint Anthony, clad in goat-skins, with long hair and beard, is seated upon the ground with legs crossed, weaving a mat. He complains bitterly of his dreary life and his self-imposed penances. "Another day gone," he sighs; "yet formerly I was not always so wretched." He used to enjoy his ascetic existence, but now all is changed. He is suffering intensely from an attack of that complaint so familiar to monks and anchorites, and called by them *accidia*—a weariness and lassitude of the spirit.

He recapitulates his life from the time he left home in order to become an anchorite, recalling how his mother in despair sank dying to the ground, and the beautiful young girl, Ammonaria, tried to dissuade him from his purpose and detain him: how he first chose for his dwelling-place the tomb of a Pharaoh and was there tormented by visions, and how the abominations that were painted upon the walls came to life and sought to seduce him: how he fled to the shores of the Red Sea and took refuge in a ruined citadel, where his only companions were the scorpions among the stones, with the eagles always wheeling over his head in the blue of heaven: how during the night he was torn by claws, bitten by beaks, brushed by soft wings, while fearful demons, shrieking in his ears, flung him to the ground: how then he made his way to Alexandria and sat there at the feet of the aged sage Didymus, learning wisdom from him and becoming acquainted with many strange heresies, which often returned to his memory and troubled his mind with their specious and plausible half-truths: how thereafter he took refuge in Colzim and lived there a life of such penance that he ceased to fear God; and how disciples gradually gathered around him. Why, he asks himself, should he lead such a miserable life as he does? Why had he not elected rather to stay with the monks of Nitria, as they had often asked him to do? In spite of their strict discipline, they were not entirely without innocent enjoyments, even good food and wine. Continuing the train of thought, he reflects that he might have done better to have been a priest, then to have been a wise scholar or philosopher, then a soldier—or he might have become a trader, one of wealthy merchants of Alexandria. For a moment Anthony indulges in reveries of imaginary felicity and is then abruptly recalled to reality, and groans at the misery of the life he has condemned himself to endure—making baskets, weaving mats, then bartering them with nomads in exchange for a crust of bread. Surely death were better!

He pulls himself together with an effort and takes up his Bible; but on every page he turns over he finds a reminder of the joys of earthly existence, which he has voluntarily renounced. He is now laid open to the assaults of the Evil One. Delusions begin to assail him: a table makes its appearance before him, laden with all manner of sumptuous and delicate dishes, the temptation of which he resists with difficulty; he stumbles inadvertently over a cup, which turns out to be of solid gold, and is gradually transformed into a cornucopia of gold and precious stones, which, when he throws himself upon it avidly, disappears; finally there comes before him the Queen of Sheba, who offers him her person and the fulfilment of all earthly passions and desires. With a supreme effort of will Anthony makes the sign of the Cross and she departs, dejected and crestfallen.

There then appears on the scene the semblance of an old disciple of Anthony's, named Hilarion, who reproaches his master with his mode of life, accusing him of burying himself in solitude in order the more fully to wallow in the imaginary indulgence of his desires. He deprives himself, says Hilarion, of meats and wine, warmth and baths, slaves and honours, but gives himself in imagination banquets, perfumes, naked women. His assumption of chastity and abstinence are a subtle form of corruption. "Was Jesus sad?" asks Hilarion. On the contrary. He went among His fellows, reposed in the shade of olive trees, and entered the house of the publican, drank many cups of wine, and pardoned sinning women. He exhorts Anthony to give up his ascetic mode of life, saying that God is not a Moloch who demands a sacrifice of flesh, and offers to reveal to him the true inner secrets of religion and philosophy.

Anthony allows himself to be persuaded, and is straightway transported into a vast basilica in which the whole army of the heresiarchs is assembled, arguing and disputing, each seeking in turn to convert Anthony to his way of thinking—all combined into a vast, vertiginous, delirious fugue.

Anthony breaks away from them and finds himself in the company of the Ancient Ebionites, withered like mummies, with dull and dim eyes, and eyebrows white as hoar-frost, who exclaim in tremulous tones: "We knew Him, the Son of the Carpenter. We were the same age; we lived in the same street. He used to amuse Himself by fashioning birds of clay, choosing the skeins of bright wool for His Mother, and He feared not the sharp tools when aiding His father at work."

The Ebionites give place to the worshippers of the Serpent, who is glorified in a grotesque parody of the Mass, which terminates in a wild invocation to the accompaniment of a flute and a tambourine. "Come, come, come! Issue from thy cave! Swift one who runnest without feet! Captor who seizest without hands! Coiled like the rivers! Orbed like the sun! Black with gold spots like the night sown with stars! Contorted like vines! Convoluted like entrails . . . Come, come, come! Issue from thy cave!"

Then there appears to Anthony the Gymnosophist, seated upon a pyre, completely naked, besmeared with cow-dung, who gives utterance to the completest possible embodiment of the ascetic ideal. "Since existence proceeds from corruption, corruption from desire, desire from sensation, sensation from contact, I have fled from all action, contact, sensation, desire . . . I have loathed Form, I have loathed Perception, I have loathed even knowledge itself; for thought does not survive the trivial fact that caused it and Mind, like all else, is only illusion."

Anthony is humiliated and impressed by an asceticism compared to which his own is as nothing, but the Gymnosophist gives place to the great mage of ancient times, Apollonius of Tyana, who offers to initiate Anthony into the mysteries of all forms of religion. "I know all gods, all rites, and all oracles. I have endured the eighty tests of Mithra. I have embraced the serpent of Sabasius. I have received the staff of the Kabyri.

I have spent three months in the caves of Samothracia. I have conversed with the Samaneans of the Ganges, with the wise men of Chaldea and the magi of Babylon, with the Gaulish Druids and the priests of the negroes."

There follows a *cortège* of gods and idols of primitive nations —of wood, of metal, of stone, of feathers and skins sewn together, intoning barbaric chants to an accompaniment of percussion instruments alone. They are followed by the Egyptian goddess Isis, who utters a grave lament to an accompaniment of harps; by the male worshippers of Cybele, whose invocation is accompanied by flutes, clarinets and castanets; then by the female worshippers of Atthis, to an accompaniment of oboes and bassoons. The chant of the Buddha which follows is set for solo voice with innumerably divided strings; that of the gods and goddesses of the Greeks and Romans of pagan antiquity for chorus with horns and tubas, and that of the God of Israel for male voices in unison accompanied by trumpets and trombones.

Each cult, in fact, is characterized by the employment of a different instrumental combination and tone-colour—each one representing a section of the orchestra, a facet of the whole, a segment of the complete circle of life and thought; each, in short, is an "ism". Finally, Hilarion, who has been at Anthony's side throughout, becomes transformed and assumes his real identity—the Devil. He represents the Spirit of Science, absolute negation, and therefore has no music at all. His utterance consists in an unaccompanied spoken monologue, ending with an imperious demand that Anthony shall bow down before him and worship him. Anthony lifts his eyes to Heaven in a supreme effort of will. His prayer is answered, the Devil abandons him, and he finds himself lying on his back on the verge of the cliff outside his hut.

A monologue follows which is in the nature of a recapitulation of the opening section of the work, in which the leading motives, both psychological and musical, are passed in review. He evokes once more, nostalgically, the charms of the girl

Ammonaria, whom he had known and loved as a young man before he determined to become an ascetic, and then violently revolts against his weakness. "My flesh rebels again! Even in the midst of grief I am tortured by desire! I can bear myself no longer! Why should I not kill myself? Nothing easier. Only one movement and all would be over."

He leans over the abyss and gazes into it, a prey to the supreme temptation of all—the desire for annihilation, oblivion, peace. There suddenly appears on one side of him an aged woman who seems to resemble his mother. On the other side appears a young woman, exquisitely beautiful, whom at first he takes to be Ammonaria. They are Death and Lust, and they sing an antiphonal duet together: the former, a contralto, accompanied by the darker-toned instruments of the orchestra—oboes, bassoons, horns, tubas, violas and double basses; the latter, a soprano, accompanied by the brighter instrumental colours—flutes, clarinets, trumpets and trombones, violins and 'cellos. And just as, in Flaubert's text, Death and Lust gradually come closer together and finally merge into each other, becoming one, and forming a kind of monster—a skull crowned with roses, set upon the pearl-white torso of a naked woman, while below a shroud, starred with specks of gold, resembles a tail upon which the whole body undulates like a gigantic worm, erect upon one end—so these two antiphonal orchestras are gradually drawn closer together and eventually coalesce into one.

The last section of the work consists in a gigantic coda, peopled with primordial figures of which the bodies are only symbols of ideas and psychological states of mind, links that exist between matter and thought. First the Chimera, leaping, flying, spitting fire through her nostrils, lashing her winged sides with her dragon tail; then the Sphinx, with its gaze constantly fixed on a far horizon that none may reach; then the Astomi, like bubbles of air traversed by sunlight; then the Blemmyes, who have no heads and are the most laborious, virtuous and happy of all creatures; then the Pygmies, good little people that swarm on the earth, like vermin that crawl on the hump of a camel, terrible on account of their infinite multitude; then the Sciapods, fettered to earth by their long hanging hair, with their heads as low as possible (the secret of happiness); then the Cynocephali, men with the heads of dogs, masters of the world through strength of arm and callousness of heart.

A vast beach stretches before Anthony. In the distance, jets of water arise spouted by whales, and from the end of the horizon come the beasts of the sea. Phosphorescence gleams in the moustaches of seals and shifts in the scales of fish. Echini whirl like wheels, ammonites uncoil like cables, oysters make their shell-hinges squeak, polypi unfold their tentacles, medusæ quiver like balls of suspended crystal, sponges float hither and thither, anemones ejaculate water, wrack and sea-mosses have grown round about.

Then all sorts of plants extend themselves into branches, twist themselves into screws, lengthen into points, round themselves like fans. Gourds take the shape of breasts, and lianas interlace like serpents; mandragores sing. Plants are no longer distinguishable from animals. Polyparies with the appearance of sycamores have arms on their branches. And then the plants become confounded with the stones. Pebbles assume the likeness of brains, stalactites that of limbs; efflorescences appear in fragments of ice; diamonds gleam like eyes, metals palpitate, insects that have no stomach persistently eat; withered ferns bloom again and re-flower, absent members grow again. At length there appear tiny globular masses, no larger than pinheads, with cilia all around them. They are agitated with a vibratile motion.

Day at last appears and, like the unfolded curtains of a tabernacle, clouds of gold unrolling in broad volutes unveil the sky. Even in the very midst, in the very disk of the sun, radiates the face of Jesus Christ.

Anthony makes the sign of the Cross and kneels down in prayer. All nature joins in a hymn in praise of the Creator.

The music, I have said, consists in variations and counterpoints on one basic motive, which is enunciated at the outset: a twelve-tone motive, incidentally, it is interesting to note, although it was not built according to the Schönbergian method, consciously and mechanically, but just happened—born naturally, and not like a homunculus in a test-tube. In fact, I was not aware at the time of its conception that it conformed to the principle of the succession of a series of melodic progressions comprising the twelve notes of the chromatic scale; and so far from being atonal in its harmonic implications it is, on the contrary, based upon the most diatonic and tonal of all possible harmonic progressions—tonic, dominant, and sub-dominant—which can be found to underlie every musical system in the world, past and present (see my book, *Predicaments*, for a development of this point), which was called by the Ancient Greeks "the body of the harmony". It may consequently be regarded as the musical embodiment of the eternal, the everlasting, the absolute; in a word, God.

Similarly, the interval of the augmented fourth, or diminished fifth, which in the Middle Ages was called *diabolus in musica*, aptly symbolizes the opposite principle, the power of Evil, and plays that rôle throughout the work. It is in the struggle between these two antagonistic principles—the tonic, dominant, sub-dominant progression representing the forces of good and light, and the interval of the tritone, which splits the octave into two equal parts, and symbolizes the powers of evil and darkness, both of which principles are contained in the twelve-tone scale motive which represents man, Saint Anthony, in whom all potentialities for both good and evil exist—it is in this polarity that the musical as well as the literary plot of the work consists. And again, it must be added, this symbolical correspondence between musical notes and philosophical and theological concepts was not consciously arrived at or deliberately contrived, but only became apparent to me after the completion of the work.

Well, it remains unpublished and unperformed. It would

be absurd for me to grumble at this. Before I set pen to paper I realized that such was likely to be its fate, during my lifetime, at any rate. But I had no choice in the matter. I only knew that I had to write it, come what might: the impulse was a categorical imperative, its accomplishment an act of faith, directed *ad majorem Dei gloriam.* I shall only say that in any other country in the world it would at least have been given a hearing, and that even in this country anyone else would have been given a chance of a hearing; but this is merely a sardonic observation. I do not complain, for in the writing of it I have been able to realize all my potentialities, such as they may be, to the fullest extent of my capacity, and therefore I am well content.

I do not even feel the necessity of hearing it in order to learn whether it sounds as I had intended. I had always thought I knew exactly how it would sound, and this belief was strengthened when Leslie Heward and Constant Lambert played it through at the piano one day while Hyam Greenbaum followed in the full score. At the end I asked him for any and every criticism of the orchestration he could give me, without any regard to my feelings, because I valued his opinion in such matters above that of anyone, and my sole concern was to make the work as good as possible. He seemed slightly distressed at my entreaty, but under pressure reluctantly consented, and pointed to a place where he had to tell me he did not think the bassoon would come through. I thought he must be joking, for in such a vast score there must surely, I felt, have been many passages that might legitimately be queried; in any case, the bassoon part in the passage in question was only there to provide a slender life-line to a choral part struggling in danger of submersion in the treacherous seas of chromatic intonation. But no: he insisted that he had no other criticism to make on the score of orchestration. . . .

The Women of Troy, on which I started work almost as soon as I had finished *Saint Anthony,* is a very different proposition. It, also, is in one long act, lasting about an hour and a half, preserving the Greek unities, and musically all of a piece; but the material demands are in comparison modest—two sopranos, one mezzo-soprano, one contralto, one tenor, one baritone, one bass, female chorus, and medium-sized orchestra. Technically, it presents no difficulties to either singers, players, or listeners. A truncated version was performed by the B.B.C. in 1944, as a result of the favourable opinions expressed concerning it by William Walton and Leslie Heward to Arthur Bliss, who was then Director of Music. That the latter should have made this generous gesture to me, incidentally, reflects great credit on him for his magnanimity, for in my *Survey of Contemporary Music*, published in 1924, I made very severe and caustic criticism of his work. I will not go so far as to say that I was mistaken then, but I should like to take this opportunity to say that since these far-off days he has made a great advance, and that now I admire some of his work very much indeed.

I first came across the play of Euripides in the English version of Gilbert Murray in 1912, when I was seventeen, and thereupon decided to set it to music some day. Twenty-five years were to elapse before I did so, but all that time it had been present in my thoughts and maturing in my mind. I soon realized, however, that Murray's translation, though admirable in many respects, was unsettable as a libretto, so I went back to the original and, with the aid of literal translations (for I had forgotten most of the Greek I had learnt at school) I made a shortened and condensed version of my own.

It consists in a prologue, four scenes and finale, playing continuously in one act. The place of action is outside the ruined battlements of Troy, after its capture by the Greeks. The curtain rises in darkness; it is the moment before sunrise. As the sky becomes gradually lighter, the figure of the god Poseidon appears outlined, in relief, against the sombre background, and utters a soliloquy over the fate of the unhappy city, "which now lies smouldering and overthrown. Forsaken stand the groves; the shrines of the gods lie drenched in blood, while on the altar steps of mighty Zeus himself, lies Priam—

dead"; and he ends with the solemn imprecation: "Accursed be he who sacks the towns of men, with shrines and tombs, for in the end he makes a desert around himself—and dies".

It is now light. Hecuba arises from the ground on which she has been lying, and intones a passionate lament in which she is joined by the chorus of captive Trojan women. Talthybius, a Greek messenger, enters and announces the fate that is in store for them. He summons Cassandra into his presence in order to deliver her into the hands of Agamemnon, to whom she has been allotted. She enters, robed in the white garments of a priestess of Apollo, carrying a lighted torch, and executes a wild song and dance, in which she prophesies the death of her captor, Agamemnon, and the downfall of the House of Atreus; after which she is led out to meet her fate by Talthybius and an escort of Greek soldiers.

After a lyrical chorus, Andromache, the widow of Hector, is brought in, accompanied by her son, the boy Astyanax. Andromache and Hecuba take part in a duet in which they lament their sad fate. Talthybius enters again with a band of soldiers and haltingly tells Andromache of the cruel decision taken by the leaders of the Greeks: that her son, Astyanax, being the son of so great a hero as Hector, is too dangerous to be left alive: from the battlements of Troy he must be thrown. Andromache bids farewell to her child in a tender and passionate threnody, after which she bursts out into a storm of invective against the Greeks.

After another lyrical chorus, Menelaüs enters and delivers a menacing denunciation of Helen, whom he commands to be brought before him. She enters, and defends herself, at first proudly and haughtily, then cajolingly, then desperately, against the accusations brought against her by Menelaus and also by Hecuba, who regards her as the cause of the downfall of her race and city; but without avail. Helen is led forth, weeping, by Menelaüs and an escort of soldiers.

Again the scene is rounded off by a chorus of captive Trojan women, and the last scene, like the first, with which it links up thematically, is an *ensemble* for Hecuba and the chorus, in the course of which the Greeks set torches to the remnants of what was once the proud city of Troy and, to the exultant sound of the victors' trumpets, the wailing women are led down to the ships in which they are to be taken to slavery in Greece.

The musical form of the work consists in a series of variations and counterpoints based upon a *passacaglia*, which consists in the chromatically descending scale of C to G, from tonic to dominant, which is one of the most fertile motives in the music of the 17th and 18th centuries, from Purcell (as in "When I am laid to earth" from *Dido and Æneas*) to Bach's B. Minor Mass. But since it is obviously all too easy to build up anything on a chromatically descending bass, in witness whereof the music of Delius, I laid upon myself certain definite conditions and limitations: firstly, the counterpoints to the chromatic bass must conform to the strictest classical canons, limited to thirds, sixths and suspensions, with only an occasional passing-note; secondly, the sequence of notes, C to G, must remain unaltered, without transposition. As a result of these self-imposed conditions some interesting technical consequences arise: as, for example, in the lament of Andromache over the fate of her son, in which the C to G *passacaglia* serves as a bass to the vocal melody in B major, always in thirds and sixths.

In the midst of the throes of composition I had occasion to visit France for the last time before the war, as it happened (and I vaguely apprehended), and the very heart and centre—Touraine, the France of Rabelais and Balzac—in the company of Constant Lambert. It was at the time when the Munich crisis was developing, and the experience was what can only be described by the French word for which there is no real equivalent in English or in any other language—*navrant*. The heart of France, it seemed to me, had stopped beating, or was beating so slowly, so faintly, so sluggishly, that one felt that death was near, or at least mortal illness; and if France died, Europe was fated to die with her.

I had then nearly completed the broad outlines of my

Women of Troy, but the music for one of the choruses had consistently and tantalizingly eluded me—a chorus for un-accompanied voices to the words, "So now thou hast delivered, Zeus, into Achaea's hands, thy shrine in Troy, thy fragrant altar, and sacrificial flame. With smoke of myrrh to heaven uprising, and Pergamos the holy, and ivy-mantled glens of Ida, watered by rills of melting snow; a holy land that bounds the world, and takes the sun's first rays—thy sacrifices, all are gone, and the glad sound of the dance; the midnight revels of the gods, thine images of carven gold, and Phrygia's holy festivals— all are gone for ever".

One day, perhaps the most memorable in my life, my companion and I visited Azay-le-Rideau, near Tours, and after an admirable lunch, embellished and fortified by many bottles of some of the noblest wines in the world, we repaired to the grounds of the *château*. While my friend indolently reclined on the green sward in the warm summer sunshine and indulged in a post-prandial *siesta*, I made my way to an exquisite spot at the farther end of the grounds, already well known to me from former visits, in order to contemplate once more the picture, so familiar, like a Chinese landscape, of the lake, on which was to be seen every day and at all hours of the day an old fisherman in a brightly painted barge, sitting motionless with his rod and line and never catching anything, and reminding me always of that favourite character of mine—the old Chinese fisherman who spent his entire time fishing, but used no bait, his object not being to catch fish.

As I was walking there, the perfect summer day, the exquisite beauty of the picture and of the surroundings—the embodi-ment of the historic glory of France, together with the deep, sad conviction of its imminent passing—all combined to produce in me one of those moments of illumination which, if one is lucky, occur two or three times in the course of life, in which one has the illusion—or the reality, rather—of becoming one with the universe; and there came to me then the music of the chorus for which I had been seeking vainly and for so long,

sung by celestial voices with absolute clarity and exact definition; and, wonder of wonders, the melody and the harmoniza-
tion accorded perfectly with the *passacaglia* on which the
whole work was based.

It is obviously impossible for me to judge the intrinsic
merits of the outcome of such an overwhelming subjective
experience. As a critic of the work of others I am only too well
aware of the fact that the divine numinous afflatus can produce
consummate balderdash, but at least I do know, and can say,
that in the moment I have ineffectually attempted to describe,
I experienced what can only be called "inspiration" in the
strict, literal sense of the word, as consisting in something
coming to one from outside—something which I was personally
incapable of producing.

Is it pride or modesty to suggest that one has known the
experience of being a highly imperfect instrument of Godhead? There may be a certain element of pride in having been
chosen rather than many worthier and less imperfect vessels,
but humility preponderates and, above all, awe, reverence, and
especially gratitude. . . .

Apart from all that, however, I was conscious of having
experienced a deep prophetic intuition of the impending downfall of France and of European civilization, with such blinding
clarity that I could not question the reality of the vision.
I returned to England with one aim in view: to finish my work
before the onset of the catastrophe which I knew to be
inevitable, like a husbandman labouring desperately to gather
in the harvest before the breaking of the storm. In this I was
successful.

The finishing touches to *The Women of Troy* were made in
August, 1939, which is the term I have set to this book.

INDEX